Zen Filmmaking 3

Expanded Writings on Creative Life and the Cinematic Arts

Scott Shaw

Buddha Rose Publications

Zen Filmmaking 3
Expanded Writings on Creative Life
and the Cinematic Arts
Copyright © 2019 by Scott Shaw
www.scottshaw.com
All Rights Reserved.

Rear Cover Photograph of Scott Shaw
By Hae Won Shin
Copyright © 2019 All Rights Reserved.

This book contains material protected under International and Federal Copyright Laws and Treaties. Any unauthorized reprint or use of this material is prohibited. No part of this book may be reproduced or transmitted in any form or by any means, electronic or mechanical, including photocopying, recording, or by any information storage and retrieval system without express written permission from the author or publisher.

First Edition 2019

ISBN 10: 1-949251-19-5
ISBN 13: 978-1-949251-19-7

Library of Congress: 2016930120

Printed in the United States of America
10 9 8 7 6 5 4 3 2 1

ZEN FILMMAKING 3

Introduction   11

Chapters:
Be Willing To Change Your Ideologies   14
Filmmaking:
    Keeping the Artist from Creating Art   18
Acting for the Camera   19
Everybody's Got the Same Hustle   22
Stand Up for the Rights of the Creator   25
What I Said Was…   27
Vision Lost   29
No Outcome   31
It Was Not Easy   33
Would You Work for Free?   35
Saying Everything That I Said   37
Part of the Process   40
When It Doesn't Work   42
The Wrong of Right Language   45
What's In It For Me?   47
Liar   50
Don't Psychoanalyze Me!   53
The Learning Annex   56
You Can Only Play
    In Your Own Playground   61
The Funky Cuts Barber Shop   66
How Little You Know of the Truth   69
Killing the Relationship   74
Seeing Yourself Through the
    Eyes of Other People   77
Do You Remember the TV Show Punk'd?   82
The Personality of Philosophy   84
Everybody Wants Something from Me
    but Nobody Ever Gives Me Anything   86
Zen Filmmaking: The Good, The Bad,
   and The People That Don't Know
   What the Fuck They're Talking About   89

Why Would I Give You Money?	93
Why Don't You Paint?	95
I'm An Artist, Goddamn It!	98
In For the Long Haul	100
This is Time	104
Everybody Talks About the Films but Nobody Studies the Films	108
Don't You Have Anything Better To Do?	111
How Do You Want Your Life To Be Remembered?	115
Is Doing What You Do Okay As Long As You Don't Get Caught?	118
Like I Always Say, Let's See What You Can Do	121
The First Time I Was Lied To	125
That's Not What I Want To Do	128
The Silence In-Between the Sound	131
Don't Say Yes	135
The Same Yet Different	138
The Scream Queens Get Old	141
Would Your Ever Make Another Roller Blade Seven?	143
Talking Pictures of Other People	146
Space Invaders	150
Nobody Really Cares	153
Nobody Remembers Their Name	157
Hollywood: The Impossible Game	160
Why Do You Believe?	162
Stirring the Pot	165
Getting it Right. Getting it Wrong.	168
DSLR Cinematography	173
Movies You Will Never See	176
Studying the Subtleties	179
The Way We Weren't	182
Zen Filmmaking: SS vs. DGJ	186
Zen Filmmaking 1973	188

Roller Blade Seven:
    Art-House Filmmaking Reality   190
Survivorman and the Search for Bigfoot   191
Open Your Eyes   193
There Is So Much You Could Have Done   195
References, Chaos,
    and the Game of Love or Hate   197
Same Old Lies   200
If You're Going To Claim the Claim
    Then You Better Be the Example   202
Don't Force the Art   204
People Are People   206
Knowing What You Don't Know   222
Remember When It Was So Important
    To Watch Music Videos?   225
Creation and Adaptation   227
Everything Has Already Been Done   231
Desire Verse Drive   233
You Weren't There So You Don't Know   235
Too Famous For All the Wrong Reasons   237
You Verses Who?   241
The Casting Couch   244
Pure Cinema Cinéma Pur   248
Perplexing…   250
How Much of What You Have is
    Because of Someone Else?   252
All It Costs is Money   255
It is Easy to Criticize When You Haven't
    Lived the Life   258
Every Creator Says the Same Thing   260
Black Hawk Down   263
What You Are Looking For?   265
If You Want Me to Be in the Conversation
    Let Me Be in the Conversation   269
The Guy Who Never Made a Movie
    The Guy Who Never Wrote a Book   273

Partners in Crime and You Think You Know What You Never Know	276
Watching the Evolution AKA Everyone's Dead	280
Been There Done That	283
Enlightenment Through the Arts	285
Roller Blade Seven: The Unseen Scenes	288
The Outside That Will Never Happen	290
Who Goes To Nude Beaches?	292
Torrent and Damn It People Give Me Something!	295
Honoring People's Wishes and What You Can Do About What You Can Do	299
The Effort That You Make	302
Cameras Everywhere	305
How Little the Critics Know	307
Roller Blade Seven The Music Video	309
Zen Filmmaking: Don't Miss the Bus	312
Zen Filmmaking: The Final Definition	314
You Never Know What You Don't Know	315
The 70s Were Great but They Ain't Ever Coming Back AKA You Make What You Can With What you Have	318
I Make Weird Movies! What?	321
Cinematic Enlightenment	324
Buy a Camera and Make Your Own Movie	326
What Would Your Do to Be in a Movie?	329
Film Distribution	333
The Roller Blade Seven: The Story of the Production	341
Max Hell Frog Warrior: The Story of the Production	366
Guns of El Chupacabra: The Story of the Production	386
The Rock n' Roll Cops: The Story of the Production	403

Fade In:

Introduction

So, you want to be a filmmaker. Okay... Why do you want to be a filmmaker? This is really an essential question. This essential question is also a question that many a would-be/wanta-be filmmaker never asks himself or herself. This is why so many a could-be filmmakers never actually makes a film. ...They do not truly know why they are doing what they are doing thus they do not possess the focused drive to push forward and get their movie completed.

Since I first entered the film industry, about thirty years ago, I have encountered so many people; especially at the independent, homegrown level, that have wanted to become filmmakers. They spend so much time and energy discussing what they will do, someday. Some even invest money. In some cases a lot of money. They talk and they talk, they plan and they plan, some even write scripts or they ask someone to write a script for them but nothing ever comes from this. Even I, in my early days in the industry, got sucked into some of this nonsense believing that there was going to be an end-result. But, there was not.

Does this happen because people do not actually possess the talent they believe they hold? No, not necessarily. But, perhaps it is that level of self-involvement that, in many cases, foils a person's filmmaking attempt in the first place. *"I am talented. I have something to offer."* If this is a person's motivation then, yes, they may expect problems based upon a self-involved approach to filmmaking. But, more than simply being driven by ego, instead of focused dedication, the reason many a film project does not find its way to completion is that many the aspiring filmmaker does not posses the clear artistic intent necessary to overcome the many obstacles of filmmaking.

At the heart of doing anything creative is a person's desire to project what is in their mind to the masses. For some, this is a truly unique and organic vision. For others, they simply want to exhibit an imitation of what they have seen elsewhere. Whatever the case, it is the one-pointed focus of the artistic vision that is in one person's mind that must be acutely honed in order to make any original creation come to life. In the realm of filmmaking, there is commonly more than one person involved in the process. From this arises the need to not only possess the perseverance necessary to bring your cinematic vision to life but, additionally, to understand how to focus and manage the other people who are involved with the project in a manner that will cause them to work in a unified and coordinated effort with you as opposed to finding yourself in an adversarial relationship, which may cause your dream of creating a film to never be accomplished.

In my previous books on the subject of filmmaking; most notably: *Zen Filmmaking, Independent Filmmaking: Secrets of the Craft,* and *Zen Filmmaking 2: Further Writings on the Cinematic Arts,* I have discussed formalized techniques that are designed to help the aspiring filmmaker get their film project created. In this book, though I do discuss some fundamental techniques; the focus of this volume is not on the *nuts-and-bolts* of how-to. In this book, I discuss the more metaphysical realities of filmmaking from a personal and psychological perspective. By presenting the writings in this book in this fashion, I trust it will allow the prospective and the already-have filmmaker with new food for thought in the hopes that this will not only inspire the aspiring filmmaker but will prepare them for what may happen; in addition to showing them what has happened. From this, not only will they be better prepared for the possible eventualities of filmmaking but they may also be able to avoid any negative circumstances and encounters all together. If nothing else, I trust the reader(s) of this book will be able to witness what other filmmakers, (including myself), have gone through while working on the independent level of the film industry and, thereby, they may come to realize that no matter what they encounter while working to bring their cinematic vision to life they are not the only one who has encountered obstacles in the filmmaking process but by continuing to push forward with their vision this will allow them to become a part of those few people who can actually call themself, *"A filmmaker."*

Be Willing To Change Your Ideologies

I received an e-mail yesterday from a young filmmaker I communicate with. He had encountered some problems finishing up his latest film and asked for some thoughts or advice.

The only advice I can really give him, in regard to filmmaking, and anybody else in regard to life, is that you must be willing to change your ideologies.

The reality is, in life, we each have a plan about how we are going to do something. In our mind's eye the situation occurs just the way we had planned and the outcome is perfect. Even if we anticipate a certain amount of problems, we feel they will be resolved and it will all work out fine.

The reality of life is, however, there are a million sets of circumstances that we can never anticipate. These may involve people, mechanical items, nature, or even acts of god. Though we may have it all planned out, life happens, and it is rarely anything that we expect.

This is true of creative projects. It is true of interactions with people. And, it is true of living life.

If you stay locked into a predetermined pattern of thoughts and existence, the minute a new, different, or unexpected situation occurs, you will be lost and you will be upset that it did not turn out the way you hoped. Some people get mad at the people around them. Some people get mad at themselves. Some people get mad at life. Some people get mad at god. But, what good does any of that do? All you do is create a lot of, *"Upset,"* in your life. And, upset is not balanced, not happy, not creative, not free. It is simply stifling.

But, if you are simply willing to accept things as they come. If you are willing to change your mind. If you are willing to change your expectations, think how free your life becomes.

Filmmaking:
Keeping the Artist from Creating Art

As most of the people who know of me understand, I've made a lot of movies. Whether or not the people reading this have seen any of them, well that's a different story...

People often ask me, (because I've made so many films), *"How long does it take you to make a movie?"* The answer is, I have it down to a science. If I have a location, a cast, and a crew, I can shoot a movie in a couple of days, have it edited, and sound tracked in a week or so. So, within a month, the whole film can be in the can. And, in some cases, already released.

The reason I can do this is that I do everything. I do not delegate the jobs. I always have ideas, my equipment is ready to go, I am always working on new soundtracks, and I keep my software for editing functional and up to date.

The problem is, *the devil is in the details,* as the old saying goes. Ever since 9/11 it has become more and more difficult to find free locations to shoot at. Everybody thinks that you are up to something bad if you show up with a camera. And, you do get shut down. So, my lack of locations, in recent years, has truly hindering my filmmaking.

An ideal and somewhat amusing example of this happened to me when I went to shoot some stock footage in the L.A. Harbor. I didn't even have a cast or a crew. I was by myself. I was grabbing some shots and The National Guard drove up and before I knew it I was in those plastic handcuff things. I thought I was on my way *Gitmo.* They were telling me, *"We are at war..."* Luckily, they checked me out and figured out I was cool, no threat, and just a filmmaker. They let me go with just a stern warning.

The other problem is, as I have detailed in so many articles and books, here in L.A., everybody thinks that they are going to be a star tomorrow. And, this mindset has continued to get worse. So, there is a lot of misplaced ego floating around.

This is not just the case for actors and actresses, as you may expect, but for crew, as well. I cannot tell you how many times I have had an entire shoot day ruined by the cameraman. Yet, they remain all full of themselves.

Though I am personally a very meticulous cameraman, as I appear in many of my films, I need someone to shoot some of the scenes.

From this, the question is often asked, *"Why do I appear in many of my own films?"* Again it goes back to egos.

With everybody thinking they are going to be a star tomorrow, you never know when somebody is going to get their panties in a bunch and walk off the set. With me in the film, I know I am going to show up and, therefore, can fix any problems with the story if some cast member leaves.

Outside of the industry, people don't realize all of these subtle particulars. This is how producers get people to invest in a film. Because somebody doesn't know what to expect, they expect nothing.

I know producers are always promising the investor everything: how much money they will make, how they are part of the greater good, how great the cast, crew, and director is. They are told they will get an executive producer credit and they pull out the checkbook. Everybody wants to be a part of the film industry, don't they? But, these words are all bullshit. Nobody makes big money on little films. Well, at least not the investors. Maybe the distributors...

The whole essence of my filmmaking style, *Zen Filmmaking,* is freedom and art. It is about removing as many obstacles as possible from the filmmaking process. But, the unfortunate reality is that times have changed. So, I do not make near as many movies as I could. Or, as some believe, I should. And, it's sad because all I need is place to shoot a film and a few competent and willing participants. I don't even need or want money.

By the way, I never take money from investors. It just makes everything too messy...

So, you see, every realm of art has it problems and its own set of unique circumstance that keeps the artist from creating. How long it takes for me to make a film is not the issue. The issue is, do I have a place and a posse?

Acting for the Camera

Unless you are creating non-narrative films, like I have been focusing on for the past few years, acting is at the heart of any film. It is the actor who gets your story told. But actors are also, many times, the thing that makes a film hard to watch; as they are the central focus, their performances are the first thing that is commonly judged about a film.

Acting has evolved over the years. If you like to watch older films from the 1930s and 1940s like I do, you will immediately notice that the acting was much bigger back then. The performances where much more exaggerated. This is due to the fact that most of the actors of that era were schooled on the stage. In the theatre their performances needed to be bigger. From this, they took this same acting style with them to the silver screen.

This is one of the reasons that I so much like working with my friend Conrad Brooks. He came from that era and he acts like he is still in that era. I love his performances.

In independent filmmaking, particularly the low to no budget genre, acting is what generally makes a film watchable or not. Now, this is a doubled edged sword because most people working at this level of the film industry are inexperienced actors—at least in terms of on-camera experience. If a person can remain natural in their performance then there is no problem. But, most people can't. Most people, at least the inexperienced, when they act, they are acting. And, this is what may kill the believability of their performance.

Also, particularly when people are attempting to make a spoof film, they intentionally overact. They believe this is how it was done. But, in actually, this is not the case. Bad acting is just that; bad acting. It is a whole onto itself. Therefore, by attempting to recreate it, defeats the entire purpose.

Now, there have been some great performances based upon spoofing an actor or an acting era. Billy Zane did a great job in the last of the Ed Wood scripts, *I Woke Up Early the Day I Died.* This film had no dialogue but the performances were great. And, of course, the spoof-based performances of talented actors like Johnny Depp have been great. But, these are very intentional performances given by highly talented actors. When one is inexperienced and doing this, it does not translate well to the screen.

If we look to the Republic Serial from the 1930s, 1940s, on into the 1950s, there was some great programming made in that era—whether it was for TV or the big screen. Series like *Commando Cody* and *The Adventures of Fu Manchu* truly defined an era and were the first to bring comic book type heroes to the screen. If we watch the acting in these serials, it was over the top. But, it was over the top, specific to that era. Just as when we watch Capt. James T. Kirk, (William Shatner), on the original *Star Trek* series, his acting is over the top but believable in its era.

To try to emulate these performances never really translates well to screen. I know, because we did this in *Roller Blade Seven.* Though the style of acting we employed did set the stage for the overall vibe of the film, most people didn't get it and did not understand the influences we were harkening back to, as times had changed and most who watched the RB7 film(s) were not aware of that era gone past or were not yet even born when it took place.

      To this end, and through the years upon years I have been making films, I find it is far better to simply be natural in all onscreen performances—natural to your era. Even if your film is a spoof, by being true to yourself, by being who you are on screen, while wrapped in the cloak of a character, the audience will find your performance far more enjoyable to watch than if you try to be something you are not and perform as those people did in times gone past.

Everybody's Got the Same Hustle

You know, there is a sad reality about life. We all have to make money in order to survive. Life is a very material place. To survive you have to live somewhere, eat, and furnish your life with all of the additional items that you feel you deserve.

To reach that end, most people work the *nine-to-five*. Many hate what they are doing, but they do it *none-the-less*. Some people love what they are doing. And, that is great. That is the best way to live life.

But, there are those, and there's a lot of them, who are willing to do whatever it takes to get other people's hard earned money in order to finance their own lifestyle. Some may call it work. But, it is not. I call it a hustle.

Being involved in the film business, I have witnessed a lot of underhanded nonsense when it comes to money and getting money from other people. The stories I could tell you... But, in brief, people do a lot of really messed up things to get money from people. As there is the promise of fame and fortune in the film industry, people are easily sucked in by the promises. They hand over their money.

One of the main things I always emphasize about this issue in the classes I have taught and in my books and articles is that, *ninety-nine percent* of the film industry is bullshit. People may want to make films but they do not have the talent, the understanding, or the dedication to actually get them completed. But, they still hold casting session, from which actors and actress get their hopes up. The hustle money from investors, *"If you give me this amount, you will make millions. I promise!"* It is all a colossal waste of time and cash.

Then there is the other side of the issue, where people get money from actors and actress. The biggest offenders of this are acting teachers. I mean come on! If these people were actual actors, making money from the craft, then they would not be teaching. They are not working actors, so that is why they teach. But, people get sucked into it everyday. They are told by the powers that be that they must take acting classes. And, a lot of money changes hands but the vast majority of actors never find themselves upon the silver screen.

Then there is the filmmaking hustlers. I have seen this so many times. For example, when I was first getting into the game, this guy who had made a few bad indie movies told me that his friend was the one who had made this super-famous actor, a star. How did he do it? He got him, (the actor), to finance a film in which he starred. Yeah right… He was obviously trying to get me to pay for his next movie. I passed.

But, I am not the only one this has happened to. It happens all the time. This is why I warn every novice actor, and particularly actress, who I come into contact with, *"Be very-very careful, who you hook up with."* Again, the stories I could tell you…

Perhaps the biggest problem with the film industry is that it is call an art form. It really is not. Like my friend Don Jackson used to say, *"The art is not in making the movie. The art is in finding the money to make a movie."*

Though, with the dawning of the digital revolution, it has gotten much cheaper to make a film, it still costs a lot of money. The bigger the movie, the more money it takes to make it. And, this is where the hustlers come out to play.

I guess this little piece is for the actors, actress, and filmmakers out there. If they ask you for money say, *"No."* No matter what the promise is, it will not happen. So, don't fall prey to the game.

Stand Up For the Rights of the Creator

I was teaching one of my classes on filmmaking earlier today. As the class only meets once a week I try to keep the student very active in actual film creation so I generally give them an assignment to make a short film for each class session. This week's assignment was to do a visual biographical piece. One of my students did, what so many people have done before, was to intermingle footage of his life with footage from very famous films. The short had him talking to various characters from various films. This is always a fun presentation as you get to peer into the mind of the person and view how they see themselves in association with life. It was a good piece.

After his presentation he asked if I thought he should upload it to his YouTube page. I said he could but he may run into copyright problems.

Now, for anyone who knows me understands, I am an avid proponent of Intellectual Property Rights. If somebody made something they are the only one who owns it and other people can only use it if they are given permission.

But, more than that... Each person should have the moral dignity to ask the creator of a, *"Something,"* if they can use all or part of it. Maybe the creator will say, *"Yes."* Maybe the creator will say, *"No."* But, every person who wants to tap into the creation of another person's creativity should have the honor to ask if they can use it. That is just the right moral code of life. And, that is what I explained to my students.

Now, not everyone who infringes on another person's copyright gets sued. It's expensive and it's time consuming. Not every copyright infraction is reported to the FBI. So, some people get away with it. But, should they?

Have you ever asked the creator of a project, that you have stolen all are part of or have downloaded it for free from an illegal offshore website, how they feel about what you have done? If you haven't, what does that say about you? And, as I always state, if you were the one creating the something that is being stolen I am certain you would have a very different opinion about what is taking place than you being the thief.

Many people do not personally create books, movies, music, or art. But, they like it. So, they want to view it. But, have you ever had somebody steal your bike, your car, your wallet, or break into your house. If you have experienced that feeling, then you will know what the artist goes through when their creation has been stolen.

Okay… Okay… I won't go off here… ☺ But, as you can plainly see, I am really against people stealing other people's creations.

What I always suggest (like I did to my class) is be more than the thieves. Stand up for the rights of the creator. Understand that it took their creative vision, their time, their money, their mental focus, and their undaunted dedication to make that piece of art. Don't steal it!

What I Said Was...

For some strange reason there is a certain group of people who, for whatever ever reason, quote me. First of all, I am not talking about the people who find inspiration in my (for lack of a better term) spiritual thoughts and put them out there. That's fine! If something helps it helps. If something inspires it inspires. What I am talking about are those people who go out of their way to use my own words to slam me. They do this by taking what I said out of context or snipping a small part of a larger understanding and focusing on a small piece of it. Whenever I hear about someone doing this it kind of makes me feel like reciting the lyric from the NWA song, *"Don't quote me boy cause I ain't said shit."*

These people may take something I said or wrote, turn it around, place their own definition upon it, and use it to their own advantage—whatever that advantage may be. From this, they attempt to paint a picture of me. A picture of what they think I am, what they think about me, or what they want the world to think about me. This never ceases to amaze me. I forever laughingly question, *"Why?"*

Why do people waste their time writing pieces and doing productions about other people? Don't they have anything better to do?

Yes, I have heard about a couple of people who have done their Master's Thesis and one person's Ph.D. Dissertation about *Zen Filmmaking,* where what I have said and what I have done were a big part of their presentation. In those cases, I totally get it. What they did equals something; namely, an advanced university degree. Those people had to write an original paper to complete their studies. All good.

But then, there are those people who want to tear a person's thoughts apart. But, to what end? Do they simply want to project their own beliefs onto what another person is saying? If so, that action seems very disingenuous.

This happens all the time to all kinds of people. I am simply speaking about me because I am me. ☺

People want to project their opinions, their beliefs, and orchestrate the illusion that they know more than the person they are actually speaking about. But, how is that even possible? If the person is living, that person knows what they are doing and to take their ideologies and falsely present them to the world, no matter whether the other people they are presenting them to believe what the narrator is saying or not, is simply a false representation of the truth. And a lie never equals the truth.

So, here's the point... Do you live your life for you and about you? Or, do you live your life based upon what someone else has done or has said? If you live your life by the latter, then you forever make yourself less than the person you quote and/or discuss. For no matter how you frame them; whether you present them in a positive or a negative light, what you are doing is placing them upon a pedestal by making them someone you feel is worthy of discussing. What you are doing is raising that person to an exalted status by making them the focus of what you are doing with your life.

Who do you want your life to be defined by? You or the person or persons you talk about? Simple question. What is your answer?

Vision Lost

I was filming a couple of scenes for an upcoming movie at one of those traveling carnivals today. You know, the kind with roller coasters and Ferris wheels that you would never go on because they look so rickety. The carnival was closed so it provided me with a very abstract apocalyptic backdrop. Plus, it was located in a junky part of the city. So, it gave me great visuals.

Actually, the title and the idea for this piece came to me last night and then was reinforced today when one of my cameramen saw me taking some still photographs of the attractions and he said to me, *"Damn, I wish I would have brought a camera so I could have captured some stills."*

This is something that I teach my students whenever I teach a class on filmmaking, cinematography, or photography, that you must always have equipment with you. Certainly, in this day and age of smartphones most people always have something to work with. My camera guy had forgotten his at home. It's not like it was back in the day when we used to shoot on 16mm film or take stills with big bulky 35mm cameras. Then, to have equipment with you at the ready, in the state of whatever may happen whenever, was much more difficult. Now, it is easy.

This being said, many people have an artistic vision. Whether that is for the creation of films, photography, art, music, whatever... Few, however, pursue and actualize that vision. Like I always tell my screenwriter friends, in the mind's eye, it is relatively easy to type out a script and have great locations with each word acted out perfectly by the actors, but actually making that happen is much more complicated.

In your mind's eye you can do anything. You can make the perfect movie, take the perfect photograph, paint the perfect painting, play the greatest music, but actually doing it is much different from simply thinking about doing it. The sad thing is, many people have these grand artistic visions, yet do nothing about them. From this, artistic vision is lost and a person leaves nothing to substantiate their time here on earth.

The only suggestion I can make is don't let that happen to you. In this world today, it is so easy to create art and then get your art out there. Forget about making money on it, so few people ever do that. But, you can create and you can get it out there. And, that has forever been my suggestion, get off your butt, stop dreaming about, and go and create art. Don't let your vision be lost.

No Outcome

You know, everybody has a design for his or her life. They have a vision of where they want to be and what they want to be doing. In most cases, it is somewhere else, doing something else than what they are currently doing.

This is the same with all projects that people undertake; whether it be drawing, painting, writing a poem, a novel, recording a song, making a movie, or repairing a hole in the wall. In their mind's eye they see it completed in some perfect state. But, in reality, it/life rarely ever reaches this level of perfection.

In Zen Tea Making, they spend hours attempting to make the whole process of making a cup of tea a meditation. The goal is to make the perfect cup of tea. But, is the tea made via that process any better than a cup that was produced in a couple of minutes?

I am so frequently bombarded by questions about what someone should do when something they are doing is not turning out the way they had planned. This may be their art, their movie, their book, their relationship, their trip to India, their whatever... They ask me, because people don't listen. I have said it *time-and-time* again, in so many ways, in so many places, *"If you have expectations, things will never turn out the way you planned."* This is the whole reason I developed *Zen Filmmaking;* because it allows the filmmaking process to become free—free from desires and free from expected outcomes. You get what you get and that is your movie. And, this is the same philosophy that should be applied to life if you wish to be happy.

Because I continue to get questions, let me say this again, *"No desire for a predetermined outcome equals freedom. Freedom equals contentment and happiness. Let go of your desired expectations and you will experience a much better life."*

It Was Not Easy

I was just discussing the old days in the martial art media industry with a person who helped me do some of the photographs for the martial art magazines I used to write for. Sadly, the publishing world has all changed and most of the magazines are gone, gone, gone. But, back then I would come up with the idea for the article, write it, and then have to get the photographs for it. Not easy…

Back then, everything was on film. So, you would do the photographs but you would never be completely sure of what you actually had until they were developed, printed, and you saw them. This was a time consuming and expensive process.

The thing was, a lot of times you, (meaning me), had to live with what you got. As you could not study the image just photographed, as you can now in the digital age, to see if it was AOK. So, you got what you got and had to live with it as reshooting was very time consuming and expensive. And, the magazines only paid me like $100.00 per article. So, a lot of the time it cost me more than that to have the photographs taken.

Most people never thought about that. I guess they still don't. They just see what they see and they never take the time to ponder what went into getting it. This is pretty much the same in all aspects of life. People just see, cast judgment based upon their limited mind frame of perception, and that is that. But, THAT is never THAT. There is always much more to THAT then can ever be known unless you know.

This process was the same with filmmaking. When we used to shoot on film, it was *very-very* time consuming and expensive. The film had to be shot. It had to be developed. It had to be transferred to be viewed, etc… Plus, you were never sure what you would come away with.

Even in the early days of filmmaking on video, of which I am told I am a pioneer, the editing was very expensive. You had to go to an editing facility, pay by the hour or the day, and once again you got what you got. All of this really taught me to work within the constraints of the, *"What you get you get,"* mindset.

Nothing in life is ever exactly the way you want it to be. This is particularly the case with artist creations. But, if you hope to DO you must learn to live within those constrains and create however you create. It may not end up perfect, it may not end up exactly the way you wanted it to be, but if you don't DO, if you don't ACCEPT what you've DONE, you own expectations will keep you from ever creating.

Would You Work for Free?

A friend of mine asked me to come and speak to a university class he teaches on filmmaking last week. When we got to the Q&A segment of the talk the subject of internet piracy of films came up as it often does. I asked the students, *"How many of you have a job?"* Some of the students raised their hands. I then questioned, *"Of those of you who have a job, how many of you would work if you didn't get paid? How many of you would work for free?"* Of course, nobody raised their hands.

The subject then shifted to some claiming that they are poor college students and they can't afford to pay to see movies and various comments like that. But, that does not change the primary premise, if you wouldn't do something for free, why do you think it is right to steal from someone else's income?

People rarely live their life based upon morality. Most, live what they live, take whatever it is they can get away with, and do not even give a thought to any one or any thing. Few people ever think about the implications of their actions and how those actions affect other people.

Now, I could talk forever attempting to get people to care about the greater good and what it right and what is wrong, but who would listen? If you don't care, you don't care. And, people never care until something affects them personally. Right or wrong that is the way it is. But, the truth is, it does not have to be that way. If you care about humanity, if you care about your rights and the rights of other people, particularly those who create something, then doing the right thing can and should begin with you.

Don't do it! Don't steal. Don't take away the income of other people. Don't steal people's artistic creations so you can save a buck or make a buck. Let doing the right thing begin with you.

Saying Everything That I Said

It is always amusing for me to listen to a person speaking, read the writings of a person, or the words that are spoken when an individual is being interviewed and they say exactly what I have already said but they claim it as their own ideology. It is strange… It is flattering, (I guess)… But, it is also a bit disconcerting…

In fact, there have been a few people who while attempting to rip on me have actually stolen a passage I have written; word for word and have used it as if they invented it. I mean, if you are going to be critical at least think up your own things to say. ☺

But, let's get more to the point... If you are writing something that means you have something that you feel needs to be said. If you are being asked questions in an interview that means you have done something/accomplished something that others find worthwhile. All good…

The fact is, if you have done something worth doing you must first have a philosophy to guide you towards doing it. Most people have none. Thus, when they try to do something they fail at it miserably. No philosophy equals no true expression of that philosophy. Thus, nothing can be created.

Okay… But, where did that philosophy come from?

We each are influenced by our time in history, other people, and the world around us. For those of us who have a creative mission in life, we do things that create an end result—an object, a thought, or a thing. Then, when we are asked how or why it is we, the creative proponent of that equation, created what we did, we must come up with an explainable logic that guided us to create our creation and how others may follow in our path if they hope to do something similar.

Certainly, I have written a lot about a lot of stuff. I have spelled out my, *"Why and How,"* for all that I do. I do that to help others overcome obstacles if they hope to follow a similar path. But, for those who take the understandings and philosophies that I bottled and then call it their own—I don't know? It is perplexing...

I think back to when my *Zen Filmmaking* buddy Donald G. Jackson was still alive and when we were interviewed, either as a team or as a separate entity, our answers were often times very similar. That was because we had created a movement together, *Zen Filmmaking*. We didn't base it on anything that had been done before. We based it on our own understanding of the NOW and the creativity of immediate inspiration; leading to cinematic enlightenment. Without our interaction *Zen Filmmaking* would never have happened. Yes, I was more literate on the subject and more focused on formalizing and presenting *Zen Filmmaking* definition to the world, but without our teaming up, it may never have been an actualized entity. So, when we said the same thing, it was expected. But, when others say what I have said, sometimes exactly—write what I have written, and don't throw me a bone, it is very surprising...

Like I have always said about *Zen Filmmaking, "Make it your own."* You don't have to do what I do, just do it. Remove as many obstacles as you can and do what works for you. But, I think I should also probably paraphrase here, if you are going to quote me, use my words and my philosophies, say what I have already said, at least throw me a bone and state where your words and/or your ideology came from.

Part of the Process

In life there is always a process. You rarely just get to go in and do it. Usually you have to set up beforehand and clean up afterwards. And, this kind of sucks.

This also goes to the bigger level of things. You have to learn how to do what you're going to do before you do it, and this generally takes time. Sometimes a lot of it... Plus, you have to finish what you started if you want it (anything) to reach completion. This too takes time.

Then, sometimes what you did created such a mess that it takes a *long-long time* to clean it up and to get past it. If you ever can at all.

It's like painting. I love painting. But, it is *very-very* messy. Long ago I realized that I could never paint wearing any piece of clothing that I cared about. Because if you paint, you are going to get paint on your clothing, and there is no way to get it off once you get it on.

And, the clean up. Awh man, what a mess... In fact, I didn't paint for quite awhile, at one point in my life, just because I hated the clean up.

Back in the day, when I was in my twenties, I used to live in this apartment in Hermosa Beach. It had a very big kitchen. What I would do is to staple gun a large canvas to the wall and paint it from there. I used oils a lot back then and the smell of oil paints and their toxic nature... Well, some believe it was what helped Van Gogh go insane... But me, I wouldn't clean up. I would just leave it. Sometimes the smell of oil paints permeated my apartment for days. I expected that it/they would sooner or later kill me. Well, not yet anyway...

Then there is music... The whole reason I quit playing music professional in live arenas is that I hated the tear down. I didn't want to end up being one of those guys at *thirty-five* or *forty* who had to cart their own amp on stage, set it up, and then carry it off once the show was done. At music shows I always think that kills the whole vibe, watching the lead guitarist pack up his own stuff and carrying it off stage at the end of a show.

Now, there is filmmaking. The lights, the gels, the setup, and the tear down. It all equals a lot of work. But, that's just the problem/the reality of life; we all have this stuff that we have to do if we want to do anything. For each person it is different, but it has to be done.

You can sit around and do nothing... As Zen as that may sound, it also equals nothing. So, if you're going to DO, you will need to set up and tear down. I guess we just each have to decide what we are willing to set up and what we are willing to tear down...

We each define our own life.

When It Doesn't Work

So often I encounter people who are chasing whatever dream it is they are chasing but their world is falling down around them. I imagine that I frequently encounter these types of people because of the fact I live in L.A. L.A. where everyone seems to come chasing the promise of a dream. But, for all those who have found their dream here, there have been millions upon millions who have not.

Whether it is people chasing the dream of acting in or directing films, playing music, dancing, doing art, doing photography, writing a script or a book, owning a business, you name it... Very few of these people ever achieve their dreams.

I have watched so many people suffer, when their suffering was brought on by themselves. They have invested in equipment they can't afford, lied about their income to live in apartments or houses they can't afford, buy cars they can't afford so they can project an image of success, they pay for classes and headshots they can't afford, or they have maxed out their credit cards producing a movie that they either do not finish or cannot sell. You name it, I have seen it.

In fact, when the team that was publicizing Robert Rodriguez's *El Mariachi* was claiming that the film that made it into the theaters cost only $7,000.00 to create, I know several people who went bankrupt over believing that lie—thinking that they too could produce a film of that caliber for that amount of money. Who holds the karma for that?

And, that's just the thing... When someone who has hurt, lied to, or deceived people goes under, there is no emotion attached to their failure. They deserve it; right? But, when people go under when all they do is try to succeed, then another avenue of investigation needs to be viewed.

Certainly, we can say that all the people who try and fail are following a path of desire. And, as the Buddha so aptly stated, *"The cause of suffering is desire."* But, most people could care less about metaphysics. All they know and/or care about is the reality of what is right in front of their nose. They want to be something. But, the fact is, being something is almost impossible. Yet, so many people chase after it.

The people I witness failing always have one commonality. That commonality is that they do not investigate other pathways of survival. They are an actor, a filmmaking, an artist, a photographer, a dancer, an author—as they ARE, they can and should not have to be anything else. Wrong!

On a slightly different variant of this pathway, there are so many people that are financed by their families or they live under the roof of their family. The fact is, if you are an adult, over the age of eighteen, and you are either financed by and or living under the roof of your parents, and are not set about on a directed course of moving out onto your own, you are a failure. Just like the drug addicts and the alcoholics need to accept, the first thing you need to do is to admit to yourself you have a problem if you ever hope to get better. Face life! Get out on your own!

The people I see failing, particularly financially, do so because they never investigate a new course of action. The fact is, if what you are doing is not working; get a job! Yeah, it may not be what you want to do. Yeah, you may believe you are way more than that. But, the fact is, if you were, then you would be. As you are not, you are not.

The true reality of life; the true spirituality of life, is admitting to yourself and to the world that all you are, is what you are. You may have dreams but never let your dreams destroy you. For if you do, how do you come back from that?

Stop pretending. Stop spending money you don't have. Stop lying to others and particularly stop lying to yourself and do what it takes to survive. And, do it consciously, without lying to or hurting others. If that means getting a job, get one. Think of all the new experiences you will gain.

The true essence of life is living within your own perfection. Not trying to be something you are not but simply being something you are.

The Wrong of Right Language

Over the past week or so there has been a major uproar about NBC Newscaster Brian Williams fudging the truth about how a helicopter he was riding in taking RPG hits when it was, in fact, the helicopter ahead of him. Okay... Remember back in the Presidential election cycle of '08 when Hilary Clinton claimed she landed somewhere and bullets were whizzing past her head? Then she got busted on that fact and she fessed up it didn't really happen. Okay...

Everybody is in an uproar about Williams. But, let's think about a couple of things... First of all, who among us has not exaggerated some thing about our life experience and ourselves at some point in time? Who among us has not lied?

Like I always say... ...First it was in association with the filmmaking industry and now it is in association with all of life, *"Everybody lies."*

If you have never told a lie you are probably the only person on the planet who has not done so.

I'm not saying what Williams did was right. I am simply saying that this is life and that is what most people do.

Many of us, like myself, try not to behave in that manner. But, lying is rampant in this world. It is everywhere; everybody does it.

The thing that sets me to pondering is how and why everybody is so upset about this issue. Is it because they know they too have lied and would never want to be caught in their lie? Is it that they too have exaggerated and never want their exaggeration found out? Maybe if they focus is on someone else, the scrutiny will not go to them?

Mostly, what I have witnessed, more and more, is that people are angry at themselves, at life, at the world, at god, and/or at not living the life that they truly wish they could live so they become angry at whatever target they can find.

The question is, what is the truth? Is it the stories that you tell to the world and then they believe your words to be true? Or, is it what you have actually lived and only you know the true truth?

What's In It For Me?

"What's in it for me?" This is a line that I have used in several of my films. It was first used in *The Roller Blade Seven* as I kind of homage' to the nonsense that many of the actors were dishing out to Don Jackson and myself during the production. But, in reality, it has come to be how I feel about many things in life.

In interviews, I am often asked very similar questions. One of them is, *"What are your realization about your life?"* I commonly reply, *"Everybody wants something from me but nobody ever gives me anything."*

When I say this, I am often asked, *"Why?"* Well, it is very simply. People always seem to want something from me and they never want to repay the favor.

Now, first of all... I am always happy to help people out if I can. I guess it is based upon my early years of walking the spiritual path; being indoctrinated into selfless-service, karma yoga, and stuff. I guess it is also, just who I am.

That being said, I am constantly being stalked by people to help them out.

People always want something from me! They want to be in one of my films. They want me to finance their film or turn them onto people who will. They want to borrow my equipment. They want me to give them something I own. They want me to introducing them to somebody. They want to be in a relationship with me. They want me to teach them how to do something. They want me to distribute their movie, or get them a distribution deal. They want me to help them with their book.

Get them a publisher. Whatever... The list goes on and on.

One of the perfect examples of this, (that just came to mind), was this one guy. He was the audio-visual guy at a college where I was teaching a course on indie filmmaking. He also took the course. Seemed like a nice enough guy...

The weird thing was, after the course, every time I went into this one store, he would magically show up and tell me how much he wanted to be a part of one of my movies and how important it was for him to get his name on imdb.com, etc. I finally realized that he was having this one girl, who worked at the store, call him up whenever I would go in. That's how he would know when to show up.

At the point I was doing a local movie that I could use him in, I gave him a call. He showed up, did his job, and it was all-good. I got him on imdb.com. His dream was answered... Then, the next movie comes along. To save myself from being stalked again, I created a part for him and cast several people to support his character. I hit him up, let him know, but nothing... The problem was, due to his absence, I had to let the other cast members go as they had no one to play their roles off of. Finally, he got back to me after the production was done. *"Sorry, can't do it."* You see, he got what he wanted out of me. He was in a movie. He got his name on imdb.com. But, why bother paying back the favor?

This is just how it is with my life. I mean, now if a girl wants to show up and have meaningless sex with me for no good reason. Well, that's a different story. ☺ If somebody wants to give me a million dollars; all-good. ☺ If someone wants to hook me up with a new *Rolex* or

D'Angelico; fine with me. ☺ But, that's the problem; everybody comes up to me and wants me to do something for them. Which, as stated, is fine, but sometimes I could use some help too.

And, this little ditty is not just about me. This is how most people are around the globe. They want what they want. They are willing to do whatever it takes to get it. But, once they do get it, they never say, *"Thanks,"* and they never repay the favor. They simply feel like they deserved it.

It's like, for example, everybody wants to get into the film business. At least here in L.A. But, the reality is, the film business is like thanksgiving dinner. Everybody is already seated at the table. There are no seats left. If you want to eat some turkey, somebody is going to have to get up and give you his or her seat. That means they are going to go hungry. Most people are not willing to go hungry. So, it virtually never happens. It is impossible to get into the film game.

But, it doesn't have to be this way. People can share. Please can say, *"Sit here with me. You take half of my chair and half of my turkey."*

From my personal perspective, I have always tried to help everybody that I could. If more of the world was like this, think how much better of a place this would be.

Liar

Whenever I teach a course or a seminar on filmmaking, I always begin by explaining, *"What is the number one rule of filmmaking?" The number one rule of filmmaking is, "Everybody lies..."*

In the filmmaking industry, people generally lie to make their project appear to be more than what it is. Or, to make themselves more attractive to potential employers—to increase their value so they will get a new gig.

But, lying extends much further than the film industry. It is, in fact, rampant through out all levels of society.

Why do people lie? The main reason people lie is, (just like in the film industry), they want to appear to be something more, something better, something bigger than what they actually are. They want to appear to be younger, older, better, more accomplished, whatever...

What is the root cause of this? The root cause is that people are dissatisfied with themselves. They are unfulfilled. They have not accomplished all that they hoped that they would in life, and they have not become that pinnacle of all that is right, great, and revered by the world. Lying instantly makes someone: something more, something else. But, it is not real.

The problem with lying, (and we have all done it at one time or another), is that you are left with the lie that you have told. All of the rest of your relationship with the person or persons you have lied to becomes defined by that lie. From this, you must struggle to keep that lie alive, which makes all of life complicated. And, a complicated life is just as mess. It is hard to live.

I mean, who wants to have to struggle even more through life, simply because you have lied? Life is complicated enough.

Many people commit what may be called a, *"White lie,"* a small lie. But, a lie is a lie, no matter the size. It doesn't make it right.

We have all been lied to. When we find out the truth, it doesn't feel good; does it? So, why do it to other people?

The fact of the matter is, there are a lot of people out there who live their entire lives based upon lies. They tell them all of the time and think nothing of it.

Most people who lie do so for selfish reasons. Guys want to hook up with girls. Girls want to hook up with guys. People want to be accepted into new groups. People want to climb the corporate ladder. And, as previously stated, people want to be more accomplished than they actually are; etc., etc., etc... It each case, a lie is defined by what is not—by who you are not. But, no matter how much you lie about it, no matter how much you may think the end justifies the means, it does not. Because if you lie, you are basing your entire existence upon falsehood. And, no truth, no true sense of accomplishment, no inner peace, no self-realization, can come from that.

If the reason you are lying is that you are not all that you want to be, do one of two things. The most spiritual of these is to simply accept who you are and embrace it. But, if that is not enough for you, continually move towards obtaining your *end-goal*. Stop making excuses and telling lies, and work hard.

The main thing is, don't lie to get there. Because, though a lie may open a door, it may also get it slammed in your face, once the lie has been uncovered.

A simple honest life is just bettered. It is easier, and more livable. Be who you are. Be what you are. Stop lying.

Don't Psychoanalyze Me!

I was sitting having an afternoon latte' on the outdoor patio at *Starbucks* the other day and I could not help but hear a conversation that was taking place behind me. There was this guy using all of this *New-School* psychological jargon. He was telling the woman he was with how she felt, why she felt that way, why she did what she did, and who she was. The suspiring thing was, after she contested his appraisals a few times, (from which he would immediately come back at her with more, *"Big Word," mumbo-jumbo*), eventually she bought into what he was saying and agreed with him. How foolish she was? And, what a loser that guy was.

Have you ever noticed that whenever someone is telling you how you feel, why you feel that way, or why you act a certain way, all they are doing is describing themselves? I mean, I first realized this when I was in high school. It came to light when I was at a small gathering of friends on a Saturday night. We were sitting around this one girl's apartment in Hollywood and after we were done playing spin the bottle, we did that game where you tell people what you think about them. First of all, that is a real party killer... But anyway, my one friend begins to describe me. At first I was thinking, *"You really don't get me at all."* But, then I realized, he was totally describing himself.

Similar things have happened to me a few times since. In most cases this type of critique is brought on when somebody is either angry or frustrated, as, I guess, it is their method to release their tension. But universally, whatever they have said, was wrong, and all they really did was describe their own psychological state of mind.

Perhaps one of the most curious or interesting times this happened when there was this middle-aged guy who took one of my filmmaking courses at *Santa Monica College*. After the course was over, he begged and begged me to let him be a part of one of my films. I gave in. Now, the reason I hesitated letting him on the bus, (as my filmmaking buddy Don Jackson and I used to say), was that I could tell he was one of those unaccomplished people who sabotaged every chance he had and every relationship he was in. I mean, he was alone and miserable, taking night classes in his fifties. Anyway, as could be expected, he got mad at me for some foolish nondescript reason. He called up my voicemail, psycho analyzing me, telling me this and that about myself, and stating, *"You really don't like yourself,"* over and over and over. How wrong can anyone be. I love myself. ☺

Though he was totally wrong about me, what he did do was ideally describe himself. And, this is life. People want to project their own misery, ideologies, and psychology onto you. They want to think they know you. But, all they know is themselves. They do this style of projection as a means to attempt to control you.

Like that guy to that woman on the *Starbucks* patio. They do this to attempt to make themselves feel like they are something more. That they are a knower. They behave like this in an attempt to gain control; which, if they do get a rise out of the person, will make them feel like a whole and more. How sad is that?

A self-actualized, self-realized person does none of this. They let all people be who they are. And, simply because they may have read a few books, took a few courses, or simply learned some *key-words,* they do not waste their time or energy attempting to tell other people who and what they are. Why? Because all they do is live in the perfection of their own Life-Time.

The Learning Annex

The Leaning Annex is company that organizes education programs and puts together classes for adults that promise to help them in their career and overall evolution through life. In the early 2000s, I taught a few classes for them. There was always a problem...

Initially, the first class I taught for them all seemed to be working out very well. It was a class on independent filmmaking, of course. They provided me with a large auditorium in Santa Monica. Over one hundred people attended the class. In fact, it went so well, I didn't even have time to show the class examples of some of my *Zen Film* work and the works of others, as I normally do at the end of a class. This was due to the fact that there was so much class interest, discussion, and participation.

One of the interesting experiences of this class was that one of the participates, a young girl from Texas, who had come to L.A. to get into films, blurted out. *"I want to be in one of your films. I'll take my top off!"* Everyone chuckled, including me.

Though the girl and I got together and had drinks to disuse upcoming projects. And man, that girl could drink! Just the way I like *'em*. She drank *round-for-round* with me. In fact, she insisted on a few more rounds. But, nothing ever came to pass with her being in one of my films, as she seemed to following a career more along the path of becoming a film extra rather than an actual actress. I through that was unfortunate, because she had a great look and presence—something that is essential for an actress.

In any case, *the Leaning Annex* promises to pay their instructors within thirty days. The preverbal check was never in the mail, however. So, I called them. They explained that the company had recently changed hands and I would be paid someday. That someday never came. Though they, of course, took in all the money from the one hundred plus participants that took my class.

A few months later, they asked me to teach another class for them. I'm a forgiving sort by nature, so I looked at the first class as simply karma yoga. I agreed.

The next class, they did not provide me with the promised T.V. and VCR, however. And, the class was located at some horrible hotel in Marina Del Rey. Plus, they gave the class no P.R. So, there were maybe fifteen or twenty people in it.

The class itself went fine. I believe the people learned something. But, I was thinking, *"No more..."*

Again, thirty days passed, and I wasn't paid. I called and they made all kinds of excuses and were pretty rude to me. But finally, a month or so later, they did actually send me a very small check. Not the amount that was promised. Whatever...

In 2002 I was teaching at *Santa Monica City College. The Learning Annex* in San Francisco had heard about me and called to see if I would teach a class for them. I told them about my previous experiences with the payment situation, but they promised it would be different up there. Reluctantly, I agreed.

The class was well publicized and it was held in a banquet room at a four star, central city hotel. I made reservations to stay at the same hotel, drove up there, and was all set. For dinner the night of the class, I walked across the street to this 50s style diner and all was good.

Class time came round and the students began pouring in. *The Learning Annex* even sent a very pretty Asian girl to check people into the class and/or to have them pay the appropriate fee if the participants had not prepaid. All good. The only thing they forget was that I needed a chalkboard to write on. But, they fixed that problem by getting me a very large manila paper tablet set upon an easel.

I kept all my scribbles on those pages for a time, thinking I would make it an artwork. But eventually, I tossed it.

The class was overly filled—over-full but it went great. The next morning, I made the five or *six-hour* drive back to L.A., as I had a class to teach in Santa Monica that evening.

The problem... Time passed. No payment. I called. Again, verging on the rude, they made all kinds of excuses. They told me they lost all the paperwork. *"What!"* I exclaimed, *"You even had a girl signing people in."* *"Yeah, but we don't remember who she was."* *"What!"*

Eventually, post a number of phone calls they decided to pay me the minimal amount for teaching a class. This, when it is their policy to pay their instructors per the number of students that attend a class. Thus, I got screwed by them again. My plan was to never teach for *the Learning Annex* again.

The funny thing is, a few years went by and they called me to teach a series of three classes for them in San Francisco. *"No thanks."* I told them the story of how they had ripped me off every time I taught for them. But, I don't think that they heard me.

A month or so later, I was bouncing around San Francisco. My friend and I were going to have lunch at *Johnny Rockets* on Chestnut Street and I saw a stack of *The Leaning Annex's* booklets in a paper machine on the street. I grabbed a copy and looked through it as we ate. There it was, a photo of me and a description of the class I was to teach. *"Are you kidding?"*

Anyway, I was obviously a no-show for that class. They called me up all angry, *"Why didn't you show up? The class was full."* I let them talk to the voice mail.

They were angry with me when they had screwed me over, not once, but three times. I mean, come on...

But, what is even more ridiculous, with me not showing up for the first class, is that they started calling me the next month, for the second class that they had me scheduled to teach. They were telling my voice mail how it was sold out, how they couldn't wait for me to teach, etc., etc., etc.

I didn't show up. Of course, I got the angry phone calls again.

But, then comes the third month, for the third class, and the same thing takes place all over again. I mean, how ridiculous is that!

You see, this is the absurdity of life and the nonsensicalness of the *powers-that-be*. They want to control you. They want you to serve them. When you get smart, and you don't serve their needs any longer, they get mad at you.

The sad thing is, most people find themselves dominated by these *powers-that-be* throughout their life.

Most people want to be something, they want to achieve something, they want to do something, but they cannot, because they are controlled by these external forces that, in actuality, have no idea what they are doing. And, in fact, these powers don't care. They don't care what affect they are having on you. All they care about is that they have a job, that they are doing what they want to do, and that they are getting paid.

Though I know it is a difficult life situation, my only thoughts on this subject are to try to step out of this pattern and devise a life where you are the only one having control over you.

The Leaning Annex... I guess, for me, it fulfilled its purpose. I learned to never work/teach for people who don't possess the honor to stand up to their promised commitments.

You Can Only Play In Your Own Playground

Every now and then I am asked, *"What do I think about Wikipedia?"* Though I don't really think about it at all, I guess, I do have an opinion.

When I first heard about Wikipedia, when it was launched, I thought what a great idea; taking all of the knowledge of everybody and putting it into one place. But, the reality of what has emerged is a bit different. Wikipedia is not based on the knowledge but the opinions of everybody, or more particularly the opinion of a person or persons who is willing to fight to get their ideology at the forefront.

It is an opinion based website. Not a fact based source of knowledge—like say a traditional encyclopedia.

For example, I was watching TMZ a few weeks ago and a couple of the people on the show were having a disagreement. One of them immediately put their opinion on Wikipedia and told the other person to look at it.

This illustrates the basis of Wikipedia. Anybody can say anything. And, if it is not challenged, it will remain there as fact.

Way back when it was in its early stages, I was popping around the site one day. I found that Steven Seagal's page was just basically a rip on him. Now, I have no feelings about Seagal one way or the other. I just found that the amount of incorrect and misleading statements that were made on the page was not right. So, I cleaned it up, added some true facts, and so on. I also cleaned up a few other pages, as well.

What I quickly came to find, however, is that there are people on Wikipedia who monitor specific pages and they only want them to reflect the way that they think—whether it is right or wrong.

It is not fact; it is simply the way they see it. And, they will fight to the bitter end to get their point across, even though it may be incorrect.

In fact, if you watch the site, some people are just going around causing all kinds of controversy. I guess that makes them feel alive. I do not know. But, though it may make them feel alive, it does not mean that their actions are justified or necessary.

I think the people who do this are the one's who are not really living life. And, Wikipedia gives them a place to have their voices heard. I mean, if these people were teaching classes, writing books, loving their jobs, raising a family, doing whatever—not only would they not have the time to fight their battles on Wikipedia but they would not care to do so.

Ultimately, I decided, *"What was the point? I have better things to do with my life than to waste my time and fight meaningless battles on the Internet."*

A funny occurrence happened in regard to me, (I guess you can say, in regard to me), on Wikipedia a few years ago.

One of my Black Belt students, from the late 1970s and early 1980s, was contributing to Wikipedia periodically. He contacted me and told me he had been banned from Wikipedia by someone who claimed that he was the same person as somebody else, using different screen names. The funny part of this was, the person who made this accusation, claimed the group of people all contributed to film pages associated with me and particularly to a *Zen Filmmaking* page.

But, the truth be told, this guy hates my films! And, he only contributed to martial art pages on Wikipedia. In fact, even the accuser said the edits were all made via different editing styles. Whatever that means... But, a Wikipedia administrator, (I guess they are called that), looked through all the contributions and said it was a hard decision to make, but bannered the entire group of five or six contributors. Some who had not been on Wikipedia in years.

What it boiled down to was, the group of banned contributors were all people who had made edits to the page about me on the site. So, the person who started this ruckus was out to jab at me, for whatever reason, not the contributors. How foolish. And, what a waste of time.

Anyway, I am told, two of the banned people made statements that they worked together at some film studio and actually liked my films and my *Zen Filmmaking* style. Amazing, somebody out there actually likes my movies. ☐

In any case, my friend/student tried to contest the block and got some harsh reprimand from an administrator. He later told me that he looked up the guy's page and the guy had since retired as an administrator as he was going off to college. And, the one who made the judgment was still in high school when it was made. So, these people were in high school when they had been given the task to pass judgment on other people.

Now, I am not saying that teenagers are not competent decision makers. When I was sixteen, I thought I was living like an adult. But, the reality is, until you get out there on your own, are living your own life, and have decided what your life actually is—how can you pass judgment on others?

I have heard in reports on the news, that it has been proven that some of the administrators on Wikipedia have turned out to be as young as thirteen years old. I mean, what kind of encyclopedia has *thirteen-year-old* administrators?

Perhaps the funniest, or most revealing, part of all this is, apparently the administrator who took down the *Zen Filmmaking* page on Wikipedia was shortly thereafter banned from Wikipedia for using multiple accounts to get their own agenda met. And, another administrator apparently hid the page where the person who worked at the film studio, and dug what I was doing, contested their block.

I am told, you really have to know how to search Wikipedia and get behind these blocks to find this information. So, somebody behind the scenes knew this was all wrong.

As for my student/friend, all he had to do was to set up another account name if he wanted to contribute to Wikipedia again. And, anybody can put another *Zen Filmmaking* page up on Wikipedia if they want to and are willing to fight for it if they run into this type of situation again.

The point of this discussion... You can only play in your own playground. The world out there is full of children and people with *child-like* egos who are willing to fight to get their point across. If you go into battle with them, you can fight and you can win. But, what will that mean to your life? Will you be able to accomplish what you really want to accomplish? Or, will you waste all of your Life-Time fighting with people that are not even worth the trouble?

Play in your own playground. Then you have some control.

The Funky Cuts Barber Shop

Recently, in one of my articles, I discussed a movie that I was in that was filmed in the Philippines but never saw the light of day. That was not the only one. I did a big movie in Japan that I have no idea of what ever became of it. Here in the States, I also did a couple of films, with fairly high budgets, and I have no idea what happened to them, as well. As an actor, I have had small roles that I performed end up on the cutting room floor. This is not unusual as big productions film a lot of footage and add a lot of small characters. Some of those characters make the cut, some do not. I would, of course, have liked it to go the other direction but it was not my rodeo so I had no say in the matter.

That fact is, there are a lot of films that are made, I have known of some productions with major stars attached, but they never found their way into distribution. It's just the nature of the beast. These facts are something that many people outside of the industry do not understand.

This is one of the main reason I got into production so early in my career, I wanted a say it what happened to the movie. This is also a lesson I teach my students as a filmmaking instructor and a warning I give to newbie actors who arrive in Hollywood—many a low budget production may go up but very few are finished. In fact, this is one of the primary reasons that I developed *Zen Filmmaking*. Yes, it initially organically arose out of the collaboration between Donald G. Jackson and myself when we were making *Roller Blade Seven* but from there I formalized it. Where Don was chaos, I was organized chaos. ...I did this so those filmmakers would have a method and means to actually get their film finished and not allow it to get lost in all of the over-reaching dreams and aspirations that many a young filmmaker has that cause them to shut down their production and not finish their movie.

All this being said, last night I remembered back to one of my first starring roles. It was a senior project made by a filmmaker graduating from USC. It was called, *The Funky Cuts Barber Shop.*

Here in L.A., prior to the domination of the internet, producers would put out casting notices in a weekly newspaper called, *Dramalogue.* Every week, all of the new and the established actors could bypass their agent and submit to these productions. I did it too. Thus, I got the lead role.

As schools like USC (obviously one of the major filmmaking school in the country) teach advanced levels of filmmaking, the students who attend need to make their own film productions. These student films were and are a great place for new actors to get their feet wet. Again, as I always tell my filmmaking students, these student films are in many ways a far better place to get your acting chops perfected because, unlike low budget films, they are assured of being completed, as they have to be if the student wants to pass the class.

Anyway, the film was a fun introduction into the realms of *No-Budget Filmmaking.* In fact, I got to work with a very established actor, who had co-starred in a number of major films. Not to mention even members of the band Parliament/Funkadelic can be seen in the film playing music. It was a good experience.

A few months after filming I got a call from Brian, the director, telling me about the screening. It was the end of the year screening for all of the graduating USC students of that class. It was a big event with a lot of people in attendance. There were several films shown and then came, *The Funky Cuts Barber Shop*. I got top billing, even over the more established actor. It was a great feeling. Afterward, people I didn't even know were telling, *"Great job. Great performance."* Total ego booster. ☺

In any case, Don and I went up on *Roller Blade Seven* a short time later. I really took the sensibilities that I learned while working on this film into the production of *Roller Blade Seven*. Realizing that you do not need big money to make a fun movie you just need people that care.

But... Back to the point of all this... Just like the films I was in that were lost to *Hollywood never-never-land,* this film too is lost to the archives of the film vaults of USC. I saw it once and never saw it again. So, if any of you people out there know about how to tap into those vaults and get me a screening, I would love to see it again. I'm thinking it was for the class of 1990?

How Little You Know of the Truth

I was having coffee with a friend of mine this afternoon and another friend of ours happened by. We are all in the film game so we were discussing filmmaking. The guy who showed up late made the joke, *"Shouldn't we discuss something else?"* His joke made me think of that scene in the industry parody movie, *The Player,* where one of the main characters suggested the same thing. In the film, everyone at the table then goes silent as they looked at each other for a moment. Then, they all laughed and realized they knew nothing else to talk about. Certainly, my friends and I are not like that but the joke did send me to remembering…

We were talking for a while and then the one guy remembered he had seen some discussion on the internet about *Zen Filmmaking* and he wanted to know if what one person said was true. He asked if I wanted to see it. I said, *"Not really,"* but he pulled it up on his phone and showed it to me anyway. Once again, as I am so often reminded, people talk and talk on the internet but they have no factual basis for their discussion; i.e. what the aforementioned poster said was false. The fact is, if the people weren't just flat out insulting *Zen Filmmaking,* Don or myself, pretty much every observation and every supposed fact they were stating was simply wrong. What else is new? Welcome to the internet.

Personally, I don't really care but it is a good thing to use an example. Mostly, I think it is so sad that people use the unsubstantiated words of other people as a basis for their own so-called knowledge. …Knowledge that is not based in fact, it is simply based in interpersonal bullshit. That is <u>not</u> knowledge!

I always believe in people but *time-after-time* I am let down as I witness that most of what people speak is nothing more then self-propelled sources of emotional outbursts based upon what is missing in their own life, (as well worded as some of those outbursts may be), and/or simply flat out unsubstantiated opinions that are presented as fact. But, these people don't know the facts! They don't know me and they didn't know Don, so how can they have any true understanding about *Zen Filmmaking* or what motivated the various Zen Films?

I wrote a piece that touched on this a little while back, *"Zen Filmmaking: The Good, The Bad, and The People That Don't Know What the Fuck Their Talking About."* But, it seems that nothing ever changes, people want to gain fame by analyzing the works of other people; i.e. in this case me. They want to improve on their lacking sense of self-importance by looking like they know what they're talking about. But, they don't! All they speak is simply based upon emotion and judgment. And, that is the most horrible place to be operating from.

If what you say or what you do causes one person to say or do one negative thing then you are the source of an avalanche of negativity as that emotion will breed. Just as if you are the source for one person to say or do a positive deed you are the source for an avalanche of positivity. Looking at your life, looking at your karma, which do you think is better? But, most people don't think, they just act and react. Again, this is not a good place to be operating from.

I don't mean this piece to be about me. Because it really is not. And, I've stated my case about what I believe a million times. But, I mean this style of unsubstantiated bullshit is all over the internet; about every subject and every person. People should be more than that! People should be caring and doing actual verbal and physical things for other people that will very precisely make the life of other people better. But, I guess some do not have the mental aptitude for that.

Anyway... If I can take it back to a personal perspective for a moment to illustrate that point... None of these people who speak about me do anything for me. Are they making my life any better? No. Do they even thank me for providing them with a basis for something to discuss? No. So, what is their purpose? What is the purpose of their life? If all you do is discuss something else or someone else, that you have no true knowledge about, that leaves you with nothing more than a life based upon someone else's reality and your interpretation of it. Thus, all you are is a slave.

You know, I always tell everyone to go out and make your own art. Do what it is in life that you really want to do. Be your own person. Find your own greatness. But, you will never do that by climbing up on the shoulders of someone else. All that does is make you bound to that relationship.

Now, people who partake in this style of internet activity generally spread their ideals and opinions all across the internet. If any of you have ever been on the receiving end of an internet lie or an internet attack, then you probably will understand what I am speaking about when I say all it does is created a lot of wasted emotional energy. But, who created that melodrama? Was it you?

Probably not. It was the other person with nothing better to do than to attack your life. And, that is just wrong!

So, what does this leave us with? If you are reading this article you are probably a person who takes caring about other people and human consciousness seriously. You are probably not out there judging and placing your faulty interpretations and fraudulent facts onto the life of others while trying to make yourself famous by dong so. Thus, you are probably not damaging the life of others. And, that is good! You have not fallen prey to the illusion of the lawless internet.

The fact is, what you do in life; what you say, effects not only you but everyone. It creates your reality and it influences the reality of those you talk to and those you talk about. It creates your karma. If all you do is waste your time judging and talking about things you do not truly understand than you will find yourself at the end of your days having accomplished nothing and having helped no one. Is that where you want to end up? Or, if you choose to be sucked into the world of not caring about what you do or whom you may hurt then your life will follow your own self-proclaimed path towards destruction. That's just the way it is.

At any point in your life have you ever taken a moment and actually put your own emotions aside and stood up for someone you were mad at or didn't like? Try it. Believe me, it will change the way you view the world.

As I always say, care more about others than yourself. Take others into consideration before you do anything. Never hurt anyone. From this, not only will your life become better but the whole world will become a better place, as well.

Care before you do. Think before you speak.

Killing the Relationship

Throughout all of our lives each of us desires to do and/or to become something. But, to become what we hope to be, we need training. In virtually all instances, someone needs to show us how to do the something that we want to do. If we listen, we can learn. If we do not, we cannot. This is the crux of why so few people achieve what they hope to accomplish in life. Their ego keeps them from being able to learn from the someone who can teach them.

I often speak about, *"Disciple Consciousness,"* and how it is a necessary element of life if you truly hope to gain the elemental insight necessary to reach advanced levels of understanding. This is the case for spiritual advancement, physical advancement, (for example in the martial arts), onto gaining the necessary knowledge of how to paint, play music, make movies, or do anything else where there is an actual craft involved. The problem is, everyone is so full of themselves that they skip this step. From this, most of the world's populous never achieves what they hope to achieve as they do not possess the fundamental knowledge to reach their higher goals. What kept them from it? Their ego.

Now, I am not saying that you have to bow down before all of those who are your senior, like say in the guru/disciple relationship. But, what you do have to do is to be able to shut your ego-driven mind down long enough to understand that there are people who have walked the path before you and may be able to guide you in how you can achieve your own dream of doing.

In terms of filmmaking, which is obviously a big part of my life, I discussed the fact in my book, *Independent Filmmaking: Secrets of the Craft,* that, *"There can only be One Captain of the Ship."* For if there are too many cooks in the kitchen not only do unnecessary disagreements arise but the vision gets convoluted. And, that is never a good thing. This, *"Too many cooks in the kitchen,"* has caused many an independent feature film to fail.

This also lends insight into the faulty personality of some people as they quest to live their dream of filmmaking. While they are still a novice, their ego gets involved and they feel like what they think they know should be taking place or that they are somehow being treated unfairly. But, this all goes back to the framework of, *"Disciple Consciousness"* and, *"One Captain of the Ship."* If the novice can't turn their ego off long enough to learn, they will never learn.

In fact, a few times people have come to me formally seeking to learn the craft of Independent Filmmaking and to have me be their introduction into the actual filmmaking process but their ego got in the way, they had a meltdown, and where are they today? They've never made a film. In other cases, people have come to me, they did learn they craft, and they did make a film.

It is important to note that I am using filmmaking as an obvious example. But, this same mindset spans to all realms of life and learning.

From a personal perspective, I was always willing to learn from the people who had something to teach me. Maybe I didn't personally like or appreciate everything that was going on but I turned my ego off. From this, when it was time, I was able to break out on my own and live my own vision. But first, I was the student.

This is an essential element to ponder as you pass through life and come upon new things that you hope to accomplish. Be willing to be the student. Be willing to listen to what someone else has to say. Be egoless enough to learn. For if you are never a student you can never be the master.

Seeing Yourself
Through the Eyes of Other People

Some people do all that they can to be liked by others. If someone they know likes something, they like it. If someone they know dislikes something, they too dislike it. Though somewhere deep down inside they may have their own opinion, they hide it from others so that they will be liked.

Other people are forceful in what they think and what they feel. From this, they are the ones that shape the mind of the weak who are too busy seeking acceptance to express what they truly feel. They are also the ones who attract very few close relationships as they drive everyone away by their pig headedness.

Most everyone else falls somewhere in between these two extremes.

Each of us sees the world the way we see the world. Some of us are more outspoken about how we perceive life, while other are most passive in their opinion. Whatever the case, inside each of us we see what we see, we feel what we feel, and we think what we think we know. Whether what we think that we know is right or wrong is almost unimportant as it is what we feel and that is what we base our life choices upon. This is especially the case when it comes to people. We think we know who people are. We think we know what other people think. But, for the most part, unless you truly-truly know a person, your opinion is a guess at best. If you truly think you know a person, the probability is you are far off base when it comes to truly understanding what makes their mind work and what is the motivating factor for them doing what they do.

I recently flashed back to a memory from high school. This memory reminded me of the first time that I actually experienced someone attempting to describe who and what I was. I was in tenth grade and I was invited to a small gathering at a female friend's nearby apartment. We were sitting around doing what teenagers do and someone came up with the bright idea that we should each describe one another the way we think that they are. In a group therapy session this may have been fine, but man, did that exercise go wrong. The host got very pissed at the way people described her. Me, I never really cared what people thought about me, but what struck me was the way a very close friend of mine described me. He was totally off base. I realized, we hung out all the time, and he didn't know me at all. And, that's the thing about life, even the people who are close to you may not truly understand you. Then, there are all the other people out there who don't personally know you at all and yet they are casting all kinds of judgments about you. Welcome to life…

As someone who has been in the public eye for a quite awhile I have heard people come to all kinds of conclusions about me. Most of them are far-far out in left field. Yet, that is what they believe. From this, that is what they speak. For me, I find it interesting to view how other people see me. This, even when they are totally wrong. It provides me with a microscope into human psychology and how certain people project their own shortcomings onto other people. For almost universally, the people who assume they know who I am or why I do what I do project their own insecurities into the equation. This is psychology 101. This is simply what certain people do.

On the other side of the coin there have been people who have used the idealized image of Scott Shaw and what Scott Shaw supposedly does as a source for parody. There was a filmmaking team, at a Midwestern university, about ten years who did a whole mockumentary on *Zen Filmmaking* using an actor portraying me as the primary character.

I had never met or spoken with any of them. The only contact I had, on any level, was when one of the participants, prior to doing the shoot, (and, of course, not telling me anything about it), contacted me via Myspace and asked about where I got the Chupacabra costume. When I told him that it was professionally created and it was stupid expensive that was the last I heard. Later, somebody told me that the series was up on YouTube. You can find a link to it on my YouTube page. But, that was the first time I heard anything about it. And, I never heard from any of the cast or crew again. I hope they made their filmmaking dreams come true. But, I don't know? I don't even know their names...

Anyway, in that mockumentary they present a certain vision of me and to a lesser degree Donald G. Jackson. It is comedic. But, is it me? No. Was it Don? No.

Again, they never met me, they never spoke to me, yet they used me to present an image of myself and *Zen Filmmaking*. Good thing I have a sense of humor.

And, this goes to the whole point, people think that they know a person. People think that they know what motivates a person. But, they do not.

A few years after the mockumentary was released somebody contacted me, as he was interested in creating a theatrical biopic film of Don and my life and our *Zen Filmmaking*. I laughed as I told him it had already been done.

In the martial arts, I have watch as some people have described me and some of the people I actually know very well through a very limited, self-motivated, perspective. Why some martial artists base so much of their life on juvenile criticism, based upon internal self-insecurity, I do not know. But, it has gone on forever and it still goes on. It is ridiculous. All they try to do is cast shade on other practitioners. They should be embracing and respecting one another. But, some do not. I wrote a couple of article on this subject over the past years or so: *The People Who Never Evolve* and *Understanding the Black Belt.*

But again, this all goes back to the fact of people thinking that they know another person when they do not... At least the *Zen Filmmaking* mockumentary was not based upon a position of mean spiritedness. It was a fun-based portrayal. But, other people just want to throw their own personal opinions around and claim that they are facts— believing they have the right to judge a person. But, do they?

Think about this... Pull somebody you know out of your hat—anybody... What do you think about them? Do you think you truly know them? Look deeper into that concept. Do you really know them or do you just think that you know them?

Do they think that they know you? If they were to describe you, the way my teenage friends and I did all those years ago, how right about you would they be?

In fact, sit down and have a comparison session with that person. Have them describe you and then you describe them. How right where they in describing you? How right were you? Were their thoughts and perceptions correct or false? Were your thoughts and perceptions correct or false? And, what did you not reveal to them? What will they never know about you? What will you never know about them?

Life is complex. Personalities are complex. People are who they are to the world, then they are who they are to their friends and lovers, and then they are who they are only in their own inner mind. You can free yourself by being only the Whole You all the time. But, that is almost an impossible feat as you have to take other people into consideration in all that you say and/or do. Moreover, instead of thinking you know another person, instead of judging them verbally or in your mind, simply let them be perfect in their own space—whatever that space may be. From this, you can focus on your own evolution of consciousness and not waste time thinking about what you think about others that is probably wrong anyway.

Do You Remember the TV Show Punk'd?

Do you remember the TV show that Ashton Kutcher did on MTV a few years back, *Punk'd?* If you don't, what took place is that he and his team would go around and create these elaborate pranks on celebrities making them think something very serious was taking place when it was, in actuality, nothing but a ruse. Anyway, it felt like that happened to me today.

To tell the story, I was kicking back on the patio having a *Venti Flat White* and eating some of their very tasty popcorn at my local Starbucks this afternoon as I frequently tend to do. And, these *Zen Filmmakers* had stalked me to the location. ...I guess I should be more secretive about what I do and where I do it but in this modern day and age it is pretty easy to find out anything about anybody unless they are totally off the grid, which I obviously am not.

Anyway, I noticed a couple of young guys going and sitting down behind me. Didn't really think much of it. There's a high school nearby and that Starbucks often attracts many a student after school. A few minutes later this young guy walks up, pulls out a chair, and sits down at my table. He then went into this whole scene about sharing a drink out of this bottle of ranch dressing he had. He took a drink and offered it to me. He was very convincing. Great actor! Never lost character. Personally, I initially assumed that he had eaten some acid and was just tripping. As I have seen many a person do many a strange thing while on acid. But, a few minutes into it, he extends his hand to shake mine. His friends step in and reveal who and what they are. I loved it! Great job!

They had filmed the scene from behind my head and they asked me if they could do the turn around shot and get my reaction. For obvious reasons I said, *"No,"* and explained there is a number of reasons why I couldn't do that. But, I totally loved what they did! True *Zen Filmmaking* in its purist form!

If they hadn't been so young, I would have suggested that we go out and make an entire film together. But, in terms of legality, it gets really touchy when you work with someone under the age of eighteen.

But, it's great to witness the craft of *Zen Filmmaking* moving on, growing, expanding, and encountering new interpretations. Rock on guys! You are great!

The Personality of Philosophy

I came upon an interview that this one friend of my longtime *Zen Filmmaking* partner Donald G. Jackson had recently given where he discusses Don. I found it really sad that this guy actually knew Don longer than I did but he simply categorized him as incompetent filmmaker. He totally missed the point...

Now certainly, Don was a psychologically complicated narcissist who, due to his behavior, made a lot of enemies. But, he was far from an incompetent filmmaker. He was a philosophy-based filmmaker. And, that is the point I think many people miss about the man—I know this misunderstanding has occurred to me, as well.

I have spoken about this a lot over the year, but most people view all movies from a place of judgment. Very few people watch simply to see the art. They watch movies with a preconceived notion of what is to come next. They judge and compare any movie that they are currently watching with all of those they have seen before—particularly those with a very high budget where nothing more than the philosophy of making money was employed. But, a true aficionado of film does not frame their basis for judgment on dollars and cents. In fact, they don't judge at all. They simply watch and witness. The fact is, if you want to truly appreciate art, (whatever that art form may be), you need to see any creation for what it is, based upon its own reality of creation, and moreover, on the philosophy that it took to create it.

And... This is where the guy discussing Don completely missed the point. Don made his films based upon a philosophy of actualization. You may like or you may not like this philosophy, and what he created due to it, that is your choice. But, if you do not understand this as the entire basis for the films that Don created than you completely miss the point about the man as a filmmaker. Then, all you become is judge and jury. And, no one should judge art, that is just the wrong way to approach it.

I think this is a very important fact to think about as you pass through life, whenever you find yourself casting judgment. Who are you judging and why? What is the basis for your judgment? Do you know the facts about the person that you are judging? Do you actually understand the motivation for them creating art in the first place? And mostly, do you even comprehend the philosophy they were operating within when they were doing what they were doing—that thing you are casting judgment upon?

People who judge generally do not know, understand, or care about the facts of a person's philosophy. If they did, then there would be no judgment at all.

That's my judgment about judgment. ☺

Everybody Wants Something from Me but Nobody Ever Gives Me Anything

I have long made the semi-joking statement, *"Everybody wants something from me but nobody ever gives me anything."* But, when it comes right down to the reality of it, that is how my life has played out.

Recently, there have been a lot of people asking me if they can distribute Donald G. Jackson's or my films. ...This, at the point in history when distribution is exceedingly easy, anyone can set up a company, and do *print-on-demand*. But, do these people ever ask themselves, *"Why would I want them to make money distributing my films?"* Like the joking statement I have made as an actor in several of my films, *"What's in it for me?"* ...I mean, I own a distribution company, why do I need you? It is not like these people offer me vast amount of money. Then, it may be a different story. But, they do not. They just want what they want for free. ...Do you have any idea the amount of time, energy, creativity, and money it takes to make a movie? And, you expected me to give all that to someone I do not even know?

Here's where we reach one of the philosophic quandaries of life; i.e., people want what they want for free. They want what someone else has. They want what someone else has achieved. They want it, but they do not want to work for it. When they see someone with it, they either want to steal it or, if they have some-what of a conscience, they ask if they can have it.

My answer is, *"No."*

Throughout my life I have always been more than happy to help people. I have always been happy to take people along for the ride. I came of age in a time and a space of doing karma yoga AKA selfless service—doing something and expecting nothing in return. But, that does not mean giving someone my livelihood or letting them make money off of something they had nothing to do with creating.

But, times have changed from the days of caring about the well-being of others and doing karma yoga… People see the vastness of life and cyberspace and how taking what someone else has done and/or flat out stealing it has become easy and, in fact, the norm. But, this is just wrong! If you achieve anything in life by doing this, you have developed exceedingly bad karma. And, then what comes next?

Donald G. Jackson was the last person I can actually put my finger on who went out of his way to help me in a focused manner. But, there was a very high price to pay for that relationship. Yet, I made him a promise to keep his filmmaking legacy alive and I have done my best to do so. So, I hope I have repaid his actions.

Most people are not like that, however. They don't want to help anyone unless there is something in it for them. They want to take; they do not want to make. …And this is where all of the problems of the world arise.

So, how do you encounter life? Are you the point of inception? Or, are you the one trying to make a name for yourself or a dollar off of what someone else has created?

To all the people who thank me as an inspiration and think positive thoughts about me, thank you! To everyone else who wants something from me and offers me nothing in return, you should really rethink your life path.

Zen Filmmaking: The Good, The Bad, and The People That Don't Know What the Fuck They're Talking About

Ever since the inception of *Zen Filmmaking,* that was heralded with the release of *The Roller Blade Seven*, people have contacted me about my method of filmmaking. In the early days, it was largely via letters but soon after that everybody climbed onto the internet and then everybody had a lot to say.

There have been a lot of people, over the years, who have actually contacted me and questioned, how do I do what I do. Those are the people I respect. Love my films or hate my films, they are the ones who cared enough to ask me what was actually going on. They came to the source and inquired. And, going to the source is the only way to gain true knowledge.

Some of these people contacted me because they wanted to follow the path of *Zen Filmmaking.* That's great! Make it your own...

Early in my filmmaking career, (which you have to keep in mind did not begin until I was thirty-two years old so I had a lot of life-experience prior to that), I also began to see people coming to conclusions about what I did, how I did it, and why I did it. These discourses where then mostly entered into magazines that discussed the low budget, no budget, and cult level of filmmaking. In some cases, they got it right. But, in many, (in fact most), cases they were simply wrong. Yet, these people had a pulpit and from that pulpit they broadcasted their thoughts about *Zen Filmmaking, Zen Films,* and me out to the world.

As a professional researcher, I always found this method to be suspect, as these people were simply discussing their feelings that were not based in fact. Yet, they were presenting their opinions, observations, and speculations as if they were fact. This is truly the wrong way to put forward information to the world and this mindset is what has given birth to the whole culture of, *"Fake News,"* we are currently living within—as from these inaccurate depictions further counterfactual statements and misunderstandings are given birth to. People heard, *"This,"* and, thus, they believed, *"That."* But, it is all based on bullshit. It is all based on somebody putting what they think they know out there but they do not have the true facts as they have not done any actual research. I know... I get it... Research is hard to do. It is time-consuming and it often costs money. It is so much easier to just read or hear something and then believe what you want to believe. But, the fact is, if you want to know the truth about a subject, (any subject), research is the only way to arrive at a factual and valid conclusion. And, you must enter into any research gathering with an open mind and not use it as simply a way to justify what you think you already know.

Personally, in virtually all of the aforementioned cases, I found the discourses to be amusing. But, that's just who I am. I easily poke fun at myself. If they weren't flat out defamatory lies or someone making money off of one of my creations when they had no responsibility for its actualization, I was good.

On the larger scale, I have always wondered why do people do this? Why do people want to spread their feelings about something or someone and, moreover, why do they want to transmit something out to the world when what they are saying is not based in fact but is solely based upon personal opinion, second-hand knowledge, and/or speculation? Sure, I understand, most people like something or someone for some nondescript reason but that reason is generally based upon them not possessing a true understanding about anything. Thus, what does that reason for like or dislike truly mean? Do you ever think about that when you form your opinions and from your opinions make your judgments which leads to your statements?

As *Zen Filmmaking* is a defined form of filmmaking, many people have also taken aim at the craft. They have taken aim at it but all they know about it is that in *Zen Filmmaking* we do not use a script. But, there is a lot more to it than that. And no, *Zen Filmmaking* is not just about showing up somewhere and seeing what happens next. So, if you've heard that, if you've believed that, if you've rebroadcast that, YOU ARE WRONG!

Also, there have been a lot of people who have seen *Roller Blade Seven* or some clips from it and decided that was the epitome of *Zen Filmmaking* and all of my films are just like RB7. The fact is, a lot of people don't get what Donald G. Jackson and I were trying to do with *The Roller Blade Seven* and they hate it. I get it! That movie is weird! If you don't like weird movies you probably will hate it. But, think about this, we made that movie over twenty-five years ago—whatever you think about it: love it or hate; we did something right because people are still discussing it.

On a more personal note, occasionally I have seen some people say, *"Scott Shaw makes shitty movies,"* and stuff like that. Okay... That's what you think... But, how many of my movies have you actually seen? Many people make this comment after only seeing maybe *Roller Blade Seven* or *Max Hell Frog Warrior*. I have made a lot of movies! Honestly, how many of them have you seen? Have you seen any of my documentaries? Have you seen any of my music videos? Have you followed my filmmaking evolution and watched any of my *Non-Narrative Zen Films,* my *Zen Film Art Captures,* my *Zen Film Movies in the Moment,* or my *Zen Film Mind Rides?* If you haven't, then you have no idea what I'm doing. Moreover, if you have not read my written words on the subject of filmmaking, if you have not seen my interviews, if you have not met me, again, you are basing your opinion on a preconceived notion that you have no factual bases to possess. Love my movies, hate my movies, I get it... But, if you haven't seen my films, if you don't know my philosophy about filmmaking, if you have not actually spoken to me, then how can you judge anything?

And, this goes to the whole point of this piece... Sure, you're just a screen name out there in the nowhere of cyberspace. You will never have to pay for your cyber crimes. But, no matter what moniker you use, you should be whole enough to know the facts about what you're talking about before you ever spew your misunderstandings out to the world. In other words, BE MORE. For me, that is the key to life. That is how the people who have truly excelled and made a contribution to the world have done it. Care enough to care. Learn the true facts. Go to the source and ask before you speak. Be more than someone who talks about someone else, go out there and create your own something.

Why Would I Give You Money?

Recently, I've been thinking a lot about the interplay of human consciousness and they way people interact—how they behave towards one another and for what reason. As can be seen in this article and the ridiculously voluminous amount of my other writings, I think people should think about the other person first and care about the other person first. Okay... Simple enough. But, now what? Here we are in life and we want to do what we want to do.

I guess it's because I've made a number of films that I am often contacted by people who want me to finance their film. First of all, I don't do that. Even if I was rich enough, which I am not, I have so often seen the downside of what happens next when somebody gives someone money to make a movie.

Personally, I salute creativity. I love it on all levels. Art is one of the greatest things of life. But, here comes the next step, how do you get that art created as, especially in the film game, as it does cost some money?

The great thing about the era we currently live in is that filmmaking has become very affordable. I often discuss the times gone past and detail how expensive it was to make movies fifteen or twenty years ago. Now, it is very cheap. Yet, people don't want to earn the money to pay for their own creation. They want someone to give it to them. Why is that? Why don't they want to own the inception, the implementation, and the ultimate result? Well, maybe they do what to own the result. They just want to live the experience on someone else's dime.

Again, this goes to the entire interplay of human consciousness and how a particular individual sees the world. I have known many filmmakers, in this current day and age, that get out there, get the money, and make their movies. And, they do it on their own. They don't go to *indiegogo* or any other place. They do it themselves. There is something very respectable in that. There is something truly artistic in that. They have an artistic vision that they want to create and they get it done without turning to people they do not know to accomplish it. From this, whatever they create is free from the karma of, *"Owing."*

As I feel that I am often forced to state, "I pay for all of my films with my own money." Do I wish someone would give me a million dollar to make a movie? Sure! Hell, even a hundred thousand could make a great movie. With my experience in the game I could probably go out there, sell myself, and ask people to give me the money to make a movie, but I don't.

I think if you want art to be true art, especially in the early stages of your artistic career, you really need to prove that you care enough about your art to make it happen by yourself. That is the mark of a true artist.

So, how does this impact the study of human consciousness? If you seek outside people to make you what you are, how can you ever be yourself? Being yourself is the ultimate statement of an artist. Caring enough about the art that you hope to create to find a way to create it on your own, that is ultimate statement of artistic freedom.

Why Don't You Paint?

There is this one statement that you always here whenever you are in a museum or gallery where they are exhibiting abstract art, *"Anybody can do that."* I certainly have heard that about my art. It always makes me smile.

I was thinking back to when I used to live at this one place in Hermosa Beach. I had a really big kitchen and I would staple my large canvases to the wall when I painted. I would paint late into most every night. When I would go out of the country, and I was traveling all of the time back then, I would give my one friend the keys to my place so he could come over and get my mail and stuff. One day he was over, just before I was to leave, and he went into this long discourse about my art, abstract art in general, *"Your stuff is crap,"* the, *"Anybody can do that,"* thing, and why bother in the first place? I could have taken offense. But, I get it… A lot of people think that way. They see the world the way the world is expected to be seen and they don't waste their time or their money on anything else. And, believe me, if you paint you understand: paint and canvas and brushes and stuff can be very expensive.

Now, I've written a lot about art over the years. Certainly, not as profoundly as say Kandinsky and others. But, I get it… Art is art only truly in the mind of the artist. And, whether your art is painting, photography, jewelry making, filmmaking, or whatever, you may not find a large audience for what you're doing, especially if what you are doing is somewhere outside of the norm and you don't have a big gallery owner or publicist marketing your stuff to the world.

The fact is, people like to judge. And, the judgment of art is one of the easiest things anyone can do, even if they love art... They can simply hate an artist or an art piece and that is okay—no further explanation necessary.

But, on a more philosophical level, I think most people really need to shake their life up. They need to do this as most, go through life so contrived, so predictable. They never take a step into the world of the abstract. They never try to embrace something new and totally different. They never try to paint.

I think most people, if they pick up a brush try to make something; they expect to paint like the old-school masters. They want to do that kind of art, if they do art at all. But, that is expecting the near-impossible unless you go through years of training. But, what you can do is do the art of feeling. You can make color swirl—you can make nothing at all.

The fact is, even this style of art takes a little practice. Just like Zen, embracing the nothing takes a little time. But, life is so full of the, *"All that is."* It is so full of it that it is already there. So, taking a moment to do the nothing allows you to embrace a moment of unexpected excellence. It allows you to BE without try to be.

Now, to the critic, the traditionalist, or to the uptight individual, whose mind is already made up, they will have a million reasons not to try. If they did try, they would probably try to fail, so that they would not have to do it again. But, try this, remove your mind and your judgments from the equation—even if only for a moment. Take a brush, get some paper or a canvas, grab some paint and, like a child, simply express nothing with no intentions upon your page. I mean, really... Try it. It truly will give you a moment of meditative freedom and you may really find a new space of peaceful, passive expression that will give you an outlet for the artist in you that you never believed was there.

Yeah, maybe everyone can do it. But, everyone doesn't do it. Try it. You never know how it may change your life.

I'm An Artist, Goddamn It!

"I'm an artist, goddamn it! I don't have to rationalize, justify, explain, or defend anything that I do!" This is a bold statement that my *Zen Filmmaking* brother, Donald G. Jackson and I used to voice whenever we ran into some negativity or controversy about what we were doing. The main thing to know, however, is that this statement was made in fun. We always said it with a smile on our face. I suppose if you read it, this statement comes off as kind of harsh. But, it was not meant to be that way.

It was actually Don who first coined it. But, it became our mutual motto. So, we said it quite often.

Don, more than I, (at least in the early days), received much more criticism for his films and his filmmaking practices. Once he passed away, it became me who was awarded the crown and I became the focus. It is essential to note, however, as has always been the case, there are more people who liked what he and I did than those who did not. But, as also always seems to be the case in life, those who embrace negativity as their primary means of communication, those who look for faults rather than merit, are the most vocal. Wrong, I believe. But, such is life…

Anyway, I believe I put this statement in my book, *Zen Filmmaking,* and I have been told it was quoted a few times, in various places, by people trying to cast shade on me for writing it. I mean come on… Those people who want to base their lives upon criticism always look for something to criticize. This is true in the film game, in the film watcher game, and everywhere else.

Me, I always question, *"Why?"* Why do you, why does anyone, wish to focus their life in seeking out the flaws instead of looking to the perfection of the process? Why??? The world is beautiful, people are beautiful, artistic creations are beautiful, if you just let them be.

Anyway, this statement really goes to the greater whole of anyone who is following the path of creation and/or art; because, as stated, there will be those people out there seeking out your flaws. If you are an artist, you need to be an artist. You need to create your art as you envision your art. That is what true creativity is all about. And, to anyone who wants to criticize it, screw 'em. Let's see what they have created. And then, let's throw some criticism their direction, see how they respond.

In other words, be strong in your art. Do what you do and not care about what others think. If they are so vocal to have the time to waste, simply talking about other people and other things that has nothing to do with them, that means they are not doing anything worth while with their own life in the first place.

In For the Long Haul

As we pass thorough life we encounter many people. Some turn out to be essential parts of our ongoing evolution and others do not. Some we believe can help us achieve our dreams while others we see as only an obstacle. It is essential to note, however, there is a fine line between someone who can help us and someone who we see as a hindrance. And, this choice between the two is commonly formulated by an untrained mind.

In life, we see something we want and we set about on a course to achieve it. Some people are very fervent in what they want and they go after it with everything they've got. Most people are not like that, however. They may have a desire to be something or achieve something but their process is undefined and sporadic at best, so their dreams are never lived.

When we want something we place ourselves in an environment where we can find it. This may mean seeking out a teacher, taking a course, or interacting in certain circles where we may meet someone who can help us on our way. In these situations, when we do meet someone who may help us on our quest, we begin to interact with this person in a very specific manner and this is what sets the stage for our ongoing evolution.

The thing that must be kept in mind, however, is that people are ego-based creatures. From this, they bring their ego into any relationship. The older the person is, the bigger and more defined their ego. From this, long term interactions with any individual becomes more-and-more difficult as one passes through their life. Meaning, the young are much more accepting and less judgmental then those with age. Therefore, when you desire to do something and you meet someone who may help you achieve it, if you bring an access amount of personal ego into the relationship it may make the interaction very short lived and from this you may never learn what you needed to learn from the person and, thus, you may never become what you actually desired to become.

Becoming takes time. Becoming takes focus. Becoming takes humbleness and self-restraint before you finally develop the knowledge and the understanding to be what you hoped to be so that you can move forward on your own.

Most people never achieve their dreams because they are ego-motivated. Many feel that they are equal to the person they initially sought out for help and guidance and from this ego-based decision making process they choose to leave the relationship before they had the chance to learn the subtleties of what they hoped to learn. Their logic for leaving can be defined by any number of reasons. And, in most cases, these people possess all kinds of self-defined arguments. They may even bad mouth the person of whom they were once the apprentice. But, if they leave via their ego, before their times of study was complete, they do not emerge with the skillset to go out on their own and actually do what they dreamed of doing. Thus, their ego kept them from achieving.

What this means is that if you truly hope to accomplish something you must be willing to put your ego in check. You must be willing to step back and let someone else dominate the situation for a time. Then, once you have learned the craft, through time, you can step forward into your own light and be what you hoped to become.

In my life, two individuals come to mind that came into my life and truly helped become who I wanted to be. Though, interacting with each of them did present a challenge. The first was one of my primary martial arts instructors, Hee Won Yoon. He was a great-great martial arts technician. But, as anyone who has ever been in business with a Korean will tell you, that relationship will be sticky at best. The guy was a problem. But, through years of interaction I truly gained an exacting sense of teaching the martial arts. The other was my *Zen Filmmaking* brother, Donald G. Jackson. This guy… A psychologically messed-up egomaniac. But, what he did have was a never ending surplus of film financing, without which we could never have made the films that we did.

The point being, there is always a price to pay if you want to achieve. Those who do achieve do so by staying the course, by being in for the long haul. If you allow your ego and your misplaced sense of self-worth to force you from a relationship, that could truly lead to your achievement, then you will never become what you hoped to be.

In other words, you have to control your ego. You may not like some (or all) of the things a person does or the way they behave but you must keep your eye on the bigger picture. You must understand that life is not all about you and how you feel in any given moment. Life is about you learning and then becoming, not about you simply desiring to be something but never truly taking the steps to get there.

What do you want to become? What steps are you taking to get there? If you feel you are already something, what foundations do you have to make your claim?

Foundations are the steppingstone to life. Are you willing to lay yours?

This is Time

As anyone who reads my writings or knows anything about me understands, I've written a lot about comprehending and coming to terms with the concept of time. Certainly, the Master Text on the subject is my book, *Zen O'clock: Time to Be.* I wrote that book in the mid 1980s. It was first published, by an independent publisher, in the late 80s with the title, *"Time,"* and later by a major publisher in '97. Since then it has been translated into a bunch of languages and distributed around the world. Donald G. Jackson, my *Zen Filmmaking* brother, liked the intro. to that book so much that he read it as the invocation for the faux-wedding in *The Roller Blade Seven.* All this being said, I believe that one of the essential questions to life, that each person must frequent ask themselves is, *"How am I experiencing and dealing with the passing of time?"*

For each of us, there is a prescribed amount of time that we will be here in our physical bodies. Many people hold onto the hope and the belief that there is some forever out there, where we will be the best incarnation of ourselves and our souls will live on forever. Maybe... But, nothing is guaranteed. As such, what we live here and now, in these ever-aging bodies, is all we have to hold onto. We, as living human beings, are elementally defined by the passing of time.

When we are young there is the undefined belief that we have forever. Many of us never think about the passing of time. We do what we do when we do it and time just passes on. For most people there comes a moment of realization when they conclude, time has passed, they are getting older, they do not have forever, and, as such, they must truly focus upon what they are doing with their time and how they are living their life. Some, however, though they may be brought to this realization through personal reflection or via the dying of someone close to them, never truly takes this concept to heart and they simply pass through their life defined only by whatever desire, emotion, or life-event they are experiencing in any given moment.

In life, throughout all countries and cultures, few people have the time to take the time to think about time. Their life-time is dominated by doing their job, whatever that job may be, in order to pay the bills to live, eat, and raise their family. They pass through life understanding that they should take some time but that time is never allotted to them. Or, perhaps better put, they never take the time to make the time. They allow life, and the responsibilities thereof, to control their entire existence.

There is the other side of the coin, as well. Some people have the time to contemplate time. Maybe they were born wealthy, maybe they received an inheritance, or maybe they personally made a lot of money that allowed them to retire at an early age. But, people in this situation are rarely any different than the average Joe. They rarely take the time to look at their time.

To understand time, you have to make the time to understand time. How do you do this? You stop the doing.

Most people never sit in silence. They never step beyond the doing. They have their desires which they pursue, they have their bills to pay, they have their friends and their family that they do what they do with them, but they never take the time to sit back and be silence in order to come to an understanding of life's realities of which time is one of the biggest. When they have a vacation they never STOP, they just DO. They go, and even if what they do causes them to relax, they never take the time to stop their thinking mind and come to terms with time.

In other writings, I have spelled out methods that may help one come to terms with understanding time. What I often witness from the communications I receive from people who have read those writings is, however, that people intellectualize them. They look to them as a method to gain a handle on time. But, the fact is, there is no method to control time. I can give you pointers to understand time but you have to be able to let go of what you want from time in order to grow an awareness of time.

Right now, if you are reading this, you have the time to study time. STOP! LET GO! This is your time. I really mean it, STOP!

Stop your mind from racing. Stop your mind from thinking whatever your mind is thinking about. Stop it and just be.

What do you hear? What do you see? What does you body feel like? This is your time. This is who you are in this time.

This time; this moment, is all that there is, stop thinking about anything else because it may never happen. This moment is all you have; feel it.

Now, take a look at what this time feels like. What is it? What is this moment to you? What does this moment mean? How does this moment feel?

How are you encountering and moving though this moment? How will what you are doing, in this moment, affect your next moment? Is what you are thinking, feeling, and doing in this moment allowing your next moment to be better or is it setting karma into motion?

How you feel here, is how you feel here. What you do here, is what you do here. How you feel here and what you do here affect your next forever for everything you do in any given moment creates what you will next encounter in the next moment, the next hour, the next day, the next year. What are you creating in this moment that will set the stage for the rest of your time?

To understand time, you must embrace time. To comprehend time, you must STOP and study time. To thrive in your time, you must become one with time.

Tick tock, this is your time. How are you embracing it and how are you encountering it?

This is your time. It is for you to decide how you live your time. But, if you do not embrace the pure essence of time, blame no one but yourself when your time is gone.

Everybody Talks About the Films but Nobody Studies the Films

I forever find it curious that whenever I hear or read about what people are saying about the *Zen Films of Scott Shaw* they are virtually always completely wrong. Some have gone to extended lengths to describe and discuss the films I have made but they are completely missing the point. Some love them, some hate them, and, all that is fine with me—that is their opinion. But, no one ever studies the films.

From a personal perspective, I can tell you that from the time I was young I would watch films very carefully. I would notice things about them that I would later realize were completely missed by others. There are mistakes in continuity, changes in lighting between the various takes, wardrobe differences, actors looking at the camera, and the list goes on. But, I never saw those as filmmaking flaws, I simply saw them as part and parcel of the filmmaking process. By observing a film in this manner, it truly makes the watching of that movie very intriguing to me.

Again, from a personal perspective, I can categorically state that I have never attempted to make a traditional film. From my experience, a traditional film, that will play well to a traditional film going audience, costs a lot of money as you have to play to their preconceived notions about what a film is supposed to be. As I have never had a high budget in my filmmaking endeavors, I have never attempted to walk down that road—though some of the people I have worked with have attempted to guide me in a more traditional direction in my filmmaking practices. But, that is just not who I am.

All this being stated, what I can say is that within the spontaneity, freedom, and magic of *Zen Filmmaking* every film that I have ever created has been done so with a very clear focus of message, (based upon budgetary constrains, of course). You may love what I do. You may hate what I do. You may issue praise or cast criticism. That's all fine with me. But, what most people never seems to do is to actually study the films I make. They never look for the subtleties. They simply look to the obvious. And, by viewing my *Zen Films* in this manner, they are really missing the whole point.

...I mean, come on! These are *Zen Films*, what do you expect to see when you sit down to watch them?

As the filmmaker, I could point to each element of what one should be looking for in each scene of my films. But, what would be the fun of that? This is *Zen Filmmaking* and that is all part of the process; finding the hidden meaning, revealing to yourself what is hiding beneath the surface and what it means to you. It is essential to know, however, that every scene in every one of my *Zen Films* has a Some Thing that is there for a reason which guides the overall vision of the film and projects an ideology to the audience whether they consciously notice it or not. This is why they are each titled a, *"Zen Film."*

So, I want to call out all you, (oh so knowledgeable), film reviewers. I want to tell you, *"You missed the point."* Simply by looking to the storyline, the sets, the acting, and the character development for guidance in your reviews you have completely overlooked what is actually going on.

As a Film-Watcher and as a Film-Maker I can say that to truly understand any film you have to look beyond the obvious. This is especially the case with *Zen Films*. So, the next time you want to find something to cast your judgment upon at least have the foresight to see what you are missing by studying the subtitles instead of simply sitting there with your mind already made up and casting judgment.

Don't You Have Anything Better To Do?

Every now and then someone will bring to my attention to the fact that there is discussion going on about me on the internet. Mostly, I'm doing other stuff and I really don't care so I don't check it out. Sometimes, however, if I'm just screwing around on-line when they alert me to the fact, I do take a moment and read them. Some are positive dialogues. Thanks! Others... What I always find is that the inception of the conversation was begun by a very articulate individual who is trying to cast shade on my life and me in a very subtle manner. Those make smile. The assumptions are false. The claims are misplaced. But, the writing is good. Some are just the, *"This guy is a fucking asshole!"* Those make me smile too because the person writing them does not know me at all. Like the old saying goes, *"To know me is to love me."* I think I'm a nice guy. ☺

Spending my life in the world of martial arts this type of attack is not new to me. It seems there is always some insecure practitioner attempting to create doubt about someone else. Sad but true. I have written about this phenomenon in the past...

But, it forever perplexes me why anyone discuses me at all. Don't you have anything better to do? I mean, I am just a very basic sort of guy who makes weird movies, writes books, makes music, takes some photographs, teaches a class or a seminar every now and then, and stuff like that.

...There was a filmmaking team who made a mockumentary about me maybe a decade back at *Grand Valley State University* in Michigan. I thought that was pretty funny. *Zen Filmmaking!!!* You can get to it from my YouTube page if you feel like it. I imagine they were doing it for a filmmaking class or something. But, at least they created something and probably earned a grade for it.

What always boggles my mind is, what does talking about and discussing another person equal? What does trying to make me or any other person look good, look bad, or look like anything equal? What does it prove and what does it do for your life—especially if you are hiding behind a screen name? Though, the truth be told, I have watched a couple of people cause their on-line notoriety to rise by discussing and/or talking trash about me (and other people). But, they never even said, *"Thank you."* ☺

As the joke goes, *"You know you can believe everything that is on the internet."* I mean any person who wants to can find a place to get their voice heard on the internet. But, why is your voice wasted talking about other people?

I remember back a number of years ago, I was watching a Run Run Shaw movie with a group of people and someone commented that his name was the same as mine. I made the joke, *"I'm half Chinese."* A couple of weeks later I was alerted to the fact that it was listed on some website that, *"Scott Shaw is half Chinese."* I mean, come on people… And, I have seen a few other pretty ridiculous things mentioned about me on the internet. But, the thing is, what can I do? This is the internet, anyone can say anything that they want: positive, negative, or just straight up bullshit. They can say it about anyone or anything.

Some of these, *"Writers,"* present their thoughts, beliefs, and accusations as though they are the truth. They are not the truth but there is a certain segment of society who believes something simply because they read it. Thus, if someone believes something, in that regard, it somehow does become the truth—at least in the mind of that individual. This is how false accusations and misguided beliefs have the potential to truly damage a person's life. And, what is the karma for that, if you are the one instigating or embellishing falsehood and hurting someone else's life? But, I guess most people who do that kind of stuff don't care.

And... I always feel thanks for the people who rise to my defense (and the defense of others) when they attempt to countermand the spreading negativity by inserting their positive opinions and/or truth based facts.

The fact is, who and what I am, what I have or have not accomplished is one hundred percent verifiable. I don't care about accolades so you are not going to find me listing mine. *"Just the facts..."* Other people may put them out there, but not me. I don't think about things like that. All I think about is what I haven't accomplished and what I've yet to accomplish. Yet, some people attempt to embellish or diminish who and what I am; what I have done. Why? I don't know. What does it prove? Some people even try to describe my life and my life motivation. But, they have never even met me, so how do they know anything about me? But, as they used to say on, *The X-Files,* "The truth is out there."

Now, all of this rambling about me brings us to the point of this piece... What are you doing with your life? Are you doing something for you? Doing something for the people you love? Accomplishing something with your life? Doing something for the greater good? Counteracting acting negativity wherever you find it? Or, are you wasting the very short amount of time that you have in LIFE obsessing about someone or something else? Attempting to either put them on a pedestal or cast them to the depths of hell?

My advice, if you love someone or something they created, support them. If you hate someone or something they created, support them, as well, because they are giving you a reason to think, study, and question life.

Ultimately, focus on your own life. Make your own life more. Then, you won't need to focus on my life or the life of any other person. You won't need to make yourself look right while attempting to make others look wrong. By accomplishing your own accomplishments, your life becomes a creative masterpiece based upon your own vision. From this, you can stop talking about other people and start being alerted to the fact that other people are talking about you. ☺

How Do You Want Your Life To Be Remembered?

Throughout my life I've watched as people continually shift the focus from themselves and what they are or are not accomplishing to placing the spotlight on others. Whether it has been in the world of rock n' roll where people would argue about who was the better guitar player, to the world of filmmaking where actors and filmmakers would criticize other actors and filmmakers, onto the marital arts where insecurity reigns supreme and low-level martial artists are constantly finding new reasons to criticize other martial artists. But, why do people do this? Why do people wish to find fault in others? In a nutshell the answer is, a person wants to find fault in someone else so that they can look like the authority on the subject—so that they can appear as if they are better and/or more. But, are they? What have they personally accomplished? And, if they are focusing on someone else that already proves that the person they are discussing has accomplished more than them because that is where their focused is being placed.

Okay… But, what does all this prove? What does one person criticizing and critiquing another person prove? It proves nothing.

Life is about what you personally create. Your life is about what you personally do. What you think and what you say about another person, be it bad or good, is irrelevant to the greater course of your life as any other person, and what you think about them, has nothing to do with who or what you create or become. For this reason, all energy spent focusing on someone else only diminishes who you are in the eyes of the world and/or what you can ultimately become, as your time has been wasted not focusing on the essential element of your life, you. You have instead spent it focusing on someone else.

Some people spend their life helping others. This is a very good thing. But, do people who live this life of service spend their time criticizing others who are also givers, stating that they are not doing enough or that what they are doing is in some manner wrong? No. They give and help and they allow others to give and help. These people are the ideal example of the way one should walk through life. Yes, they may know about the existence of other helpers but they do not waste their time criticizing them. They simply continue to do what they have chosen to do and that is to help the world in whatever way that they can.

At each juncture of your life you truly need to take a long hard look at yourself and what you are doing and why. This is perhaps one of the biggest flaws of humanity, they do not look at themselves. Instead, they find it much easier to focus on something or someone outside of themselves.

The fact is, criticism is easy. It takes no effort. All you have to do is criticize. But, what does that equal? It equals nothing. You have not done anything, you have not accomplished anything. All you have done is place further focus on the person you are criticizing.

Do you want to be remember in life? Do you want to do something good? Do you want to be seen as a contributor to the great whole? If you do, then there is only one way to do that and it is not by critiquing someone who actually has accomplished something, it is by actually doing something good in your own right. For this is the only way that true life-accomplishment is actualized. This is the only way to been seen as a true contributor. This is the only way to be viewed as some-one who did something other than simply a person who talks about other people.

Who are you? How do you want your life to be remembered?

Is Doing What You Do Okay As Long As You Don't Get Caught?

There is this video that has been circulating around Facebook and I imagine other places that shows Neil Young going into a record store in the 1970s, getting upset that they are selling a bootlegged record of one of Crosby, Stills, Nash, and Young's concerts, telling the young cashier (who has no idea who he is) that they can't sell that record as he wrote the songs, giving him his contact info to give to his boss, and walking out the door with it. From a filmmaking perspective it is not shot very well but it was obviously done on a 16mm camera and the audio is really good so they obviously had a sound guy in tow. Meaning, this encounter was totally set up. Why? I do not know. Maybe Young was planning to use it in a film? Maybe it did?

Overall, it is a bit painful to watch as it is long and drug out. The cashier chases Young out to the street. ...Can't blame the kid for that... You can see where the cameraman had to change his mag as four-hundred foot loads only shoot for twelve minutes. Finally, it ends with Young going back into the store, talking to the owner on the phone, and leaving with the record after not paying for it.

Okay... What does all this tell us about life? First of all, if I was Neil Young I probably would have just paid for the record and left behind all of the melodrama. I'm sure he had the money. But, on the other side of the issue, I totally get it. In this modern digital age, people steal my creative work from me all time. People watch my movies for free from illegal download sites, read my books, and download my music. Though me, the creator, is not getting paid, the people who have stolen my stuff are getting paid or they would not be doing it. Just as is the case of the people who recorded, pressed, and released bootleg records back in the day—they wouldn't be doing it if they weren't getting paid.

In the modern world, very few people ever think about any of this. As they are not creating anything, they don't care. At best, they hope to create something someday… But, someday never comes. Thus, they take from the lives and the bank accounts of those who do create and they do not care. …They do this because they will never be caught.

I believe most people would not go into a store and actually steal a DVD, a CD, or anything like that. But, stealing on the internet… They never even ponded the overall consequences of their actions. As long as they get away with it, they don't care.

Growing up on the wrong side of the tracks as it were, in my early years, I knew a lot of seedy people who did some very bad things. Luckily, my mind was focused on other things and I never went down that path. But, they would be all proud and bragging about what they did. They were proud and bragging until they got caught and ended up in jail. And, we all know what happens there. Some, I never heard from again.

In my adult years, I have known a few people were drug dealers. They all thought it was a cool way to make money while staying high. One friend of mine ending doing five and half years in an Arizona prison. He got out and died a few years later. Was it worth it? Losing your life-time?

People who are in the game of taking for free never think about any of this until they are forced to think about it. Though I doubt the law(s) will ever focus very prominently on people who rob people's livelihood by stealing their creations via the internet, you as a thinking person should be more than that. You should decide that simply because you will not be caught and held to task, that does not mean that it is okay to steal.

The good in all life begins with you deciding to do the right thing. The bad in all life also begins with you deciding to do the wrong thing. Thus, you are the source for all that is good and/or bad.

If you see something bad, you should call it out. You should tell the person to stop. You should make it stop. You should try to replace and fix anything bad that was done by doing something good.

You know what is good or bad. You know what is right or wrong. Choose to only do good, stop allowing other people to be hurt by people who do bad things just because they won't be caught. Make the world a better place.

Like I Always Say, Let's See What You Can Do

I was talking to a buddy of mine at the *Rose Bowl Flea Market* last Sunday. He's a big fan of *No-Budget Cinema* and he alluded to the fact that I must be spending twenty or thirty-thousand dollars to make my films. I told him no, my top budget is three hundred dollars. He was a bit surprised, like most people are when they hear this, but he's a savvy guy who's been around so he immediately understood that I can produce films for that budget because I own my own equipment and do much of the stuff myself.

I must paraphrase here and state that some of the films I did earlier in my career and many of the ones I did in association with Donald G. Jackson had much higher budgets. They were shot on film and shooting on film is very expensive. This being said, we shot all of them as if we had no budget. We never paid for locations, never got permits; we just went out there and got it done.

Every now and then, as an actor, I've been called up to *The Bigs* by some great filmmaker: Brian De Palma, Robert Altman, James Cameron, and most recently Adam Sandler. Whenever I am on those sets it is just scary how much is going on... I mean, in my most recent experience in the Steven Brill, Adam Sandler film, *Sandy Wexler,* the vastest of the production was just dumfounding. They literally shut down Sunset Blvd., on the Sunset Strip, so they could film there; midday. I can't even imagine what it took to do that. When it was time for my lunch, they had a driver take me from my trailer at basecamp and drive me a mile or two over to the old Tower Records building where they were serving the food. Then, they had a driver take me back. I even had my own stand-in. A guy who was a younger better looking version of me. ☺ I mean, on every level, what it takes to get these productions accomplished is scary.

I think back to when I was in the Stallone film, *Stop or My Mom Will Shoot*. There was a scene in that film, shot on Hollywood Blvd., just off of Western, at night. (Just a couple of blocks from where I grew up). The scene had a large garbage truck, supposedly driven by Sly, crashing through the walls of the building—literally crashing through, into my character's supposed art gallery. As I have never been one of those actors to just sit around in my trailer doing nothing, I had been out there watching them set up for this shot. When the shot happened, Sly, his handler, another actor, and my self were the only ones up in loft above what was supposedly my character's gallery. Sly hadn't seen any of the set up for this shot so when the truck came crashing through the walls, he didn't expect it, and jumped back. Me, I had been out on the street and saw that the truck was chained down so it could only travel so far. Afterward he joking exclaimed to other people, *"That guy,"* (meaning me), *"Was scared but I was all good."* Sly, great guy. ☺

Now, that scene never made it into the final cut of the movie. Why, I don't know. I think maybe it would have helped. As the movie was kind of a flop, I doubt a director's cut or any DVD version, with the unused footage, will ever be released. But, that's Hollywood… And, this goes to the whole point of this—tons and tons of money is spent on these films. I don't think the average person can even fathom the over all goings on of what goes on.

Do I wish my film's had a bigger budget than three-hundred dollars? Sure. But, it is a little late in the game for me—I'm kinda old. So, I doubt I will ever be at that high-end level as a producer or director. But, that's okay…

After my part was done shooting on Sandy Wexler I thought to tell Adam or one of the producers, *"Hey, I've done some production work, maybe I could help out."* But, the level of productions I have worked would probably be way below their expectations. So, I never said anything. ☺

In any case, this all goes to you—you, the person out there… The wanna-be filmmaker and/or the critic. Like I have long said, and something that has been quoted many times, *"What is a film critic? With very few exceptions, (i.e. Bogdanovich), it is someone who doesn't have the talent or the dedication to actually make a movie."* But, you can make movies! You can get them done! They can even have some production value, even if you only have a budget of three-hundred dollars.

Throughout my career, either in writing or in filmmaking, I have been told so many times, *"You stuff is shit. I can do better."* But, not one time, in all of these years, has anyone who said this every went out there and wrote a book and got a publisher or actually made a movie that received distribution. It's easy to cast shade. It takes no effort. Creating is hard. That takes focus. That takes dedication.

Now, on the other side of the issue, there are a lot of people out there who have used my philosophy, adapted it to their own understanding of filmmaking, and made some fun films—even if they had no budget. But, like my aforementioned friend, there are fans out there of No Budget Cinema. So, it doesn't have to cost big money to get your project done. It doesn't have to cost big bank to get someone to watch it. Just shut up about other people and DO IT! Create something! Give your art to the world! You never know where it will lead.

The First Time I Was Lied To

I've noticed that recently whenever I turn on a program on TV or pull up a movie on-demand that someone will be giving somebody their music demo CD. This sets me thinking…

Back in the 1970s when the personal 4-Track Reel-to-Reel Recorders were released I was one of the first to buy one. They were great! For the first time, multi-instrumental musicians like myself or bands could actually record their own music via multi-track performances and actually create a fully orchestrated presentation. Certainly, they were no where near what can be done today on your PC but they were the first step in true home recording.

I was in my early semesters at college and I met a girl in one of my classes. We got to talking, hung out a bit, and she told me that she knew some music producer who was looking for a new performer. I guess it was due to the fact that I had grown up in Hollywood and had interacted with a lot of people who were actually family members of some really high-end people in the film and music business that I didn't doubt what she told me. I bought into it… With this, I set about creating a demo tape in my apartment.

I was totally focused and totally in a state of belief that this could be my ticket. As anyone who is a young musician (or once was a young musician) understands, there are all the dreams of musical stardom. From this, I became highly focused and recorded the demo tape. I mixed it and gave it to her on cassette…

After that, though I would see her around campus, it seemed like she was avoiding me. Finally, I needed to know what was up. As it turned out, the only person she knew, who had anything to the with the music industry at all, was her ex-boyfriend who was in band and he didn't like my demo tape. Of course not. But, would have gone through all that time, focus, energy, and process to create a tape for a guy in a post-high school hard rock band? Hell no! I got pulled into the lie.

Now, the fact of life is, some people lie all the time. But, why? Mostly, they lie because they want to seem like something more than they actually are. They tell lies so people like me (back then) will believing them that they are something more than nothing. But, what is the desired end? I don't know… I guess each person has their own definition or undefined reasoning. But, a lie is just a lie. All a lie does is to mess with someone's life. And, that is never a good thing.

As I have long detailed, *"The number one rule of filmmaking is that everybody lies."* Lying is so rampant in the film industry that it is almost unfathomable. But, you almost expect that. A bunch of bullshit, self-involved people trying to climb up or stay on top of the heap. But, that is the film industry. In life, why do people need to lie?

I guess it really comes down to lacking a defined sense of self. If a person, no matter who they, where they came from, or what they are doing, is not whole and complete onto themselves then they may find a reason to lie as they wish to appear to be something more/something else. If they accept who they are, however, then there is no need to lie about anything.

I can tell you not to lie as it is not good and it messes not only with other people's lives but with your life, as well. …If you are found out to be a liar than a liar is all you will ever be. I can tell you this, but if you are a lair you will still lie. It is a pathology that some people develop and never get past.

But, lying is bad. Be who and what you are—whole onto yourself. Accept who you are. Be proud of who you are. Don't lie.

That's Not What I Want To Do

One of the first things I realized when I entered the film business is that I could edit a movie very quickly. Most people, (at that time), would maybe get five minutes of raw footage put together per day. Me, it was very common that I would edit an entire feature length film over a weekend. I guess this has something to do with possessing an eidetic memory. Which is actually more of a curse, in life, than anything else, in that I remember everything. But, once I saw a scene I would remember it and I could put the best scenes together very quickly.

Many of the *Zen Films* Donald G. Jackson and I created were edited in this manner. We would go and rent a video-editing bay on Friday night and we would come out with a movie by Sunday. *Armageddon Blvd., Ride with the Devil, Lingerie Kickboxer* were all done in this manner.

From this ability, the people who financed Don, (in that time period), had high hopes that I would jump ship so they could finance my films instead of our films, as Don was very mentally chaotic. He never got things done. Or, it took him a long time to get things done. Me, I am bam-bam; see it, shoot it, edit it, soundtrack it, and done. They thought they could make a lot of money off of me.

But, I was born in the *Year of the Dog,* (in the Chinese astrological calendar), from this, I am told; I am supposed to be a very loyal person. Which, I guess I am. Also, one of my curses. ☺ Anyway, I said, *"No."*

Back in those days, Don and I would meet at our offices in North Hollywood everyday, seven days a week, at about eleven; hang out, cast movies, talk with other filmmaker, shoot footage for films when the inspiration struck, go to screenings, see live bands, eat, and basically hang out and have a good time. This went on for a few years. And, we did make a few good films during that period. Most of the time, we had fun. Good memories, good times. But, times always change.

Though Don and I took, literally, more than a year to film movies like *Guns of El Chupacabra,* this was not the pattern I preferred. Ever since I made, *Samurai Vampire Bikers from Hell,* (which we made over a weekend), my philosophy has always been to get out there and do it. Make that film. Get it done. Because it will be no better if you take two years or two days. Sure, if you need some pick-up shots after the fact, go out there and get them. But, the body of the film; get it done!

It's all about focus and organization.

From this ability, I have also had people coming at me wanting me to make films for them. But, I don't make films for money. I don't do exploitation. I do Art—at least Art as I see it.

As time has progressed and I have become more and more filled with distaste for the meaningless egos and the innumerable promises and lies prevalent throughout the film industry here in Hollywood, I have continued to minimalize and acutely focus my film productions. …Bringing in fewer and fewer cast and crewmembers and focusing on specific characters to get the story told. This has been a very freeing experience. It has also lead me to create the next generation of *Zen Filmmaking,* the *Non-Narrative Film.*

So, though I still hold onto the belief that if you are filming a narrative film, that it should be done to get it done, I have also retreated to one of the practices that Don and I employed with *Roller*

Blade Seven and *Chupacabra*—creating a film over time. For example, I have been filming the next *Max Hell Frog Warrior* installment for over two years. My feeling is, it will be done when it is done. So, for all of you out there who ask me what is going on with that project, there is your answer.

Don and I used to always say that the most important element of filmmaking is that, *"Fun is what it is all about."* Though working with Don, due to his numerous psychological quirks, was not always fun, I have personally held onto that belief. From this, it is has guided me down the road of removing as many obstacles as possible from the filmmaking process. And, the fact of the matter is, filmmaking is not easy. Dealing with the egos of people is not easy. Paying for a movie is not easy. Getting things done and making things happen on a set is not easy; nor is it always fun. But, as I hold onto the belief that filmmaking can actually lead to a state of *Satori* or *Cinematic Enlightenment* and that a film should not be based solely on the desire(s) of the filmmaker or the actors to feed their egos and/or their careers, or for financiers to fill their pockets, I continually have to tell people who want me to make a traditional film, *"That's not what I want to do."*

I'm about freedom. I'm about a happy experience. I'm about obstacle removal. I'm about art. So, ultimately, I'm about one thing, *Zen Cinema!*

The Silence In-Between the Sound

I was woken up by some noise outside on the street this morning. It made me think back to another time...

I had this condo in Redondo Beach for about six or seven years. The building was right up against the water. So, it had specular views and the sound of the waves caressing my ears. When I first saw it, I feel in love. I felt it was exactly where I should be.

When the real estate guy showed it to me, it was in the evening. I noticed on the other side of the building that there was a bunch of scaffolding. I asked about it. He told me that the building cooperative was cleaning all the windows. Okay... That sounded all right. I put my money down and I moved in.

I had previously been living about a block away so as soon as the deal was done I grabbed my Mac, a couple of pillows and blankets for my lady and me; walked them over, and I was there. I was in heaven.

AM rolls around. I start to hear all of this loud pounding and cutting off in the distance. It kind of made the building vibrate. As it turns out, the real estate agent had lied to me. They were not cleaning the windows. They were retiling all of the patios. Now, this was a big tall building, there were several hundred units, and they had just started the job. I got screwed.

I thought to sue the real estate guy, as it would have been an open-and-shut case of deception but I pulled back. My lawyer was mad at me. He gets mad at me frequently as I always stop him from suing people even though he knows he will win. I'm his worst client. I know this because he tells me I am.

The big problem in the equitation was, they had started on the other side of the building. As they moved around to my side of the building the pounding and the tile cutting got louder and louder until it reached a fever pitch when they were working near my unit. It was really deafening.

During this period I was teaching a lot of classes at the university. For those of you who may not know, it takes a lot of time to prep a class; especially a class on filmmaking. You don't just go in there and spit out wisdom; you have to have it all well organized with lots of cinematic examples. The noise killed me.

I was also writing a lot. I was working with this publisher that really liked what I wrote. Pretty much once I finished one book, they would ask me for another. This, plus, I was writing articles and making movies. So, the noise was not good.

If you were one of those nine-to-five people, like my lady, it was no problem. She never understood all my complaints. She would leave before it started and come home after it ended. People like her never had to experiences the blunt force of the trauma. It killed me.

But, I had to exist. I had to create. All I could do was to formulate a plan.

The tiling would start every morning around 8:00 AM. So, I would get up prior to that, try to get some work done, and then go out and have breakfast, shop, visit friends, and do stuff like that, once all the chaos began. The crews would go to lunch from 12:00 to 1:00 so I would come back and try to get some more work done for an hour. They would re-start. I would re-leave. I would work out or teach some MA (martial arts). They would quit around 4:00 PM. I would come home and get busy. When I was filming movies, during this period, it wasn't so bad because I would be out doing it. But, when I had to do stuff at home, it was very problematic. This process of retiling the patios took about six-months. It was bad!

Now, when they were done, when all the tiling had been completed, life became better. But, then arose a new problem. This was at the time when every one was getting into hardwood floors. I've never liked hardwood floors very much. I like carpeted floors. But, to each there own.

In any case, many people in the building began redoing their floors. The way this building was constructed, out of concrete, I believe, sound vibrated through the structure—especially the sounds of construction. So, every time I thought it was all over and I was back to simply listening to the waves and creating: bam, bam, bam, cut, cut, cut. Heaven again became hell.

When construction wasn't going on it was a great place to live. When it was, it was not. Eventually, all the noise caused me to move. But, I was there for a lot of years. The noise and my figuring out ways to work in-between it makes me think to the old Zen proverb, *"If a tree falls in the forest and there is no one there to hear it, does it make a sound?"*

I think if we look at this a different way, the sound would be the distraction in the solitude of the forest. It would be disruptive to the peace and the serenity. So, when the tree falls, the noise it makes interrupts this peace and serenity. But, once it meets the ground, again there is silence and all things can return to being as they naturally are.

This is the place of meditation; of *Zazen*. This is the place we all seek. We may have to wait until the world around us becomes silent. But, if we wait, we can find it. Even if it only lasts for a moment; in that moment, *Satori* can be found. It can be found if we do let the disruption of the noise linger in us and control our inner-being.

Don't Say Yes

On a funny note…

As you can imagine, I am asked to be interviewed quite a lot. …All the crazy movies I've made, the *Zen Filmmaking,* the martial arts, and all that…

Do I say, *"Yes?"* Sometimes… But, I'll get back to that in a minute.

The first time I ever saw an interview take place, (and what can go right or very wrong with it), I was like seventeen. A few of the close disciples and I had gone to a local TV station, here in L.A, with my teacher, Swami Satchidananda. He was to be interviewed by this longtime L.A. newscaster and talk show guy, George Putnam, for one of those morning shows. Putnam was a real conservative but I had seen him on TV my entire life. So, I expected only the best.

Now, *Gurudev* was a fairly important guy. He was the one they had asked to open *Woodstock,* he was giving lectures all over the world, writing books, you name it. So, when he went in there I am sure he was simply expecting the usual questions. But instead, Putnam went after him. Said things and when *Gurudev* attempted to respond, *"Oh the Swami is upset…" "I'm not, feel my pulse,"* was his response. But, it was real hatchet journalism.

After seeing that I was always a little leery about what can happen during an interview—particularly a live interview. Certainly, I think we all have seen when the interviewer goes after the interviewee on TV or heard it happen on the radio. And, so many hatchet job articles have been written about people who simply thought they were going in to talk over whatever they were about.

For me, I have always been pretty lucky. Everyone who has interviewed me has been fair and has done a good job. In fact, I think back to an interview I was asked to do in the 90s for a martial art magazine. I said, *"Yes."* Then, the editor contacted me and said, *"Why don't you just write it yourself and put my name on it."* Of course, this made me smile. I wish all of my interviews could have been like that—getting out there what I wanted to get out there.

The things that go on in journalism that most people never know about...

Anyway, since the dawning of the age of the internet a lot of people have gotten busy and that is great, I always appreciate people who go after making themselves more. There has been a lot of internet journals go up, then came podcasts, and internet radio shows. And, of course, there been cable access shows around forever. There are a lot of all of those. So again, I get asked to be interviewed quite a lot. And, I always appreciate the offers.

It terms of the journals, those are easy. They email me a set of questions and I answer them. But, podcasts and internet radio shows kind of worry me. You know, it is very easy to say something that can be taken the wrong way or something that people well read their own meaning into. So, I walk that road very-very carefully. And, if I don't know the person who is asking to interview me, (as there are so many people doing podcasts and internet radio out there nowadays), I don't want to lead myself into a bad situation like my guru did.

So, to the funny part... When I am asked to be interviewed, I am way too congenial and accepting. I am, until I am not. So, people ask and I generally say, *"Yes."* But then… Then, I rarely show up for the show.

My manager had a long talk with me the other day… *"Scott, don't say yes,"* came the words… So, I have been trying to turn the eternally nice guy off and say, *"No."*

In fact, this one guy, who is a successful independent filmmaker onto his own right, recently asked me to do his internet radio show. He had actually taken one of my seminars on filmmaking way back in the way back when. Good guy! And, I certainly did not want to mess with him. So, there was the test. In times gone past I may have said, *"Yes,"* but not shown up. So, instead, I said, *"Thanks but no thanks."* □

So, to all you internet entrepreneurs out there, I'm not saying, *"Don't ask."* Because I may do it. Just please understand if I decline.

I'm making progress…

The Same Yet Different

As an artist, when you are painting a painting, there is always the question, *"Is it done?"* Sometimes you look at a painting that you are working on and you are just not one hundred percent happy with it. Then the choice must be made, do you go back and rework it or do you let it live in its own perfection?

The thing about this question is—yes you can redo it. In some cases, as an artist, you can redo it over and over and over again. But, at the end of the day, it is still what it was; a painting with paint upon a canvas—the same, yet different.

Life and the way you act in life is very similar to this. There are chances for a redo—most of the time. In other cases there are not. But, one way or the other we are left with our life. It can be seen as having been lived within its own perfection, to the best of our ability, or it can be viewed as if something is missing, something is wrong.

You know, the world has changed a lot over the past two decades in terms of art and creativity. For example, what was once very-very expensive to do, like create a movie, is now relatively cheap due to digital technology. I recently read this piece where Quentin Tarantino stated that digital is the death of cinema. He stated this even though his friend and confidant Robert Rodriguez has used it extensively.

I won't go into this debate because I see both sides of it and I have already written extensively about it. I will say that as one of the first people to ever create a film on video that received international distribution, *Samurai Vampire Bikers from Hell,* that I saw the future early. Years before me, look at Frank Zappa's, *200 Motels,* if you want to see a really early contribution to the genre.

Anyway, early in the digital game, everybody wanted their movies, that were shot on tape, to look like film. Enter, Film Look. A very expensive process of adding controlled noise to the video movie. Was it film? No. Did it look like film? A little bit. It was the same, yet different.

When Donald G. Jackson and I created, *Guns of El Chupacabra,* we filmed it with a combination of 35mm, 16mm, and digital videotape for the scenes with the reporter, to change the look and feel of the various elements of the film. One day when we were on the set filming with Julie Strain and her then husband Kevin Eastman, we had our videographer along so we had him shoot the scenes on video that we were shooting on film as a backup. When I edited *Guns of El Chupacabra* I used the footage we shot on film. When I did *Guns of El Chupacabra II: The Unseen,* I used the video footage of the same scenes. Did you notice that? Did anybody? It was the same, yet different.

Now, when digital photography came along, I hated it. Just as with video, gone was the depth of field, that myself, as a filmmaker and photographer, loved to work with. But, just like with filmmaking, digital photography made photography insanely cheaper and easier. So, with the changing winds of time, you have to change or be left behind.

Thankfully, now, many of both the new video cameras and still cameras, (which are pretty much one in the same), achieve really nice depth of field. Case in point, I purchased this new Nikon a little while back and was shooting it as digital had been. I expected everything to be in focus, it was not, there was depth of field that I didn't realize until I looked at the shot later. Though I lost the shot I had in mind, I was happy to see the improvement. The same, yet not different.

This is life. It is all about the availability of your options and what you do with that availability and those options. Options are out there, if you want to work with them. Life is out there, if you want to live it. But ultimately, it is you who must decide when what you are doing is done. Are you making it better by working and reworking it? Or are you simply making it the same, yet different?

The Scream Queens Get Old

Though there have been *Scream Queens* in each era since film upon the silver screen occurred, there was no greater era for *Scream Queens,* at least in my opinion, than during the 1980s into the 1990s. At least not yet…

The women who inhabited this era were the stunningly beautiful Brinke Stevens, Linnea Quigley, who is such a sweet person that I have worked with, and then it spreads out to actresses like Michelle Bauer and Monique Gabrielle, and even onto actresses who went mainstream like Jamie Lee Curtis. If you want to expand upon this inner circle just a bit further, there are actresses like, Jewel Shepard and certainly the incomparable: friend, former-filmmaking partner, and force to be reckoned with, Julie Strain. (And, this is just to name of few). Filmmakers like Fred Olen Ray, Jim Wynorski, and David DeCoteau took this this film genre, in this era, to the max.

"Youth is beautiful." That is true. There is a beauty in the look and the innocence of youth. That, *"Youth,"* truly feed into the roles these women played. But, time ticks on for all of us—as it has for these actresses.

Now, this is not a criticism at any level for all of these actresses are still beautiful in this stage of their life. (I am in the same age group). But, with these actresses moving on in time and in space, there has been a vacuum created. It has come in combination with the changing of the independent film industry in general and the lack of emerging talent. Though there is a never ending supply of beautiful, young actress out there—but with the combination of no filmmakers, in the indie industry, truly addressing this genre, and none of the new actresses moving up to the forefront, all we are left with is what once was.

Times change; that's just life. People get older, that too is life. Many try to hold onto youth, as they get older, that is very understandable. But, I forever find it sad when, in life, a great era comes to an end and nothing better replaces it. This, at least so far, is the case with, *"The Golden Age of Scream Queens."*

Would Your Ever Make Another Roller Blade Seven?

"Would you ever make another Roller Blade Seven?" I get asked this question fairly frequently. In fact, as RB7 was just named number twenty-seven of, *"The One-Hundred Best B-Movies of All Time,"* at *Pulse Magazine,* (thanks guys), I have been asked that question several times this week. Last year the question was asked a lot when I was named number ten on the list, *The Best Movie Trash Creators* on imdb.com.

To answer, *"Yes, I would."* In fact, I would love to make another film of that caliber. The problem is, what we did then for relatively little money would be very-very expensive to do today.

Don Jackson and I made *Roller Blade Seven* and *Return of the Roller Blade Seven* for about thirty-thousand dollars. We shot it on 16mm and doing that, in itself, is not cheap. During the production, our executive producer had us add extra, *"Name Talent,"* which wasn't in the original deal. We had set the Name Talent standard at two: Don Stroud and William Smith. But, she kept getting new ideas so the money went out: Karen Black (RIP) was $3,000.00 and Frank Stallone was $6,000.00. Now, I was happy to work with both of these people, as they are both very talented actor, but they did cost money.

More than that though, when we made RB7 it was a different time in the film industry. People wanted to be a part of something. So, virtually every person who was in the film, including myself, was paid no money for his or her participation. But, they were happy to do it. I mean if you look at some of the scenes, there were upwards of over fifty people in one shot. They were all great and very nice people.

Also, we shot RB7 with no filming permits. We would simply go to the locations we had picked and film.

It was a different time. You could do things like that. At one point, when we were shooting out in the desert, a sheriff's helicopter landed to check us out. As long as we had no guns, which we didn't, they were all good. They flew off and filming continued...

Since 911, everything has gotten sketchy. It is much harder, if not impossible, to shoot with that many people with out getting filming permits, renting the location, and all that entails... Hell, it's hard to shoot with even a couple of people nowadays. Which means, it would cost a lot of money to bring a film like RB7 up again

Now, RB7 was not without its problems. Though I wrote a long chapter about the production of the film in my book, *Zen Filmmaking,* I plan to write another article, *"Roller Blade Seven: Darkness in the Light,"* on the subject about all the negative and bad things that took place during filming and post production; including the fact, I was totally broke by the end of the production, so much so that I had to sell my *1934 D'Angelico New Yorker,* just to survive. A guitar I have never been able to replace. And, that's just one story... A lot of shit went down.

But... All this being said, people still watch and talk about the film and that is great! Many hate it. Calling it one of the worst films ever made. Maybe... But, many also like it. They love the bizarre, psychedelic, abstract nature of the first *Zen Film.*

In closing, I would love to do another *Roller Blade Seven*. In fact, Don and I planned to do the next chapter as, *Wheelzone Rangers*. But, we got distracted and made other films; both individually and as a team and never got back to doing it. Then, he passed away and all that is left of the *Zen Filmmaking* team is me.

All this being said, if someone out there has the money, (I know I don't), and would like to finance another bizarre wild ride into the *Wheelzone,* give me a call. I am willing and I am available. ☺

Talking Pictures of Other People

I just finished up the filming of a music video this past Saturday. We did this whole Bollywood thing at this Hindu temple set. It was cool. I love Bollywood productions!

Every now and then I get brought on to direct one of those real high-end union music videos. It's great. I don't have to do much but just sit around and guide the ship. The crew does everything else. Not like *Zen Filmmaking* where my hands are on and in everything from directing the actors, to doing the lighting, to shooting the camera, to whatever…

At one point on Saturday, I had a vision. I wanted to go handheld in amongst the dancers. My cameraman freaked. That wasn't in the schedule or on the storyboards. A cameraman can give me his opinion but he can't try to overrule me or he's off the set. This is the thing about filmmaking. The D.P. or cameraman can be your biggest asset or your worst curse. They can make your vision look great or they can totally fuck you over. Most are cool and are happy to work with you. They get the art. Some, however, particularly film school geeks, get the idea that it is their show and they are the one in control. Wrong!

This guy almost got to that level. He was a newly graduated USC film school guy. Nice enough. But, full of all the bullshit film school teaches you.

Now, I must preface this with the statement, I've had some good experiences with USC film school guys. One of my first films, *Samurai Ballet,* was filmed by me, (of course), and this guy in his last semester at USC. Good guy, great job! Hell, probably one of my first starring roles was for a USC student film, *The Funky Cuts Barber Shop*. Fun and great experience. I saw it on the big screen at USC, at their end of the semester fest, but never got a copy as 16mm transfer was big money back then. If any of you people out there have an in at USC, hook me up with a copy; I am sure it is their archives.

But, back to the point... Cameramen are really your lifeline to film production. If they mess you up, they can really kill a picture. I've had bad cameramen that shot on autofocus and, as such, the walls behind my characters looked great and in focus, but the characters were totally out of focus. One of the most poignant stories I like to tell is when I was helping this one friend put his first film together and on the first day of production the cameraman back-loaded my *Arri,* meaning the emulsion of the film was on the wrong side. That obviously killed all the footage, which killed the film. A lot of money, gone to nothing. He was a film school grad. And, these are just a couple of examples. I've done a lot of films and music videos; I've got a lot of stories...

Taking pictures of people is an art and an art form onto itself. And, in most cases, photographing people is at the heart of any film production. Now, I'm not talking about taking headshots, that's just mindless bullshit. Any monkey with a digital camera can do that. I am talking about capturing your subject(s) with art attached. And, the more people in the shot, the harder that is to do with vision and with art.

It was like I was at the *Rose Bowl Flea Market* yesterday. There are always thousands of people there. As we were walking, up ahead I notice this guy taking a photo of my lady and me with a long lens. Now, this obviously pissed me off, but what can you do about it? It's a public place and as much as you want to raise a stink and kick their ass, the law is the law. They can do it. But, *"Why,"* is my question? What is a photo of my lady and me in a crowd going to mean to the photographer?

This is the same up in Santa Barbara. Everywhere you go on State Street there is always someone talking pictures of people. I was up there a little while back and there was this older guy with a camera around his neck, high up on his chest. I could see he was snapping photos with a remote control that he had in his pocket. Most people don't know cameras; so most people didn't even know it was happening. But why? You can take all these shots but what is it going to prove? There is no art in them. Simply a mishmash of images.

Just like the paparazzi at places like, *The Grove.* Like I always jokingly tell them when they take my photo, *"I doubt you'll make any money trying to sell a photo of me to TMZ or Radar Online."*

This is the thing. There is art everywhere. There is art, if you have the eye for it. But, most people do not. They just want to take snapshots. This is true of many cameramen in the film game, as well.

Sometimes in restaurants or bars or clubs there will be a person etched in perfect lighting. It would make the perfect photograph. But, even though I carry a camera with me everywhere, that image I see probably would not translate to the captured image, especially in this digital age. As digital camera are well… They just have their own mind of image interpretation. Meaning, taking that photo would not only encroach on a person's privacy but it would also, most likely, not be what is seen by the human eye. ...I've written a lot about, *"Seeing What the Camera Sees."*

Anyway, what all this equals is that, first of all, you have to have the artistic vision to see the vision. Then, you have to have the skills and the tools to recreate what you saw, when you saw that perfect vision of a person in some place and some time and then capture it in it's orchestrated perfection instead of invading a person's space and not getting it anyway. Mostly, if you have art in your blood, you need to remain free to change and adapt as necessary to capture that art. You cannot let yourself be held back by what they taught you in school or your ego, as this will only keep you from capturing that perfect image.

That is art. That is what the reason to take pictures of other people, to make that art.

Space Invaders

I think it is very interesting how in certain periods of our life we continually encounter the same time of person or a similar type of situation. I don't know if this is based upon our *karma*, personal projection, or being tested by the powers from the great beyond. *None-the-less,* in certain times we interact with a certain type of person over-and-over again. This is why people move to religious community, I suppose. So, they will only interact with people of like mind.

Recently, I have been forced into interaction(s) with a type of person that I would call a, *Space Invader.* Meaning, they come into an environment and take it over either knowingly or unknowingly via their unconscious actions—messing with the lives of all those around them.

Today, I was speaking with a smoker. He believes it is his right to smoke anywhere he sees fit. Thankfully, laws have been put into place, and are continuing to be put in place, to curb this type of activity. But, these laws leave him unfazed.

I asked, *"What about the damage you cause to others with your second-hand smoke?"* His answer, "What if I don't believe in that?" I said, *"It doesn't matter if you believe in it or not; facts are facts!"*

I remember when *Starbucks* instigated their no smoking policy a couple of years ago. I saw some customers literally throwing fits when the staff, (who mostly smoked themselves), would go out there and tell these people they couldn't smoke on their property. *"It is my right!"* *"This is public property!"* Well actually, no it isn't. It is private property.

For those of us who don't smoke, I think we can each remember times when we were enjoying a cappuccino, a cocktail, or a meal somewhere outdoors and then somebody lighted up and ruined it for us. *Space Invader!*

Now, I am a sinner too, (in more ways than I can count). I mean, back in the '80s and '90s we rode our Harleys with straight-pipes. Meaning, they had no mufflers. This really added to noise pollution. This is probably one of the primary factors that lead to the tinnitus I suffer from. …That, and standing in front of one too many blasting *Marshall* amplifiers. (That's my *karma*, I guess). Of course, I ride with a muffler now.

Anyway, I remember I was cast for an *Orange Crush* commercial back in '90 or '91. My Harley and me. Also cast was this blonde girl who also had her own Harley.

The commercial was for South America and I guess they wanted to present the whole long blonde hair California thing. Anyway, after we drank our *Orange Crush(s)* and did our dialogue, we rode around Hollywood behind a camera truck while they filmed us. Every time we would set off a car alarm with our tailpipes, the girl, (I forget her name), would get all excited and give me the thumbs up. Man, bikes were loud back then and some of them still are. When I saw the commercial they had edited in a lot of her thumbs up but made it look like it was all about the *Orange Crush*. Funny… Very *Zen Filmmaking.*

From a psychological perspective, the modern proponents talk a lot about owning yourself and owning your space. But, owning your space does not mean invading the space of others. I think this is something we each have to be cautious of.

Because, not only do we not want to create negative *karma* for ourselves, but we want to be thought well of. If we mess with people's space, either via things like smoking, noise, or whatever, then negative thoughts are directed towards us. And, nobody wants this, because negative thoughts are the sourcepoint for negative actions.

We, as conscious individuals, want to be good. We want to do good things. We want to think good thoughts and have good thoughts thought about us.

Don't Space Invade!

Nobody Really Cares

People claim they care about things. They say they care about global warming, saving the whales, freeing Tibet, immigration reform, art, music, cinema, but they do absolutely nothing about anything. They simply dance through their life, living whatever momentary reality they are living, and that is that. They may even get into long discussion about what they believe to be right or wrong, write some comments on some webpages, but still they do nothing—as talking is not doing.

There are certain instances in life when people congregate. There was this big immigration rally; focused on providing citizenship to illegal immigrants held here in L.A. several years ago and it drew large crowds of Latinos. Sure, Latinos make up most of the illegal immigrants here in the U.S… There were even signs at drive-thru restaurants like *El Polo Loco* during this rally stating that you may have to wait a long time because several of their staff members went to the rally. Some places even closed.

I won't go into the logistics or the right or wrong political ramifications of what this rally was or was not. But, I will discuss, what came from it—nothing. Sure a large group of people congregated, speeches were given, they marched, it gave the newscasters something to talk about, some police got in trouble for doing things against policy, but whatever… Mostly, it was a large street party, now forgotten. Same with occupy, New York, L.A., Oakland, etc.

People congregate to get their adrenaline agitated. It is the same as going to a nightclub. But, then they go home and fall back into mundane existence.

People care until they care no longer—though for a moment in their mind they believe that they do. In your mind is not in your life.

When you actually find somebody caring and getting out there and actually doing something to actualize a desired end goal, virtually always it is based upon something that will benefit them personally—even if they may falsely claim it is for the good of all.

There are places in the world where you have to care or die. It is not like that in the West. Here, caring is, at best, about something that makes the individual feel better, more empowered, or in a position of authority and control for caring about what they care about.

Think about when you were young, you probably really liked a singer or a musical group. Their posters were on your wall. Maybe you really liked an actor. You discussed them all the time with your friends; had fantasies about them. But, then you grew up. Do you still have posters of your favorite band on your wall? Probably not.

I have witnessed people get into arguments and fights over one person believing in one thing and the other person believing the opposite. They believed, sure. They argued, they fought, okay. But, then what? Neither one of them did anything to make anything happened. All they did was believe, which lead to meaningless violence.

This happens in religion and in politics all the time.

On the artistic level this is no different. People like what they like, don't like what they don't like based upon whatever momentary reality they are basing the existence upon. They feel this is a basis for caring. But, do they really care?

I receive questions all the time about what I do and why. Most people are cool but there are even some people who take the time to attack what I do. Okay, but why? How does that change anything? Why do you care? I am me, you are you. I do what I do based upon a philosophic premise. Why do you do what you do? And, how does attacking me or anybody else equal anything? Art is such a ridiculous medium to instigate controversy over.

Life is about doing, not undoing. And, if your caring is based on hurting, damaging, or negativity you are really caring about the wrong thing.

It was like when Donald G. Jackson passed away. I cannot tell you how many people kept asking me, *"Who was he? What was he like? Please make a documentary about him!"* Some people he knew actually contacted me and wanted me to give them the footage I was in possession of so they could make a documentary. Like I was going to do that! ...For I have long ago realized that though people have great intentions, nobody ever does anything. Anyway, I did do a documentary, more than one, in fact. Nobody has seen them. Except for a few very hardcore people who actually truly did possess an interest in Don, how his mind worked, and our filmmaking process—very few people ever viewed the film(s). They may have thought that they cared. They may have believed for a moment that they cared. But, they did not care.

This is an ideal example of life and the life of caring. In your mind you may believe that you care. But, in your life you can't really be bothered unless something is handed to you on a silver platter.

People care when they can care from home. People care when they are discussing things with their friends of like-mind. People care when it doesn't cost them any money. People care when it doesn't cost them any time. People care when they don't have to do anything but believe they are right and you are wrong. People care when they receive personal empowerment by caring. People care when what they care about benefits them. People care when they can go to a street party, get adrenalized while being surround by people who are screaming the same slogan. People care... Wait, people only care about themselves.

Nobody really cares...

Nobody Remembers Their Name

I often jokingly tell stories about some of the calamities I have encountered while casting a movie. Nobody ever believes me until they try to do it themselves. There have been so many times I have discussed this subject with students in my classes or at a seminar and there is always someone who is dismissive if not downright argumentative about the realities of casting an indie movie. Then, they try to bring-up a film and I always hear back from them telling me, *"You were right!"*

Hollywood is a strange beast. And, I use the term, *"Hollywood,"* to describe the film business in general. But here, in actual Hollywood, people come to be stars. They come to be stars on the big screen. And, they expect to have it happen overnight with no effort. They feel they have a look or talent and that should be enough. From my experience, I can tell, you it is not.

In any case, I have discussed some of the situations that have occurred while attempting to cast in a film in many other places. There is extensive discussions of the subject in my books: *Zen Filmmaking* and *Independent Filmmaking: Secrets of the Craft*. But, one of the ideal examples that comes to mind is when Don Jackson and I were originally going to film *Lingerie Kickboxer*. We planned to shoot it on 35mm and do it in a twenty-four hour period just to show the world that it could be done. We had shows like *Entertainment Tonight* and reporters from industry magazines like *The Hollywood Reporter* scheduled to meet us throughout the shooting day at various locations. At 4:00 AM, the night before the shoot, I receive a phone call from the actress who was to play the lead role in the film, she told me she couldn't do it because she had to go to a family reunion with her boyfriend. Thus, the production came to screeching halt.

There have been numerous other times where I offered actors and actresses the lead or a supporting role in a film and they either didn't show up for the production or called me the night before saying they decided not to do it or their agent told them not to do it.

I won't even go into the bullshit-ness of agent here...

So, there went their roll. One of the more amusing phone calls I received was from one actress who called me up and rudely stated, *"I'm not going to be in a film just so you can have somebody make-out with me!"* What? She sure had a high opinion of her self. In any case, I had offered her the female lead in a film where all she had to do was kiss a guy to establish they were in a relationship. Not too much to ask for a starring role. And, this chick was a stripper by trade and had never been an actual film—even though her resume said she had.

Remember the number one rule of filmmaking, *"Everybody lies."* Anyway...

Aside from not showing up or not showing up on the next day of a shoot to complete their role, some people have left my set before they were even filmed due to the fact that they arrived and discovered that we were not a major Hollywood production. Though I certainly never claim to be.

Just a side note here: This is one of the problems that occurs from people being an extra in a movie or on a T.V. show. In those situations, the productions are BIG. Thus, the novice actor or actress comes to believe that all productions should be that big. From this, what happens is that their minds have been mislead into believing that the BIGS are the only real productions. They are not.

All this being said, let me get to the point, because I could go on for hours upon hours about this subject... I have worked with a lot of very talented actors and actress since I enter the film industry many years ago. The majority of them are nice, professional, and came to do their job and did it with excellence. At the end of the day, they were in a movie. In fact, some have used this on-camera experience to springboard their careers. Others did not move up the ladder, but at least they have one film that they were in to show their family and friends.

I had a realization while I was driving this afternoon... It was, all of those people who turned down the opportunity to be in one of my films, (for whatever reason), I do even remember their name. And, nobody else does either.

You really need to accept opportunities when opportunities are offered to you in your life.

Hollywood: The Impossible Game

People come to Hollywood everyday hoping to become stars. Once here, they pay hundreds of dollars to get headshots, pay thousands of dollars to take acting classes from teacher who, themselves, have never appeared in film, T.V., or commercials to any substantial degree, if at all. Then, if the person is lucky enough to get an agent, they will buy clothing for auditions that they have no hope of getting, believe that they are actually appearing in something when they are only an extra in a film or on a television show, (FYI it is very easy to get extra work), buy video cameras to practice in front of, and this list goes on and on.

As someone who was born in Hollywood, I have a bit of unique perspective. In fact, I used to walk to Hollywood High School down the boulevard of the stars everyday until I got a car and then I drove down Hollywood Blvd. to get to school. I lived between Hollywood and Sunset Blvd. So, I saw all of it, the whole Hollywood game from a very inside perspective. This is what caused me to never want to be involved in the film industry. But, I too fell prey to many of the drawbacks once I gave into the curse when I thirty-two years old. In other words, I know what it's like. The stories I could tell you...

All this is also why I go out of my way to help young actors and filmmakers wherever I can— because I know that most who come here will never achieve anything except maybe an overextended credit card bill.

Like I always tell young actors and actresses who delve into the indie film market, ninety-nine percent of the people who hope to make a film will never complete it because they do not have the focus, the finances, or the dedication to do it, so be careful. This same premise is why I developed *Zen Filmmaking*. To help those young filmmakers get past some of the hurdles and actually make their dreams become a reality.

But, let's face facts; Hollywood is an impossible game. Sure, some people do come from nowhere and actually make-it. Good for them! But, what is the truth behind their success? We will probably never know.

And, think about this, how many actors who had a T.V. series that you really liked or where in a movie that you remember, disappeared and were never heard from again. They had success for a second and then they were gone. Where did they go?

That is the truth about Hollywood; many people come here, most leave with only broken dreams. The others may have a moment of success and then they are gone. The few who make it, by talent, luck, *karma*, whatever, are the blessed ones. But, the main thing is, if you come here; never fall under the illusion that anyone or anything—that any about success will make you more than you already are.

Success is internal. Everything else can be taken away from you or it can simply fade away.

Hollywood, it is an impossible game. Fortunately, or perhaps more than likely, unfortunately; it is where I am from.

Like the line I fed one of my actor's in the *Zen Film, Samurai Vampire Bikers from Hell*, *"Hollywood? Hollywood's just a state of mind."*

Why Do You Believe?

Whenever I teach a course on filmmaking I always begin by explaining the number one rule of filmmaking to the students. The number one rule of filmmaking is, *"Everybody lies."* Meaning, that in the film game everybody lies about everything. They lie about their credits, their abilities, their training, their film's cast, crew, equipment, budget, EVERYTHING.

It is pretty easy for the students to understand this concept when I detail this fact. But, let's think about life. How different is it? Not much…

People lie. It is a simple fact of life. They lie for an untold number of reasons. But, the fact of the matter is, they do lie.

The problem that arises here is that the average person is schooled to believe what a person says is, in fact, the truth. Unless an individual is caught in an outright lie, what they speak is believed to be true. In fact, most people want to believe what another person says. But, people lie… They distort the truth to use it to their own ends. They lie to gain power, control, self-worth, wealth, fame, whatever, in order to gain whatever it is they hope to gain by altering the boundaries of the truth.

This lying goes on everywhere in life. Whether it is a small white-lie or a massive deception; lying is one of the dominant factors of life. It exists in *person-to-person* relationships, certainly it is abundant on the internet, and it also flourishes within religious and spiritual communities, even though most would hope and think this is not the case.

All lying begins with one sourcepoint. It begins with you.

Ask yourself, *"How many times have you lied?"* Also, question yourself, *"Why did you distort the truth? What did you hope to gain?"*

To each person there will be a somewhat differing answer. But, the root action is the same, a lie was told.

Let's think about this for a moment, *"What happens when you lie?"* The answer is, another person makes a choice, based upon a false set of facts. From this, though you may gain what you had hoped for, the other person's life is altered forever.

Let's also question, *"What is the consequence of your lies."* If you are not caught, most people feel they got away with it. They gained whatever it is they hoped for. Thus, they won.

If you are caught in a lie, however, most people lie to get out of their original lie. But, it all ends up in the same place. People's lives are altered due to your falsehood and in many cases these people are left to progress through the rest of their life less than they would have been had you not lied.

And, I use the term, *"You,"* meaning everyone…

Some will say, *"Everyone lies. So, what's the difference?"* True, but all life begins with you. And, all life ends with you.

While you are here, in human form, you are an instrumental element in all the reality that surrounds you. As such, what you do affects EVERTHING. Thus, it is your choice how you want to create not only your world but also the world around you.

It is very simple; if you lie you hurt people. If they lie to you, they hurt you. The circle needs to be broken. Tell the truth.

Stirring the Pot

There are some people who like to create controversy and disharmony. I believe that we have all met people like this. The say things and do things that are either distorted or not true simply to get people to believe things about life-situations or other people in order to cause them to become angry at that situation or that person. Some call this practice backstabbing but it is actually much deeper than this.

The reason that people commonly behave in this matter is that they hold a low sense of self-worth. Where this comes from can be anybody's guess. But, early in life they have discovered that they can gain a false sense of control over others by guiding them with misinformation and/or lies. The result of this type of behavior causes all kinds of interpersonal disharmonies that can lead to confrontations, arguments, fights, and on a larger scale, wars.

The problem with people who behave in this manner is that the people they are telling their stories to commonly are not aware that they are being lied to and strung along in order for the person to gain a sense of control and self-worth. In other words, people believe the lies.

I believe that most of us want to trust people and believe the things that we are told are true and valid. It is human nature to believe that others are the same as us—speaking the facts, as we know them. It is only after encountering people of the aforementioned type that we then begin to become less trusting and are forced to begin to critically analyze the words of others before we move forward with what we have heard.

From a person perspective, my friend and *Zen Filmmaking* associate, Donald G. Jackson, was notorious for this type of behavior. He would tell people all kinds of things about other people, simply to get a rise out of them. He would, in fact, totally break apart film production teams simply to satisfy his need to gain misguided control. There was several times when I was associated with him that people I considered friends would either shun me or accost me due to false words that Jackson had spoken. It was very strange.

For me, I saw through this character flaw early on and, as such, took his words with a grain of salt. I heard them but I did not allow them to influence me as to my judgment of a person's actual personality. Sadly, other people were not so astute and, as such, he caused our relationships to fall apart.

The causation factor for this type of behavior is rooted in a person's desire for power, dominance, and control. You can commonly see this type of behavior in the workplace when something has gone awry and higher management challenges middle management as to their actual management skills. From this challenge, the person in middle management begins to take out their lack of control on their underlings. They shift the blame, they blame others, they may even make up lies about their coworkers in order to shift responsibility, but the outcome of this style of human interaction is all the same—they have created disharmony due to the fact that they are not whole, confident, responsible for their actions, and complete onto themselves. Thus, they create havoc in order to shift the focus from their own inabilities to manage towards someone else. This type of behavior is commonly titled, *"Saving their own ass."*

Ultimately, (and perhaps sadly), we are all going to be forced to interact with this type of person as we pass through life. There is no way around it. In fact, in the workplace environment, this type of person may actually have a certain amount of control over us. But… We do not have to let this type of person control who we are, how we feel about ourselves, and how we make our life decisions about others.

We must each listen to all that we hear and then make our own choices about the truth and/or validity about what is spoken to us. Then, we must move forward, without judging, and make our own decision about people and this life-place free from the domination and control imparted by the words spoken by others.

Life is full of many people who embrace low human consciousness. In fact, we are more likely to encounter that type of person than one who actually embraces refined higher consciousness. This is life and that's the dilemma. But, by being whole and true onto ourselves, we can exist in a space of peace, knowing that we embrace the truth and are not dominated by the psychological inadequacies of others.

Be silent. Don't try to control or alter the consciousness and understandings of others. Don't desire control or admiration. And, this world becomes such a better place.

Getting it Right. Getting it Wrong.

When you create something, it is always curiously interesting to find out how other people view it. When you create something with art as a basis; be it a painting, a piece of literature, a photograph, or a movie, mostly people describe how they feel about it—if they like it or if they do not.

As we all come at art from our own preconceived notions and personal tastes, I always find it curious how other people come to define my work. Sometimes they get it right. They understand what I was doing. Other times they get it totally wrong.

I guess that is the basis of art, at the sourcepoint the creator understands what they are doing and why they are doing it. And, in most cases, the creator likes what they have created. Someone who was not involved in the creation—someone who has no vested interest in the work, may not understand the creative source-process and they may not like it. That's just life. That's just art and the interpretation thereof.

As I have written in various places in the past, and even in an article I wrote, *"Film Reviews: Fact or Fiction,"* as many of my films have been reviewed in magazines, books, and on the Internet over the years, I find it very interesting when the reviewer gets things right and more particularly when a reviewer get things wrong but presents their words as facts.

Now, I'm not speaking about when people hate my films and totally rip them. That's fine with me. If you don't like it, you don't like it. Whatever... I'm speaking more of when someone does not possess all of the facts, but writes as if they do, and presents the overall process incorrectly.

Recently someone sent me a copy of a book where the author mentions a couple of my films and one film made, (at least in part), by my *Zen Filmmaking* friend, Donald G. Jackson (RIP). The book was pretty good. My stuff got discussed in the, *"Honorable (and Dishonorable) Mention,"* chapter. That was fun and amusing. But, the author got a few things wrong. Let me explain…

In one chapter, he discussed Don's film, *Pocket Ninjas*. I believe he got his source information from the Internet, because he states that Don and the executive producer were trying to make *The Roller Blade Seven* for kids. This is not true. This was not at all the basis for that film—though I have seen it detailed as such on the Internet. Don was simply obsessed with roller skates and later roller blades from the 1970s forward. He came up in the era of pretty girls on skates. So, he would integrate that into his films whenever possible. Plus, though he never personally trained, he loved the martial arts. As such, he would also feature the martial arts in his movies wherever possible. Thus, was the basis of *Pocket Ninjas*.

The author also attempts to detail the relationship between the executive producer and Don in the book. Again, I guess he got the information from the Internet because it mirrors what I have seen but it is essentially wrong. The executive producer did not come to Don; Don had our friend Mark Williams (RIP) write a script based on an idea he had. He then took the script to the executive producer.

I had previously worked with the executive producer and he is a very nice guy. Don had also known him for years.

The executive producer was a formalized filmmaker; he had no intention of making a *Zen Film*. *Pocket Ninjas* was in no way a *Zen Film*. Bad, yes. But, not bad because it was a *Zen Film*.

In the book, the author details Don's removal from the film. But, he gets it wrong. The reason for the relationship collapse and Don being pulled was that the executive producer felt Don was letting production fall behind. Don, on the other hand, blamed the producer, who became the credited director. It was one of those common Hollywood dilemmas. Nothing new here… But, we all still remained friends.

That's the story. I hope the world will finally get it right.

The author also discusses, *The Roller Blade Seven* and *Max Hell Frog Warrior*, explaining that they are two of the best-known *Zen Films*. Maybe…

Roller Blade Seven is certainly, without a doubt, the most well known *Zen Film*, as it was released theatrically, on T.V., and by other methods around the world. Actually, *Max Hell* is somewhat lowered down the list. Here in the U.S. there has been a certain amount of talk about the film. They even mentioned it on the HBO T.V. show, *The Newsroom*. Thanks! But, the fact is, other *Zen Films* such as: *Samurai Vampire Bikers from Hell, Guns of El Chupacabra, Undercover X, Hitman City, Vampire Blvd., Vampire Noir,* and *Super Hero Central* have all been much more widely distributed. But, that fact would be impossible to know unless someone asked me. …Which no one did.

The author also makes an attempting at describing *Zen Filmmaking*. Certainly, I realize that is a bit of a complicated matter. ☺

And, the problem is, most people who talk about it, don't really get it. But, this author provides a fairly good overview. Good job!

In his description of *Zen Filmmaking*, however, the author details that in *Zen Filmmaking* shots are often repeated. The fact is, to date, this is only true in the two films he mentions. It is not a common trait of *Zen Filmmaking*. The basis for this technique being used in the two discussed films is, *Roller Blade Seven* was the first *Zen Film*. We set up that film-style in that movie which we created in 1991 and 1992. Don and I did not make another film together until 1996 when we created *Toad Warrior,* which later became *Max Hell Frog Warrior.*

When we reconvened as filmmakers, we decided we wanted to capture some of the essence and energy of *Roller Blade Seven,* which is why I wore basically the same outfit and we again employed that editing style. But, no other *Zen Film* that Don and I made as a team or that I have made employs that editing technique.

This is one of the things that those who watch a *Zen Film* commonly misunderstand—particularly the two films that were detailed in the book; *Zen Filmmaking* is constantly evolving, it is never a stagnant art form. Each film brings with it its own unique sense of creativity and artistic expression. And, the two discussed films are very different from every other *Zen Film* ever made. Ultimately, that is the essence of *Zen Filmmaking, embracing* the moment and allowing the creative environment of each film to guide you down the road to cinematic enlightenment.

But, as was embraced by P.T. Barnum and Andy Warhol, *"You may have gotten a few things wrong but thanks for the publicity Mr. Author."*

DSLR Cinematography

Over the past several years many people have taken to using their DSLR cameras to film their independent films and music videos. The reason for this is twofold: One, the cameras are generally much cheaper to buy than a good camera that is actually designed to shoot live action video. Two, due to the fact that you can easily change the lenses on these cameras they give the would-be filmmaker varying cinematic options. Though, on a basic level, these cameras do provide a fairly good video image, there are also several problems with using them as a tool to film a competent movie.

The initial problem that arises with using a DSLR, as a filmmaking tool, comes from the way in which it focuses. Whereas the focusing mechanism in a video camera is designed to find, focus, and capture a moving image, this is not the case with a DSLR. DSLR focusing is designed to capture a still image, (as they are actually designed as a still frame camera). To this end, if you are going to use your DSLR camera to film a movie you really need to work with lock-off shots. Meaning, set up a tripod, get your actors in place, and then let them do their stuff with little or no spherical or to-and-fro movement. If you work within a standardized lock-off shot format then your DSLR can capture a nice image.

For me, personally, I find the lock-off shot very boring. I like visual movement. To this end, whenever I use one of my DSLR cameras to film people, I very precisely lock the focus and keep the subject(s) at a static and standardized distance. From this, the figures appear to have movement while keeping them in focus and preventing the camera from attempting to find focus.

The second problem with using a DSLR camera, as a filmmaking tool, comes from its capability to record sound. Almost every digital camera from the point and shoots up to the high end DSLRs now have built-in microphones. The problem is, these microphones are terrible. They produce horrible sound. In controlled internal situations you can get okay audio, but never good. If you go outside, forget about it.

Most higher-end DSLRs do have an external microphone input. If you are going to shoot with a DSLR get a high-end mic and use it! This being said, the way a DSLR processes sound is also not as good as the way a camera designed to shoot video does.

Now, I'm not going to go into a long discourse about sound here. If you want to read the everything about the superiority of the XLR microphones and the appropriate microphones and cables that drive them you can read my book *Zen Filmmaking* or find information online. I will say, high-end mics are not designed to be feed into a camera through a mini plug, as the DSLR provides. Your sound will be altered. It will be much better than using the on-board mic but it will be altered. So, expect that.

On the other side of the issue there are some microphones that are designed to mount on a DSLR camera and provide you with superior sound. Yes, they do give you better sound. But again, they are not a professional XLR microphone, driven through an XLR port, so you must keep that in mind.

Personally, whenever I use a DSLR, as a filmmaking tool, I use it only to capture a visual image. I never expect the sound to be usable.

The fact is, the DSLR is, no doubt, going to continue to be used in filmmaking situations. But, if you use one, you must keep in mind that though they can capture video, that is not what they are designed to do. It is an after thought. If you plan to shoot a visually stimulating film, the best thing to do is to actually go with a camera that is designed to shoot video. The best cameras for that purpose have always been the ones created by Sony. Though Canon is a big player in the market, their cameras forever have underlying issues. Sony is a much better product.

At the end of the day, if you want to be a filmmaker, I always say, get out there and do it. Make your movie in the best way (any way) you can. So, if you have a DSLR to work with, do it. Even if you just have a point and shoot or your phone—if you want to film visual images, use whatever you have.

This being said, it is important to keep in mind that every medium has its limitations. Work with what you have but understand the limitations.

Movies You Will Never See

I just read a very interesting article about films that were pulled from distribution or never released. Some of them were very big dollar productions.

With all that is going on with the debacle of the film, *The Interview*... And, I understand all sides of the issue. Sony (a Japanese company) got hacked. North Korea is pissed and they have nukes and are very close to Japan. And, the distributors, at least at this moment, pulled back from its distribution. So, there was no way for Sony to get the film out there. In the process of all this, a lot of people were hurt, however. So, who is ultimately to blame? I don't know? As everyone in the film game is a participant and a player. So??? I will just leave that question to the annals of karma...

Back here in reality, there are a lot of reasons why films are not released. The biggest one being, they turned out bad and the main creators of them would not let the film get out there. Back in the day, the name Alan Smithee was use by filmmakers who had made a film and ultimately didn't like its outcome. As too much money had gone into it to simply bury it, the creators, to hide from all the shame of it, used this pseudonym.

There's a great group of people who do a project called, *The Smithee Awards*. They track down, screen, and provided awards to the best of the worst. Some of my films have made it. Thanks guys!!!

But, more to the point... A lot of films are lost to the changing tides of time. Look for the film, *London After Midnight*. Gone... All copies disintegrated to *never-never-land* with the passing hands of time.

  Another causation factor is that a lot of films that were made back in the day, before the age of video and digital, were made at a time when a film was only going to be a film. Thus, they never contracted for the rights to use the music or various other elements of the film when new technologies were born. With no release for the music, and the copyright holder refusing to let the music be used in new media, the film was lost. I know this held up the great film, *Two Lane Blacktop* from being released on video for many years. There are others that you will never see in any new medium.

  And, this is just one example. People own the rights to their creations; whether it is the character, the screenplay, the music, you name it. And, this is a very litigious society. Have you ever been sued? It is not fun nor is it cheap. So, people wisely choose to not release a product, that they do not own the rights to, over getting sued and losing—which is what happens if you don't own the rights...

  I realize that in this digital age people believe that they can grab anything and do whatever they want with it. Of course, this involves grabbing somebody else's something... And, this is the key to the equation. You don't care if it's not yours... If it is yours, you may have a very different ideology. But, this is life...

  I too have had films lost to *never-never-land*. The main one being, *Lingerie Kickboxer*. Done, but never seen. And, that's the thing when you collaborate with other people; each has their own ideas. Don Jackson and I were all-good with the film, our partners wanted a few high-budget

changes, that we never got around to making. So…
I think it's a great film and a perfect example of true *Zen Filmmaking* but you will probably never see it. Of course, if you wanted to pay me a lot of money I may go and take it out of my film vault at Paramount and set up a private screening for you. ☺

And, this is the thing, simply because you cannot see a specific film as you may want to see it: via video tape, DVD, or streaming, does not mean that it is not out there somewhere and with the right incentive you may view it.

On the other side of the issue, there are tons-and-tons of films that get started and are never finished. Then, there are the finished products that the filmmaker doesn't know what to do with them so they are lost to the viewing eye and never seen. I know several films and filmmakers who have followed this path even thought they had made a really good movie.

So, I guess it all gets back to the Zen of life. If a tree falls in the forest and there is no one there to hear it, does it make a sound at all? Or, if you heard it fall once what happens if it never falls again?

Studying the Subtleties

Rather amusingly, I received an email today from a guy who has written a long review about the *Zen Film, Max Hell Frog Warrior*. For some reason he wanted me to read it before it was published; though the review is already on its way to press. Every now and then people do this. Why, I don't really know?

It amazes me, but we made *Max Hell* almost twenty years ago, yet it is still receiving press. I guess we did something right. But, that is not really the point…

The point being, and this is something I see so often with film reviewers, is that they do not study the subtleties of a film as they write their reviews—long or otherwise. And, this is true whether they like the film or not. From a filmmaker's standpoint, I can tell you that all of my *Zen Films* are full of subtleties: from the dialogue, to where the scenes are shot, onto the camera movement, the set, the set decorations, the lighting, the music, the editing, and beyond. You may need to look for them (as that is the point of subtleties) but they are everywhere. But, reviewers oftentimes overlook this fact.

For example, in *Max Hell Frog Warrior* AKA *Toad Warrior* many reviewers (as did this man) mention the fact that we return to one scene several times. That scene is a Kurosawa influenced moment where my character is on a ridge and the sun has left the sky. My character and my opponent charge at each other with samurai swords in silhouette. It's a beautiful scene. We used this scene several times as a moment of transition between various other scenes in the film. What most everyone fails to take note of, however, is that it is not simply a one-take scene. We shot that scene several times. Thus, what you see in the finished film, if you care enough to study it, is that there are different versions of that scene used for different transitional moment. Thus, equaling filmmaking subtlety.

For me, I don't care if someone bags my films or not. (Though this reviewer wrote a fairly fair appraisal). We all like what we like and don't like what we don't like. What makes me have a less than ideal attitude about some reviewers, however, is that they miss some of the most elemental moments of a film, as they are watching the whole and not studying the intricacies.

And, I believe this goes to life, as well. Most people do not study the subtleties. They plow through any new environment, situation, life experience, or work of art they may encounter with their mind already made up, doing and saying what they have forever done. They are who they are! Their mind is made up! And, the world be damned! But, this is not a good way to live life. Because by behaving in this manner you miss so much of the elemental magic that is available if you step beyond yourself and your preconceived notions and take the time to experience each thing you encounter as new and whole—not simply as something you believe you have the right to pass judgment upon.

I believe that everywhere you go, everything you do, the first thing you need to do is stop, listen, see, and embrace the wholeness of the environment or the work of art. Let it define itself. From this, you will have allowed yourself to take note of and embrace the subtleties. And, this is where the magic is born.

The ultimate truth about life is that you are not in control of anything. At best you are simply a conscious participant. Seek to know the subtleties. Then all life becomes MORE.

The Way We Weren't

I had this interesting flash, as I was getting up this morning. The song, *"The Way We Were,"* sung by Barbara Streisand, came to mind. Why, I don't know? Weird... But, the title of the song did set me to thinking...

Before I get to the whole point and realization of all of this, the thought of the song and the aftermath caused me to ponder the film. I know everyone is speaking about the upcoming film, *Fifty Shades of Grey*—which is soon to be released. But, I think the casting for that is all wrong. Dakota Johnson is no where near homely, as depicted in the book, and Jamie Dorman is not all that. They should have cast it like, *The Way We Were,* with a young Robert Redford and Barbara Streisand. That's the visual dichotomy expressed in the novel. Anyway, on to the point...

I have never been one of those people to look back at people, relationships, (failed or otherwise), and life events, and question what would have happened if only... I never felt like someone or something got away. I have always simply viewed life as life and relationships as what they were, when they were, and have moved on. This being said, in each of our lives, mine included, if I would have gone this way with that person instead of going the other, certainly my life would have turned out differently. But, different how?

I mean there were more than a few girls who came knocking on my door but I was locked up in the arms of someone else and couldn't answer. There were a few that were totally into me and I treated them like shit due to my dissatisfaction with the relationship. Not their fault, but mine. There were a couple that I was just too young and arrogant to appreciate. Others that I felt I had nothing to offer so I stepped away. There were one or two that some self-righteous, so-called friend trashed the relationship by telling them his appraisal of my truth and killed what should/could have been. And certainly, there has been a psycho bitch or two—the kind of woman that men just love because they pour a bucket of adrenaline over your head and you become enthralled in passion and all its consequences—at least for a time. Luckily, I was (eventually) smart enough to leave those women behind...

But, it is not just love affairs that define a life. It is the people(s) that you interact with and what they have the potential to do for and/or to your life. I mean, I too have been fucked over by people in business relationships. Certainly, in the martial arts there have been a few people that really messed with my life. This, after I helped them for years... The film industry, forget about it... The stories I could tell you. The future that could have been in my life had it not gotten trashed by the hands of other people more than a few times.

As I speak about my *Zen Filmmaking* buddy, Donald G. Jackson periodically, I can tell a story about one such incident. Don had briefly worked under the auspice of Roger Corman when he first moved to L.A. We heard that Corman was thinking about moving from film to digital for his productions. Who better to help him make this transition than Don and myself? Don set up a meet between the three of us. On the morning of that scheduled meeting, Don calls up my voice mail and tells me that he was going to the meeting alone. He stated, *"This is Donald G. Jackson and Company and you are just the, and company."* What an asshole. Fuck you! If it weren't for me, you wouldn't have finished a film in years!

For those of you who did not know him, Don was a very self-involved, selfish, childish individual. He could be a real asshole. More than a few people questioned why I was his friend. Me too...

But, I knew what was going on. Due to my age, (compared to his), my vast knowledge of technology, and my natural enthusiasm, he knew Corman would hire me and not him. I didn't speak to Don for over a year after that, though he called and called my voice mail. Finally, when he was getting near the end of his days he contacted me as he knew I was the only person who would keep his legacy alive. Which I have done. But, this is an ideal example of someone killing the what could have been in another person's life and doing it for no good reason.

In some cases, I, like everyone else, do get pissed off about what people have done to me and how it has affected my life. Like many of us, (especially in this internet age inhabited by trolls), people have said untrue things about me. Some have even written them in books and magazines. Of course, it pisses me off. And yes, it does affect the evolution and the what could have been in my life. But, you can't let yourself be defined by a retaliatory mindset—allowing people who do things like that to control your emotions. As is the case with all of us, what you do leads to what happens to you... They will get theirs.

But, back to the central premise...

The point is, and the thing we must all keep in mind: what is, is—what is not, is not. We will never know what would have been, if only... In some cases, people try to rechart their past. I know people from my past have contacted me years later to see if we can reenact a moment. You can't! Yes, it can be a different moment, if you choose it to be. But, it cannot be that ideal dream-space of what, *"Should have been,"* that is locked in your realm of fantasies.

So, ultimately we are simply in a state of living our life to the best of our ability—doing what we can with what we have available to us at this point in our Here and our Now. Yeah, our lives would have been different if... But, that is just wild speculation. It may have turned out great, if... Or, it may have turned out really shitty.

So, all we can ALL do is just live to the best of our ability. Make our choices of people, relationships, and the where, how, and who we interact with and what we do, as best as we can. Leave the past as the past and live now, with what and whom you have.

This is life. Live your moment as this moment is presented by what you have set forth in your past.

Don't look back. Look forward.

Zen Filmmaking: SS vs. DGJ

I am so often asked this question that it used to annoy me, now it makes me smile... The question being, *"What is the difference between your Zen Filmmaking and that of Donald G. Jackson?"* I just got hit with that question again this morning when I was doing a Skype interview for Italy...

So, here we go again... Don, unless he was working with me, virtually always based his filmmaking around a screenplay. Me, I never do. Why did he do this? I do not know, as he was one of the most random, crazy, disorganized, discombobulated people I have ever met. He was a mess! *Zen Filmmaking* was perfect for him. But, he virtually always chose to base his films around a screenplay. Though in the press he rarely revealed this fact.

His mind-mess is what led to him starting so many films but never finishing most of them. It also led to his filming a project and then either losing the film footage or hiding it away somewhere. In some cases, he didn't even know what he did with it. This is why, while he was in the hospitable, shortly before his leaving this world, he had his wife give me all of the film and video footage he and we had filmed. He knew who and what I was, a finisher. The minute I received them, I started editing. This is why so many more films he produced or directed came out after his death than while he was alive. I still a have a few more pieces to put together over a decade since his passing.

The biggest difference between the films Don made, the films he and I made together, and the films that I make, was money. Don would get investors and some of our films had major dollars behind them. And, Don would freely spend that money. He would buy tons and tons of stuff. He would feed everybody. He would pay for everybody's gas and buy them gifts; especially if they were girls. He paid a lot of rent for a lot of young ladies… He would even pay some people.

My *Zen Films* are just the opposite. I never take money from investors. So, my films are made with no money.

Don and I did, however, follow the same path of spontaneous, spur of the moment production, either when we were working together or apart. We would film like we had no money, even if we did. This is what leads to the fact that it is hard to tell which of our films had a big budget and which did not.

Mostly, Don and I functioned very well as a team. Though we had very different personalities, and he did bring in a large dose of melodrama to every film we ever made together, (something that I trust is absent from my productions), we were friends and from our abstract mindset we did create some interesting pieces of filmmaking.

So, were we different filmmakers? Yes, we were. But, when we made *Zen Films* together the magic did occur.

Again… There, the question is answered. ☺

Zen Filmmaking 1973

Flipping channels, the great Blaxploitation film, *Black Caesar* was just starting on one of the movie channels last night. With nothing else on worth watching, my lady and I took the time to rewatch the film. Good movie! I remember first seeing it when it was theatrically released back in '73 at one of the theaters on Hollywood Blvd. (Back then, my friend Steve and I would walk down the street and ask the person in the ticket booth if we could get in for free. Whomever would let us in, that is what we would see. We didn't need to do that. We had money. But, for whatever adolescent logic, that is what we would do). Anyway...

One of the interesting things I noticed that I had completely forgotten about was that when they were filming this movie they must have been doing it *Zen Filmmaking* style—with no filming permits. For if you watch the scenes shot on the streets in New York City near the end of the film, where Fred Williamson's character is shot, he is walking around and everyone is looking at him, looking at the camera, trying to figure out what is going on as he is supposedly bleeding—walking around all injured and stuff. It is pretty amusing. You can even see one guy walking up to him and trying to help him.

Now, I don't know the actual facts about the filming of this movie but it is a very interesting experiment in crowd interaction. And, I guess the director, Larry Cohen, was willing to have, and/or did not care about, the crowd looking into his lens. ...As we all understanding this is the absolute no-no in traditional filmmaking.

When you compare this movie to arguably the best Blaxploitation film ever, Super Fly, you can see the budgetary differences. When Ron O'Neal's character, Priest, was interactive in NYC he didn't have the staring into the camera of the massive bypassers going on. More budget obviously buys a better produced film but not necessarily a more unique production to watch.

One way or the other, *Black Caesar* is a great view into cinematic history and how *Zen Filmmaking* was working way back in the way back when. ☺

Roller Blade Seven:
Art-House Filmmaking Reality

As I discuss way more than I probably should, I am continually asked questions about and receive an insane amount of comments made about, *The Roller Blade Seven.*

That's All Good. I have stopped questioning why. And, I am happy to discuss the film even though it was created over twenty years ago.

It is one of those films that anyone who sees it will be set to questioning. I understand...

One thing I don't understand, however, for those of you out there in the wide-beyond of abstract *Art-House Filmmaking Reality,* is why no one sees the films that answer a lot of the questions about *The Roller Blade Seven.* Namely, *Interview* and especially, *Roller Blade Seven: The Unseen Scenes.*

Now, I am not trying to sell you a movie here. But, what I am telling you is that, particularly with, *Roller Blade Seven: The Unseen Scenes,* there is a lot of facts, never spoken information, and tons of unseen film footage in that documentary. So, for anyone who cares or anyone who really wants to know the truth behind RB7—know more than the average viewer of *Cult Cinema,* you should really check that movie out.

Okay... I'll shut up now. Keep asking your questions... ☺

Survivorman and the Search for Bigfoot

If you ever watched the show, *Survivorman,* with Les Stroud, you realize that guy is pretty hardcore. He goes out into the wilderness, for a week or more, and survives in some pretty intense environments. Good Show!

The other night I wish flipping channels and I came upon a show he did for the *Science Channel.* It was about his quest to find out the truth about Bigfoot. I won't go into what I think about the legend of Bigfoot but I will say, as all of his productions are, it was a very well photographed and produced television show. I guess part two of it will be on next week when we find out what Les finally discovers.

The reason I write this is that during the episode Les would go into long discourses about his past experiences with what he believed may have been Bigfoot and he also talks about strange occurrences like the way trees have fallen, forming a shape, and how others were broken in a very specific manner. He believed these happenings may have actually been orchestrated by Bigfoot.

During his discourses, I could not help but laugh. Everything he said, the way he described possibilities and circumstances, was so much like the way my character, Professor Andre' DuVena', spoke in the *Zen Film, Witch's Brew,* that it was scary.

Witch's Brew was one of the final films Donald G. Jackson and I collaborated on before he became too ill to film. He did his bit. I did mine. Of course, Don being Don, he never finished his part. So, several years after his passing, I put together his end of the footage and finished up the film. I believe that *Witch's Brew* is a great example of *Zen Filmmaking* though it is one of the *Zen Films* that has been virtually completely overlooked.

Anyway, it was like Les had taken his cue from that film and followed its evolution. (Though I would imagine he has never seen the film).

Anyway… It is simply funny how life and art parallel one another sometimes. And, how what was filmed, as a farce, has now become cinematic pseudo science. I smile…

Open Your Eyes

As a filmmaker, photographer, and instructor of both, I am often asked, *"What is the best way to compose a shot."* I have talked and written a lot on this subject and I think one of the main things you must keep in mind, (like I have long said), is that you must learn to see what the camera is seeing.

A camera does not see reality the way you see reality. And, each camera captures reality a bit differently.

I won't go into all of the technical reasons why, but each is different. The only way you can begin to understand how your camera views reality and how you can best use it to capture your vision of said reality is to practice with it.

With that as an initial basis of understanding, it must also be understood that a lot of times, with modern technology, you may not even be able to view what the lens of your camera is seeing. This is the case with both certain digital still cameras and the cameras that are designed to shoot video, as they only provide you with an LCD screen display to view your images instead of an actual view finder. Try shooting on a very sunny day and most likely all you will see is the screen and none of the information provided on it. Though the LCD screen is a great tool in controlled light, when you take it outside it is often times unusable. But, this is the modern world so you have to work within its definitions.

Many people when they go into a situation and know what they are going to shoot, all they end up trying to do is to capture the information—whether that information be a person's face, body, an external attraction, or in the case of filmmaking, human interaction. All they want is the information, plain and simple. But, more often than not, this information is static and boring.

From my perspective, what you truly need to do if you hope to create your own style in your photography or your cinematography is that you must open your eyes. You must never simply try to provide the information you need. Instead, you should integrate that information with your unique take on reality. To do this, take the time to study the environment, even if this is only for a moment. Integrate your subject(s) with the art that inhabits the space where you find yourself. And mostly, keep your eyes open all the time; actually look at and study the world around you, see what there is to see. If you witness something that moves you, photograph it. If you don't have a camera, simply witness the scene unfold.

If you want to understand how to best capture any image, always be a witness.

There Is So Much You Could Have Done

When I was teaching at *Santa Monica College* this beautiful Japanese girl took one of my classes on digital filmmaking. One evening I asked her about how she had come to the U.S. She explained that she had initially traveled here on a tourist visa, set up a business under a pseudonym, and then hired herself as an employee of that business when she returned to Japan. From this, she could stay here, with no expiration date, on a work visa.

OMG, I thought that was the greatest idea and it truly illustrated the creative ingenuity of some people.

Most people sit around and talk and talk. What does it equal? Nothing.

They may want to do something, they may wish they were something more, doing something else, they may even talk and talk about how special they are and what they are accomplishing, but what they are actually doing is that they are doing nothing, they just talk.

Some people even try to do something, but they do it in such a half assed, haphazard manner that all they end up doing is creating a mess in their own life and in the lives of those around them.

People are driven forward by their own inner nature. Some people want nothing from life—they want to do nothing. Okay... That is very Zen. Others want to do something but in their doing, they do it all wrong because they either have no clear achievable end goal or they hurt people in their process of obtaining their desired end; thus their karma becomes a mess and little can be achieved with a messy karma.

Doing can only be done when it is done from a state of pure mind. Pure mind is a focused end goal for the betterment of all.

The girls I speak of, she came here with vision of moving animation forward. She achieved it. Thus, she served all, not only herself.

If your ego is upfront, all you will ultimately do is fail. Ego is the defining factor of that. Surrender your ego to the greater good and then the greater good can be achieved.

References, Chaos, and the Game of Love or Hate

I have always found it a curious process that when you apply for a job they ask you for a list of reference. ...People who will vouch for you and your goodness. Now, what does that mean? Of course, you are only going to give them a list of people who are going to say good things about you. So, how does this add anything to the process of finding out who is right or wrong for the position?

More than a decade ago I taught this seminar on filmmaking. It was right at the time when indie filmmaking, due to digital technology, was taking the world by storm. The seminar was highly attended and it went very well. The next day I received a fax (remember those?) supposedly from the head of the film department at a local college. He wanted to speak with me about teaching for his school. I called him a couple a times but each time was told he was not available. Strange, I thought. I called back until I realized that it was not the head of the department sending me the faxes at all, it was probably one of the students in the department, who liked my seminar and wanted to push me into teaching at the school. A recommendation? Or not?

A few years after this I received a somewhat snarky letter from a local university, telling me that they were staffed up and did not have a position for me as an instructor. Accompanying the letter (remember those?) was a copy of the letter I had supposedly sent them. The thing was, I never sent them a letter! I never asked for employment. Also in the envelope was a copy of my pseudo *Production Resume*, which looked like it came straight off of imdb.com, and my academic credentials. The problem was, the list of schools that were listed were totally wrong. So, again... A recommendation? Or not? And, how would something like this affect my life in the future if I ever actually apply to this university for employment? But, more than that, why does anybody bother wasting his or her time doing stuff like this?

But, I guess those people liked me... A recommendation?

The film industry is a very strange game, as is the academic world. Once upon a time, way back in the way back when, the whole reason I went to grad school was so I could teach. Then, I got my first position and OMG; the backstabbing that goes on among professors at universities and the subtle realms of bullshit is unbelievable. So, I left all that behind for a long time. Then, after making (some would say) way too many films, I decided to teach again. And, I discovered that there was still a lot of behind the scenes bullshit going on. Stuff that, unless you are there, you would never know about... But, I have the credential, and like everybody, we all need to make a living. So...

In the many years I've been in the film game and an instructor of said, I have met some great people and a few horrible people. One of my students turned out to be a great cameraman and became a great boon to several of my films. I would give him a glowing recommendation. Another of my students produced a couple of films with me; great/talented guy! Then there are the other students (and people in general) who have begged and begged for me to usher them into the film business. Me, being the person I am, always wanting to help, I showed them the ropes; let them get their hands dirty. In this process, some decided to hate me. This, after going far out of my way to help them in the first place. I doubt that they would give me a very good recommendation. But, then I wouldn't recommend them either. ☺ But, that's just life… Especially life in the film game.

The problem with recommendations is that no one ever lists the people that hate them. But, here comes the kicker… You like or love a person because of the perceived nice or good things that they do for you. You dislike or hate a person because of the perceived nice or good things that they do for you. But, perception is based in your own personal level of reality; how you see and interact with the world. So, love or hate is all based in you. As such, the same actions performed makes one person happy and another person angry. Thus, where is the difference? The difference is in you.

So again, I don't know what recommendations mean? I've worked with people that other people hate. Me, I liked 'em. I've worked with people that other people revered. Me, I thought they were a jerk. So, the ball is all in your court. You see the world the way you see the world. You see people the way you see people. You judge the actions of people the way you judge the actions of people. The only defining factor is how your view(s) affects your life and the lives of the people whom you intact with and/or the entire world around you.

Who would give you a recommendation and why?

Same Old Lies

I was at my studio today having a sit down with a young filmmaker. Thankfully, his project was going to be financed by his father. A lot of times people ask me for a meet, telling me that their project is all ready to go, but when we get together it turns out that all they are doing is looking for money. I DON'T DO THAT, OKAY!

Anyway, as we sat there talking all I could hear was the same old language. *"My film is going to be a big success. I'm going to get it into film festivals and from there major theatrical distribution."* And, the promises went on... The problem was and is, this young filmmaker was making the same mistakes made by so many first-time filmmakers before him. He is going to shoot a very contrived script. The seen it all before kind. He is casting actors that due to their names and the numerous low budget projects they have previously been in will kill any hope of wide distribution he has for his film.

Word to the wise, just because a person is a known actor does not mean that their name lends anything to a film project. I told him all this, but the young man was undaunted.

Now, I often speak about the number one rule of filmmaking that I discovered many years ago, *"Everybody lies."* But, it is more than that, *"Everybody believes."*

I cannot tell you how many young filmmakers I have watched walk down the same road as this young man and make exactly they same mistakes, while stating the same expected outcome. Some of them ended up bankrupted. Most ended up very disillusioned. Few finished their films.

On the other side of the issue, I have seen some young filmmakers who go out there and do everything right. They get down to business, (with money behind them or not). They get their piece of cinematic art created. They do PR and get their film out there. Most have not made any money on their films. But, they DID IT! And, that is the number one thing to be proud of. They didn't talk for hours upon hours about what they were going to do. THEY JUST DID IT!

As this is the thing… And, one of the main reasons I developed *Zen Filmmaking*… If you lock yourself into a desired dream, it is most likely never going to happen. If you lock yourself into a, *"Done a million times before,"* formula script, you are probably going to fail at achieving your vision for that screenplay. If you believe you can make a film that looks like it cost several million dollars for ten thousand dollars, expect to be disappointed.

The point is, and this is what I told the young man I met with today, *"Free yourself! Forget all the bullshit that you are telling yourself and the promises you are making to everyone else. Focus on cinematic art as you see it and get out there and create the best film you can make with what you have available to you."* Then, what will be will be. But, by following this prescription, what you will have actually created is your first calling card and the only thing that really matters in the filmmaking game, a completed film.

If You're Going To Claim the Claim Then You Better Be the Example

It is no secret that the reason I am so down on all those who claim to be spiritual teachers (of whatever breed) is because they play the game of pretend. They are one thing when they are talking to people who don't really know them and then they are another thing when those people are not around.

Most people don't give two shits about spirituality. So, they don't think about it. Thus, they are not lured into the web of deceit that these modern proponents propagate. And, that's a good thing. But, as most of his have been indoctrinated into formalized religion in our youth, it is not hard to believe the promises of the lie. So, sometimes people get sucked in.

Me too. I was there. When I was young and first walking the spiritual path as a teenager, I believed. Luckily, I was allowed inside certain secret circles when I was very young and got to witness the process. The process of pretend.

But, bullshit is everywhere. I often discuss how at the beginning of any course on filmmaking that I teach, I detail that the number one rule of filmmaking is, *"Everybody lies."* But, it is much broader than that. People lie all the time. They pretend to be something they're not. They do it to GET. GET whatever they want. The fact is, unless it is proven to you, you cannot believe anyone.

Today, I was having breakfast and a guy was auditioning another guy for a position at the table behind me. First of all, don't go to auditions if the person who claims to own a big business does not have an office. Anyway... The prospective employee was hungry for a new job. The economy is shit right now so he obviously needed one. He listed his skill. The employer then went into his spiel, telling this guy all this bullshit about how much he would make via commissions and the like. He told him how he, himself, had just made a two hundred thousand dollar commission. Okay, all was as it was… They finished. Thank god! And, left… As I was leaving, I see the guy who was running the audition getting into his 1980s old, junky Toyota. Where's the two hundred grand?

This is the prime example. It is easy to talk the talk. The guy sounded very convincing. He had all the key words memorized. But, it was all a lie.

There is one truth. That truth is the truth of you. You know what you know. And you, and only you, know the true you. You are what you are. And, though you too may be one of those people who lie, deep down inside you cannot hide from the truth of you.

I can say, *"Don't lie. Don't play the game of pretend."* But, if you are going to do it, then you are going to do it. Does it make the world just a little bit worse if you behave in that manner? Yes, it does. But, I can't change you. Only you can be the true you. Only you can be the truth.

What are you going to do? What world are you going to create?

The number one thing I would recommend is to shut the fuck up and quit lying. Stop the game of pretend at its source.

Don't Force the Art

Because I have made a long list of *Zen Films,* people often bring to my attention the artsy films made by others. Many of them are very good. Some... Well, they try to force the issue.

It is hard for me to see it or understand it but many people tell me that my films and my filmmaking philosophy have been an inspiration to them. *"Thank you,"* I guess... And, that's great. I am glad I could be of help in any small way.

But, there is a long list of indie filmmakers that I have noticed who really miss the point. They try to make their movies look bad. Bad, in the sense that they over do the doing. For example, I have seen many a film where they intentionally leave the lights in the shot, the actors try to act badly, they try to make their movie look like a crappy low budget production, and the list goes on... Or, they simply mimic the films that have come to be considered schlocky from the past, instead of creating their own wholeness; their own uniqueness of project and of style.

They say, *"Imitation is the greatest form of flattery."* All good... But, when you look to some of the works of someone like say, Warhol... Yes, he did things that could be seen as poor filmmaking technique in some of his *Art House* pieces, but he did it first. He did it to do it. Thus, he was undoing what was done. Not mimicking anyone.

Art is about making it your own. Art is about creating your own style. Certainly, in art and film art you can reference those who have come before you. But, there is no reason to make something intentionally look less.

If you want to do *Art House* do it. But, make it your own.

People Are People

At the root of all conflict is the desire of an individual. All conflict is based upon the simple fact that a person wants a situation to happen in a specific manner. When it does not, they become upset. Some people are conscious enough to simply realize this fact and understand that the particular situation in question is not going to turn out the way that they hoped—they realize this, take note of it, and move on. Others, however, who live their life from a very unaware perspective and base their existence upon achieving their desired ends, by any means possible, will create conflict when things are not going their way.

Now, this happens on all different levels. For some when they are not happy with a particular situation's outcome, they become sad or depressed. Others become very hard to get along with. Some become angry and throw a fit. Others still, become violent.

Ultimately, you must understand that all of these individual reactions are a choice. It is you who chooses how to behave in any given situation. It is also you who chooses how to behave when someone is encountering you with a conflict-based mindset, based in the fact that his or her individual desires are not being met.

An example of this happened to me early into my immersion into the film industry—when I was creating one of my first feature films. I had invited this guy to come onboard and help me produce the movie. We had several cast and crewmembers at our downtown Los Angeles location.

Now, it must be understood, on a film set, there can be only one captain of the ship. Though you have people helping you on many levels, there can be only one guiding force or a project becomes convoluted.

On this day the shooting was progressing and we had planned to meet up with this one, non-actress, girl that my associate was infatuated with and wanted to put into the movie. Though I was happy to have her in the movie, I had a realization that due to time and location constraints we should wait until the next day to use her because I realized that we could shoot her character's scenes at a much better location. I explained this to him and he completely freaked out. He started yelling and screaming—which ultimately upset my cast.

One has to question, where does this kind of reaction come from? Because most people would not react like this. They would simply understand and readjust their thinking.

Where it comes from is a very childlike mind-space. A place where, as a child, this person learned that if he yelled and screamed long enough, he would get what he wanted. In fact, this type of behavior is very common. Many adults use it. And, in some cases they do get what they want. In other cases, like the one I am describing, this person's behavior simply made everyone one else ill at ease by his actions. But, it must be understood that in some cases that is exactly what a person wants—to take control over a situation by whatever means possible.

In regard to the film, ultimately, we did what I suggested. The movie was completed. And, the man realized that my choice of shooting the girl at a different location was, in fact, the best thing to do.

But, the damage this type of behavior unleashed is never repaired.

By nature, I am a very forgiving person. So, this person vacillated in and out of my life for the next decade or so. Every now and then, however, I would see this same behavior emerging. Why? Because people are who they are.

"People are who they are." This is one of the most important understandings to come to when studying the nature of conflict. There are certain people who avoid conflict. If you associate with them, your relationship will be relatively conflict free. Then, there are others who seek it out—for whatever reason. If you associate with them, there will be conflict. And then, there are those who exist somewhere in between these two polarities.

Each person has the choice to react to any situation in whichever way they want. This, *"Choice,"* is based in so many elements: Biology, Sociology, and Psychology. How they were born, how they were raised, how they were indoctrinated into life, who they grew up around, what was their societal environment, etc., etc., etc.

This being stated, again, people are who they are. But, few ever choose to consciously define who they TRULY are. They simply exist in the body they were given and the mindset they were indoctrinated to believe is theirs. Few ever choose to truly define themselves as a complete person. Thereby, if they are locked in a mindset of, *"Me," "That's what I want,"* or basing their existence upon generalized desire, they are at the heart of causing a conflicted world.

As I am speaking about the film industry, another revealing story about human nature affecting the realms of conflict comes to mind…

An amusing, interesting, and revealing situation occurred on one of my films.

One of my older college students, who had taken a couple of my classes and was very interested in working with me, continued to contact me. He called and he called. I finally gave in and let him come onto one of my sets.

On the first film he worked with on, he simply was the boom operator. The shoot was simply an afternoon gig and there were no problems. On my next film that he worked on, I let him shoot some of the scenes that I painstakingly set up, as he wanted to become a cinematographer. Again, no problem. On the third film, however, he had purchased a camera, had been practicing, and I allowed him to be one of the camera operators. The problems began to arise when he decided that the movie was his production—which it was not. This was due to the fact that I allowed him to help me with casting.

Perhaps the most interesting element of this casting equation came into play when I found out that he was a professional drug dealer. I guess I should have known because several months earlier we had met at the *American Film Market* and he did one of those things where you shake hands and, as we did, he put some pot in my hand. I laughed and gave it back to him.

In any case, we were having a casting meeting at a Starbucks in Santa Monica, California one afternoon. The funny thing was, he had also invited one of his buyers to the meeting place. When the buyer arrived, he literally went over into the nearby bushes to make his deal. Now, as amusing as this was to my production manager and myself, this was very uncool because if he had been arrested, that would have put my production manager and myself in the path of law enforcement for something we had nothing to do with it.

I overlooked this fact and continued on with the production. On the final day of principal photography this man, apparently attempting to demonstrate his immersion into the industry to his friends, had invited a guy on the set to help with boom operation—which was fine with me. The problem was, the guy was one of those wanta-be film industry types who have never done anything but think that they know more than you and can do everything better than you. But, I just let his negative attitude go and kept moving forward. He also invited a professional cameraman he had meet at the Apple Store. This professional cameraman had brought his own equipment. He asked if he could help with filming. *"Of course,"* was my answer.

Immediately, I saw this cameraman's prowess and put him into the primary camera position. This set the problems with ego into motions...

Combine this, with at the end of that day's shoot, a cast member asked me if I knew any one who sold pot.

Because I have long hair, I guess everyone assumes I do drugs. I do not.

But, I referred him to the aforementioned student/cameraman. As drug dealers tend to be a very paranoid bunch, this set the man into a world of denial. Combine this was the fact that the guy held some false belief that I had sabotaged some hidden deal he had made with another of the cast members. And, all this set him into a rage. Luckily, he did not bring it up until the next day.

The next day, with principal photography complete, my *father-in-law,* who I was very close to, (as he was one of my best *drink'n* buddies), entered into the last stage of his life. He was dying from lung cancer. As I drove to be by his side, I get a phone call on my cel. I answer. I hear, *"Mr. Zen..."* My student then hangs up on me. But, instead of letting it go at that, he continues to leave me voice mail after voice mail, (on my separate voice mail/pager number), telling me what an asshole I am and making all kinds of threats against me. So, there I am, dealing with all of the emotions of watching my *father-in-law* slowing drifting from this world, as my pager continues to buzz, fed by this man's irate and meaningless conflict based behavior. He also proceeds to call and tell all of my cast and crewmembers what a jerk I am. This, when I was the only person to ever attempt to give this guy a break in the industry and to help him out.

But, in Hollywood, and in life in general, people don't see things this way. They see themselves as the center of the universe and even if they possess minimal abilities, they expect to be treated like stars or they will create conflict. Furthermore, this is the way people who wish to instigate conflict behave. It is never enough for them to discuss their dissatisfaction solely with the particular person involved. Instead, they want to drag as many people, who could care less about the situation, into the matter as possible. From this, they gain some misplaced validity to an emotion that is based solely out of the desire(s) of their own ego.

As a lifelong martial artists, one of the most essential elements I have learned is that, just because you can kick a person's ass doesn't mean that you have to do it. And, this is one of the best definitions to hold onto when you are forced to deal with an individualized conflict like the one just described. Instead of getting in there and throwing punches, just realize the limited reality that the person who is causing the conflict is embracing. In other words, become more and rise above it and them. Because by descending to their level and beating them up, all you do is grant them a sense of validity for the way they are behaving.

How did I react to the aforementioned conflict? I just let it go and I moved on. I mean the guy had sealed himself into his own wasteland. He made his choices about how he would choose to react to life situations and there was nothing I could do about it.

The moral of this story is that we each have the ability to realize who a person is and what is their individual personality. For example, the background of this guy was, this man was in his late forties/early fifties, single, never married, and taking courses at night.

The reason I mention this is that this says a lot about his ultimate character development. It is important to note that an individual's character development is something that can clue you into possible upcoming problems with conflict. In addition, when we were out looking at filmmaking equipment, he couldn't go into a certain camera store because he had a conflict with one of the employees. He also couldn't walk past this one restaurant because of a disagreement he had with a former friend who worked there, and so on.

What was obvious is that he was a person constantly creating conflict. I observed this and yet, I overlooked it. So, it was my fault that I allowed him to cause conflict with me.

Now, this is one of the most essential details to realize about the reality of conflict—though you cannot protect yourself from every level of conflict, because life is too chaotic and uncertain to predict anything, what you can do is to not let a specific person, who bases their life upon conflict, into your realm of existence. When you see who a person is, and they are not living in a pure space, it is best to move along.

Though it sometimes takes time to realize a person's true personality, once you do, you must make a very conscious decision whether or not you are willing to let them into your life. By practicing this simple observation technique, you will save your life-time from a lot of unnecessary conflict.

The ultimate questions is why do people like the previous detailed individual, cause conflict. There are obviously a lot of reasons, but one of the primary ones is adrenaline. Adrenaline is an addictive hormone in our bodies. It accelerates our minds, our cardiovascular system, and provides us a sense of hyperawareness. It is a drug. And, just like any other drug, some people are able to take it, have some fun, and not get hooked on it. For others, this is not the case.

Some people find that in the midst of conflict their adrenaline is pumping. Though they do not make this happen, from a conscious perspective, *none-the-less* they come to crave this adrenaline and they discover that conflict is one of the primary sources of this drug. So, they create conflict to get high.

One of the primary locations where conflict(s) occur is in the workplace. Though I have never had a traditional job, for any length of time, I have heard *story-after-story* about how bosses and superiors berate their lower level employees and shift blame to them when it is not deserved. I have heard from so many people who tell me that the workplace is one of the primary points of life changing conflict.

Personally, I had an amusing situation happen to me when I was teaching a class on filmmaking for the University of California, Los Angeles, Extension Department.

I had taught a class for U.C.L.A. Extension the previous semester. The class, itself, went well enough, and I believe the students came away with some new knowledge. In fact, one of the students became a friend and we ended up making a couple of movies together. During the class, however, I saw inside the true structure of U.C.L.A. Extension and witnessed how flawed it was.

An ideal example of this flawed system happened when we had our class shifted from the Westwood campus to the campus at Universal Studios. There, I was to teach my students about editing. We all arrived, pay the expensive parking fees, only to find out that the individual who ran these editing suits would not let us use the equipment. While we all stood there and listened, he called up the course coordinator, at the main U.C.L.A. campus, screaming at him about even allowing us to be there. In any case, after witnessing that, I swore I would never teach for U.C.L.A. Extension again.

The next semester rolled around, however, and they asked me to teach another class. Though I did not really want to do it, we all need to make a living. So, I accepted the offer.

The first day of the class I walk in and was overwhelmed. There were over forty students in a class that was specifically designed to be taught to no more than twenty. Then, I was hit with the next news. There was only going to be one camera to use in the class. What!

In the previous class I had taught for U.C.L.A. Extension, I had ten students and two cameras. With this, there was plenty of time for each student to get hands-on experience and get a true feel for filmmaking. In this new class, however, that was going to be impossible.

I complained to the program coordinator, who was this interesting lady from France. I am using the term, *"Interesting,"* to be kind. This lady possessed one of those *devil-may-care* attitudes, as she was the boss, and emanated all of the *all-knowing, power-fed* arrogance, of her position.

After I expressed my doubts, she told me that I was a professional and I should be able to teach the class just fine. In other words, she completely dismissed any of my concerns about what the students would actually be receiving from the course. This, when the students were paying in excess of one thousand dollars ($1,000.00) to take the course. Which means, that U.C.L.A. Extension made over fifty thousand dollars ($50,000.00) from my teaching the class. Think about that for a moment...

Another interesting caveat is that U.C.L.A. Extension offers only a limited refund when a student drops a course. So, I knew there was going to be problems. But, interesting business plan, don't you think?

A few classes in, this very large, very gay female student, asks if she can bring her girl friend into the class. *"Sure, why not."* I should have known something was up...

In any case, she sits down in the front row, with her arm around her lover, occasionally giving her a kiss. Weird, for any class. But hey, I'm an opened minded guy...

About half way through the session, she erupts. There was this Armenian porn producer/gun dealer also in the class. Actually, a very nice guy. But, he was prone to speaking his mind. He said something. She exploded at him. She then exploded at me and everything went to hell. She stormed out of the room, *hand-in-hand* with her lover. I shook my head, smiled, and somewhat dismayed, attempted to carry on.

The next day I get a call from the aforementioned French program coordinator. She tells me that the girl wanted out of the class. She wanted all of her money back. Plus, she still wanted the ability to film on the U.C.L.A. campus, with the promised camera. To achieve this end she had filed some kind of stupid misconduct charge against me for discussing the fact that there is nudity in the independent film industry. I mean, come on, who doesn't know that and hasn't seen it a millions times on the screen? Plus, she had her girlfriend to back up her charges. I realized that I had been sucked into the middle of a total set-up.

You see, this is one of the problems with modern life—it doesn't matter if something is true or not, simply a person making the claim, has the potential to derail another person's life.

But, it was my fault. I should have seen it coming—the high cost of the course, the too many students in one class, and only one camera. I should have walked away and not taught the class.

I explained to the program coordinator that this was at least partially her fault, as she overbooked the class to make as much money for the department as possible, and she did not provide me with the appropriate and promised equipment to teach the class correctly. Of course, she dismissed everything I said. Frustrated by not being heard, *"That's it. I quit."* I hung up the phone.

The next day I get a call from the head of the department. She put four of us on a conference call: herself, the program coordinator, the course coordinator, and myself.

I had never met her, as she was new to U.C.L.A., but she was actually a very nice person. I explained to her the situation, as the French program coordinator claimed to have not understood that there was any problems. Basically, it was so blatantly obvious, even to the head of the department, that the program coordinator was simply trying to save her own ass.

Me, I continued to state my resolve to quit. But, the head of the department was so nice that I gave in and completed the class. (She obviously did not want to refund all of that money, to all those students). The French program coordinator lied and kept her job. And I, of course, have chosen to never teach for that program again.

The U.C.L.A. *powers-that-be* blinked and gave in to the woman who threw the fit. She got her refund and got to shoot the final weekend of the course on the U.C.L.A. campus with a camera provided by the department. The false allegation against me were obviously dismissed. So, who won? And, what was gained by any of it?

Well, I believe the woman who stormed out of class lost out, at least on the learning experience, because she did not learn all of the secrets of the independent film industry and independent film production and distribution that I taught the class—which is why she signed up for the class in the first place—right? But, in the process she tarnished my reputation as an instructor.

Did I really care? No, not really. Because I knew the truth. But, that is just who I am...

I suppose if being a university professor was my ultimate goal in life, it may have matter more. Because it could have crushed my career.

The ultimate question of any conflict is, *"What do you gain and what do you lose?"* Before you engage in any conflict, you have to ask yourself, *"Why are you doing it? And, is any of it worth it?"* Plus, if you instigate one of these situations, you have to ponder what kind of karma are you creating simply to get your own way and fulfill your own momentary desires.

This is the primary problem with conflicts in general. As detailed, they are all based in a person's desires—as momentary as they may be.

Think about it, how many of your desires have lasted for more than the moment they were felt? How much of any anger you have may have felt has lasted for more than the few moments it was experienced?

Emotions go by the wayside. This is simply a fact of life. What is felt today, will not be felt tomorrow. What you do with emotions, while they are being felt, is what defines you either as a conscious spiritual person or simply a person who bases their reality around the limited perceptions of the world.

The next semester I taught at Santa Monica College—a much more laid back environment. In the first class of the session I was speaking to a student and she said, *"I don't know how you can teach, everybody is always out to get the teacher."* I smiled.

You see, this is life. There is going to be conflict and it is going to come at you from a direction you never expect. Conflict can happen, even when you are trying to do a good thing and a good job. Why? Because, people only care about themselves and their own momentary reality. And, they are willing to do whatever it takes to fulfill whatever desire they have in that moment. Plus, they could care less what effect what they are having on the life of another person.
As you now see, it even happens to me.

So, what is the answer? Just as with the examples I have given you—had I listened to my inner-voice, the conflict would never have occurred. Had I listened to my inner-voice and either not chosen to interact with a specific individual or allowed myself to be put in a less than ideal environment than I would not have gone through the experience. Furthermore, had I just walked away, once I could see that the situation was going South, then the ultimate conflict orientate outcome would not have occurred. So, the main point in avoiding conflict is you really have to trust your inner-voice and not put yourself in situations where a conflict is waiting to happen.

In the fighting ring and on the chessboard, the first rule is to unleash a powerful offense. The basis for this is that you want to take your opponent out with a rapid and precise first-strike. Though few people who instigate conflict know this rule, this is what they are doing. They hope by creating a crisis that they will defeat their opponent before they even have the chance to compete. But, here is the secret to defending against this style of offense—do not compete.

If you do not care about the outcome of a conflict, than how can you be dragged into it? If you do not care, you will not argue or fight to win. Just like with the previously discussed examples, the movies were being made with or with out these problematic people. So, why would I care if they participated or not? It was out of my kindness that I offered them the opportunity to come on-board. Regarding the teaching assignment—I didn't want it anyway. I was the one offered the position, and I accepted it solely as a means of helping the students. So, if I never went back, who cares? Not me.

This is the mind-space you must live your life from. You must orchestrate your reality to live in a space of refined consciousness. You do what you do, and hopefully you can help some others in the process. But, never put yourself in a position where you must rely upon others. By living your life from this perspective you are free and you will never be drawn into a conflict.

People each have their own life, lifestyle, and psychological makeup. They each have the potential to come at you, cause conflict, and mess up your life in ways you never expected. This can easily derail anything you are working towards. So, you really have to be careful whom you bring into your life and where you place yourself in this Life-Space.

Trust your feeling and if you are getting weird vibes from a person, (or if a crewmember is making drug deal during a casting meeting or a student brings her girlfriend to class and puts her arm around her), steer clear of them as they have the potential to mess up your life. Move away, move on. And, if you find yourself engulfed in a conflict situation, it is far better to nip-it-in-the-bud, close-it-out, and walk away before it ever has the potential for escalation.

Knowing What You Don't Know

I always find it very amusing when someone who has no idea about how the independent film industry actually works tells me how I should be doing something or that am I doing something totally wrong.

Over the many years I have been involved in the film industry I have received messages telling me how virtually everything I have done is wrong. These messages generally come from someone who has never made a film and most likely never will.

It all began when Donald G. Jackson and I were making *the Roller Blade Seven*. Don and I knew we wanted to create something very different. We initially hired an editor to help us create our vision when we had completed the filming process of the movie. The man edited the movie for us for a couple of days with Don and I guiding his every action. But, he didn't get it. He took Don off into another room one day and told him, *"You are really pushing the envelope too far."* When Don relayed his message to me with both laughed. We knew exactly what we were doing. And, as I have previously mentioned in my writings on the movie, the mistake this editor made was that he taught me how to use the equipment. We were gone. We rented an editing suit. I became the editor. And, we took the movie to the level we hoped it would reach.

We must have done something right. People are still talking (and criticizing) the film over twenty years later. In fact, most of the people who are criticizing this movie were not even born when we made it.

People also have told me that *Zen Filmmaking* is all-wrong. Wrong? How can anything be wrong when the entire premise of *Zen Filmmaking* is based upon the concept that there are no mistakes? But, I won't get all-philosophical on you here…

People also have contacted me detailing that my story structures are all-wrong. Again, to understand my filmmaking style you must understand that I don't care about stories. The stories have all been told. I care about visional images, with occasional dialogue, taking the viewer on a mind-ride. The fact of the matter is, most people have only seen my most talked about films. They never go and investigate all my other work.

Some of my films actually have defined storylines. Can you believe it?

Also, I have heard random comments about the fact that I don't pay actors. First of all, that is not true. For actors who bring no name value to a film I may not pay them in cash. But, I do pay them in other ways. I give them a chance to be in a film that will be completed and will be distributed—which is not the case of many independent films. During their time on the set they get hone their acting skills for the camera. Plus, they get to have a film, (a calling card), that they can show to their family, friends, agent, and the world.

For only asking a few hours of their life, I think that is quite a nice payment.

Hell, the entire time we were making *the Roller Blade Seven,* which took months-upon-months, I got paid virtually nothing in terms of cash. But, at the end of the day, I was happy to have donated my time. And, in the early stages of my career, I acted in several films where I was not paid.

In fact, this is the case with most of the low-budget, independent film industry. The cast and the crew are not paid in money.

But you see, people don't know these facts. People who watch films, particularly independent films, want to armchair quarterback the production. As has long been the case, my suggestion to everyone is, before you throw in your two cents about something that you know nothing about, why don't you go and make your own movie.

Remember When It Was So Important To Watch Music Videos?

I was sitting around flipping channels last night. There was nothing really worth watching. Of the hundreds of channels I have, nothing... *"Pretty amazing,"* I thought. I popped over to one of MTVs remaining music channels. There was a good song playing by an obscure band that I heard on KCRW. I didn't know the name of the band, but it caused me to stop and watch. The video was okay. Not great. Just okay...

I looked over to my lady and realized/asked, *"Remember when it was so important to watch music videos?" "Oh yeah,"* she responded. She continued by naming the list of shows here in L.A. that actually used to play music videos at various times of the day and night in the early 1980s. There was this one show on at three in the afternoon, one on at midnight on Friday, and the etcetera. I smiled. That was a long time ago.

When MTV came around a bit after this, it really changed everything. (I know... I know... I'm dating myself here.) But, back then, it was really important to watch music videos and watch for new music videos. It really felt like an accomplishment.

I remember back in my twenties when MTV broke through. I was living in Hermosa Beach and I had this big kitchen that I used to staple canvases to the wall and paint. I'd have the coffee pot going and MTV on. If a new video came on, I would run in and tape it on my video deck. I never really rewatched them. But, it was just a feeling that you had to catch that moment.

Really... A lot of revolutionary filmmaking was being unleashed in the genre of music videos at that time in history. But now, that has all changed. The funny thing is, in many cases, I will hear a song I like on the radio or something but then when I see the music video, (if I ever do), I will wish that I did not know what that person or that band looked like; as they're just not very appealing and the video isn't very good.

And also, and probably more importantly, the craft and the art of pushing the boundaries of filmmaking seems to be gone in music videos. It has just become rehashed versions of people posing for the camera. Nothing revolutionary in that…

I don't know… Watching music videos every now and then is something to do. But, it certainly no longer seem very important or educational.

Creation and Adaptation

You will forever be defined by what is available to you. This is particularly the case in terms of creativity.

If you don't have a paintbrush, you can't paint. But, that does not mean you cannot do something else.

In all aspects of creativity there are things that you may want to create. The reality of creativity is, however, you can only work within the realms of what you have available to you. This goes to all levels of creation.

For example, if you want to paint you will need a canvas, paints, and paintbrushes. These items are pretty easy to come by and are relatively inexpensive. Once you have acquired those basic elements you can move forward. But, what if you desire to use the color blue in your painting and you do not have it? It is at this point that many people will stop, (or never start), the painting and dream of the day when they will have some blue paint.

This is obviously an analogy but this is what most people do and why they never succeed in being the creative person they hope to become. They stop before they ever begin.

The other way to handle this situation is to use whatever color you have on hand and move foreword with your painting. By employing this method you get your painting competed.

As an artist, I say all the time, if you have expectations your painting will never turn out exactly the way you expected it to. This is the case even if you spend day-upon-day, month-upon-month, work and re-work it—the painting will still ultimately come out different from what you anticipate.

This is good. This is what True Art is—letting the Art be the end-all of what you create—not simply your domination over the canvas. By allowing yourself to accept the art as it presents itself, it is free, it is True Art. But, this not the way most people come at art.

A personal example here is, I recently bought a large quantity of acrylic paint from this art supply warehouse in Orange County. Normally, I like to start and finishing a painting in one sitting. But, this paint is a little watery. So, I have no choice. First I have lay-down the backdrop of the painting, let it dry, then return and paint the central subject matter later. That's not ideal for me, but it is what I must do if I want to use the paint and create the painting.

Being dominated by external circumstances and situations goes much further than simply paint upon canvas. When you go into the more complex realms of art, such as the creation of music and cinema, things get even more complicated. Sure, a guy can go and play his acoustic guitar anywhere. Sure, an actor can go and actor anyplace. But, if you want to capture these creations for eternity than you must deal with technology. And, as I have long stated, *"In a mechanical world there are mechanical problems."*

It is a simple fact of creative life, you probably are not going to have all the technology that you want at your disposal and you probably will run into some problems along your path to creation using technology. You can let that stop you, as it has many would-be creators, or you can move past your limitations and get something done.

As a filmmaker, pretty much since I began, I have run into limitations of what I have had available to me in the process of film creation. Mostly, this has been dominated by money, or the lack thereof. I mean, we can look to people like Francis Ford Coppola when he was making *Apocalypse Now*. The stories have long been told how he would do take after take of the same scene which cause all kinds of cast and crew problems and forced the film to go insanely over budget. Or, Michael Cimino's, *Heaven Gate,* which followed a similar path of creative obsession. Great movies, but most filmmakers do not have the ability to take filmmaking to that level of obsession. Again, this is why most would-be filmmakers may have an idea but never get it completed because they refuse to understand when enough is enough and that you have to live with what you have if you actually want to complete a film.

As an indie filmmaker for more than twenty years I can say with authority if you want to get your film made you need to do it with what is available. If you do not want to be one of those people who simply talks about making a film forever, you have to make your movie with what you can get a hold of and then, more importantly, you need to accept and appreciate the finish product for what it is. It is probably not going to be Apocalypse Now but it will be a film that you have competed.

You can obsess if you want. But, if you desire to get anything completed, you have to be willing to accept. You have to let it be what it is. For example, one of the first films I produced was *The Roller Blade Seven.* Don Jackson and I took the film's edited footage with time code to an online editing facility to have it constructed for final output. We spent quite a lot of time there, days-upon-days. In one scene we had Don Stroud's character continuing to laugh off-screen as the lead actress skated off into the desert. It was really very dramatic. But, when we sat down for the final watch, the laugh track was gone. The online editor looked at us. He knew he had blown it. The problem was, going back and putting it in would have been very-very time consuming and expensive. Though it was the online editors fault and we could have pushed the issue, we did not. We had a delivery date, so we let it go. Not ideal, but it was the choice that we had to make.

That is the ultimate point of all this. You can choose to create; you can decide to be a creator, and move forward with whatever limitations you possess in order to get your vision out there. Or, you can sit back, waste your life, and always be the person saying, *"I am going to do that..."* Or, *"I always wanted to..."*

Everything Has Already Been Done

Whenever you throw your work or your ideas out there in the public, people are going to have thoughts about what you say or what you do. That's just life... For me, it forever amuses me when people take the time to watch one of my films, grab screen pulls from it, and then write a review totally bagging it due to *Zen Filmmaking*, lack of storyline, bad acting, crazy edits, weird credits, and all the etcetera...

Since I began making films over twenty years ago, my work has been reviewed a lot. It used to be predominately done in magazines and books, now it is on the Internet. All good... Kind of like what P.T. Barnum expressed, and Andy Warhol embraced, *"Any publicity is good publicity."* Well, maybe...

Anyway, what I have found is that the seasoned journalists and film reviewers get what I am doing. Many of the other people do not. Yet, they still take all the time to grab frames and write their thoughts.

Here's the thing... I'm an abstract artist. With that as a basis, it must also be understood that, everything has already been done. What I am attempting to do is something different. Defined by budgetary constraints, of course, do you not think that every element of all of my films are created with intent and focused consciousness? They didn't just happen. It was meant to be that way.

That being said, it actually amuses me to read the reviews that rip my films, because most of these reviewers do not take the time to understand what I am doing. If I may borrow a few words penned by the great Robert Allen Zimmerman, (Bob

Dylan), *"Don't criticize what you can't understand."*

The fact of the matter is, you can't come at something without understanding its basis or it just makes you look cretinous. If you want to go see a normal film then go to the movie theater and see whatever is on the big screen at the time. My films are intentionally not normal. Why even bother viewing them if you expect them to be like everything that has been done before? They are not. Creating seen-it-all-before visual arts was never my intention.

What I am saying is that... And, this goes to everything in life, not just films; before you draw a conclusion, you need to understand the basis, the focal point, and the reasoning behind a creation; once you know that, you can leave behind your personal ideologies and judgments and perhaps enter a new space of abstract understanding.

This is life; don't always base your opinions upon what you already know. Instead, take the time to turn off your mind and see things for what they are, not what you expect them to be.

And, like I have said forever, if you can make a better movie than me or anybody else why don't you quit wasting your time piggybacking on the creativity of other and writing reviews and instead get out there and do it, and let's see it.

Desire Verse Drive

There is a group of commercials currently in rotation where a kid of about ten is lecturing their younger siblings, *"Back in my day..."* Though this is an amusingly exaggerated example, as time passes on I believe we each have witness how things have become easier and more doable.

For example when I was a teenage musician, if I hoped to make an album I would have had to go into a recording studio, cut the record, and then have it pressed at a professional facility. All very-very expensive...

In recent years, there are a lot of people who have recorded an album on their computer in their apartment, put it on the Internet, and have become very successful. There are also some people who have simply made a video of themself singing a song, uploaded it to YouTube, and fame and success have happened.

In terms of filmmaking, when I began it was very-very expensive. The cost of the camera, the film, the sound equipment, the processing, and then the editing all were fairly astronomical. Now, you can buy a point and shoot camera go and film something, put it on the Internet, and there is a chance that your movie will open all kinds of doors for you.

There are a couple of people I have watched in recent years that have really taken this new level of relatively inexpensive technology and began to create their dreams. They have written and recorded music, gone out and made music videos to back up their songs. Some have gone out and made film shorts or even features. But, there is one element that is common among all of these people—they have done it.

All this being said, there is one very big reality about creativity. You have to do it. If you sit around and dream about something happening, it probably never will. You have to get out there and do it.

Does your Drive equal your Desire?

You Weren't There So You Don't Know

I often become very amused, (and even occasionally annoyed), when I read stories that people have written about what took place during the creation of some of my films. These people have these whole elaborate dialogues taking place. The only problem is, they are universally wrong.

Those actions were never taken. Those words were not spoken. Those ideas were not discussed. And, those ideologies were never attempted to be actualized.

People have even gone as far as to write entire articles amount my films, my self, and my filmmaking partners—all in an attempt to totally berate and slam me. Dudes… If you are going to do that, at least get your facts straight!

You know, there has been something truly lost with the creation of the Internet. Sure, a lot has been gained. Everybody who wants to have one, can have a voice. And, that is great. But, what has been lost is the quest for TRUTH. People say anything, and they do not even care if they are right, wrong, lying, or simply presenting what they think and wish occurred. It all is sounded with the same voice and it is all consumed without the presence of mind to confirm whether or not what a person wrote possesses any validity.

People hide behind the mask of fan, film geek, reviewer, intellectual, whatever… But, by whatever name they assign themselves, what they propagate is falsehoods hidden behind the guise of someone who has actually taken the time to write something. And, once they write what they write, someone else reads it and believes it, thus the lie is perpetuated.

The number one thing I have to say in response is, I spend my time creating self-developed art. What do you spend your time doing?

People… You weren't there, so you don't know. Stop writing about a subject where you have no factual basis for your conclusions.

Too Famous For All the Wrong Reasons

I had an audition early this week for a Midwestern commercial. They had only called in a few people for the audition. I believe there were four others and myself. So, this was a tight call. A lot of times production companies will see hundreds of actors for a role. For this one, that was not the case—they were seeking someone with a very specific look.

A kind of interesting thing happened to me at that audition. I went in and they slated me. That is where they take a digital photo of you, they do an upward pan of your body, you show your profiles, and you tell them your name. All common stuff...

In the room of this casting session was the cameraman, (doing the filming), and over on the couch were the director and a couple of other people. They were probably representatives from the company that this commercial was being created for.

In any case, as always occurs, the cameraman asked for my name. *"Scott Shaw,"* I reply. I noticed when I said my name a guy on the couch nudged the director and gave a little point. He whispered, *"That's Scott Shaw..."* They looked at each other and then at me. Once the cameraman was done with his duties I receive a question from the director,

"You're Scott Shaw?"
"Yes."

A strange look comes over his face, and a moment or two passes.

"I really liked your book, "Zen O'clock."
"Thanks."

At that moment, I knew I was not going to get the gig. I knew this even though I still went through the motions and read for the role...

Obviously what had happened is that my agent had submitted me and the casting director had brought me in due to my appearance. But, the casting director probably didn't read my name.

Here's the thing... Everybody who is not a part of Hollywood believes that fame and accomplishment is the end-all. Let me tell you, it is not. In fact, many times it works against you.

For example, this role called for a New Age Guru type. All good, I look the part. But, the problem is, they could never cast me because then it would look like the company was endorsing my books and me. Thus, I lost the role.

This is the same thing for the type of films that an actor does. For example, when I first stared out in the industry, (at the ripe old age of thirty-two), I initially worked in A-market roles or on indie films that were geared towards the mainstream. When Don Jackson decided he wanted me to star in *Roller Blade Seven,* I knew my career would be changed forever. Though that style of film was and is much more in-tune with how I see the cinematic arts, it is the kind of film that sets a precedent for your career. In fact, my friend Joe Estevez once said to me about *Roller Blade Seven,* *"I'm surprised either of our careers survived after doing that film."*

That is true. That film and that style of filmmaking has defined me, in the film industry, since the day it was released. Though I have occasionally been brought in to do roles in mainstream films, T.V., and commercials here in the States since RB7, those castings were more based upon the way I looked rather than the anti-fame I gained from that film and the other *Zen Films* I have created.

This is an important thing to understand about Hollywood. The casting directors are not seeking talent. They are either going to cast people that are sent to them by powerful agents, who set the standards and pretty much define the film game, or people who have a very specific look needed for a specific role.

Though this is the case with Hollywood, Asia is a bit of a different story. For the most part, the *powers-that-be* there do not view the kind of films I make as a detriment. They simply see them as Comic Book Action Adventures. A style of film that is very common throughout Asia. And, my films have done very well there.

This being stated, the other side of the coin is that due to the type of films I make, I continually receive offers to be in obscure indie films made by other filmmakers. I always turn those offers down, however. As I forever jokingly state, *"The only bad films I'm in are my own."*

Plus, I believe Joe Estevez is the king of that genre. I certainly do not want to infringe upon his territory.

Ultimately, fame and notoriety is an evil master. I remember back when Dennis Rodman was just veering off from the top of his game. He had done a film with Mickey Rourke and Jean-Claude Van Damme. Though around this time he had been released from the Lakers, he was still everywhere—all over the media. Some reported asked him, *"Why don't you get more film and television work?"* He replied, *"Because I'm too famous."* He would later use this same statement to define why the courts severally punished him for his illegal deeds. Maybe that is true. I don't know. But, it is true that fame, no matter from which area it comes, defines your life and it keeps you from moving forward because you will forever be defined by that definition.

In terms of Rodman, I'm glad he has found success in Reality T.V. And hey, he's now a friend with the leader of North Korea. ☺

Anyway, it is important to think about what you are doing. Many people come to Hollywood and only focus upon the A-Industry. I wish them all the best, but that is a near impossible nut to crack. As for the world of indie, the opportunities are greater if you have a look or a skill or if you are a woman willing to take off her clothing. But, whatever you decided to do, remember; once it is out there in the public eye; it is out there forever. Any noteworthiness or fame you obtain will define you. And, that will dictate your next set of available opportunities.

You Verses Who?

Whenever I teach a course on filmmaking I always begin by detailing the number one rule of filmmaking, *"Everybody lies."* From actors onto filmmakers, in the film industry everyone lies about everything; from their age, to who they know, to the budget of their project, to who is involved in the project, to the process they are using for the creation of the project, to what is coming next in their career, and on and on… But, the fact of the matter is, throughout all aspects of life, pretty much, everybody lies. People lie about who they are, what they are, where they are from, where they are going, what they thinking, what they are doing, etc. This is life and that is the truth, most everybody lies.

One may think on the spiritual path that this would all be different. But, coming from someone who has been walking the spiritual path for the better part of my life I can say with some authority that lies abound on it, as well. The thing is, there is no degree for being spiritual. There is no school you must graduate from where you receive a certificate of authenticity. People just become. In many ways that is a good thing because spiritually is based upon self-realization but this is also where it gets very messy.

There are a lot of people out there who claim spirituality, who claim to know; they claim to be teachers, mediums, psychics, priests, yogis, whatever… But when no one is looking they are a complete emotional and psychological wreck on the inside but they are too locked into their own egos to go and get the psychological guidance that they need. Though they may have spirituality in their heart, they have stepped up to pulpit in an attempt to fill a hole in their being. Why? They desire admiration.

The problem is, from actions based upon these principals, spiritually has become so convoluted and so many people have followed these false teachers, expecting to find inner truth and answer but since the source was so misguided this could never occur.

Desiring admirations is not spiritual. Do spiritual teachers who desire admiration tell their students that is the reason they are doing what they do? No, because then they would have no students. Yet, they are still out there deceiving people. They are lying.

On the more physical levels of reality, people lie all the time. They lie about who they are, what they are, how much money they have, what their desires for another person truly are, they even lie to themselves about why they are doing what they are doing.

In the realms of physical reality, lying is justifiable because we are all taught that we must go after a goal and gain it no matter what. But, no matter what, commonly injures a lot of people in the process.

So, I guess, not only in filmmaking but also in life in general, the number on rule is, *"Everybody lies."* For better or for worse that is it. That is what we have to deal with. We can try to be better ourselves and that is a good start. ...For all the world beings with us. And, we can also embrace the knowledge that we now know the number one rule. From all of this we can attempt to be forgiving when we encounter it. An absolute answer, no. An absolute solution, no.

Welcome to life where there is no absolute answers or solutions.

The Casting Couch

Recently, the experiences of actresses and actors experiencing sexual exploitation at the hands of powerful industry professional has been at the forefront of the news. This is a sign of the times and it demonstrates the changing and refining mindset of people and what they are willing and/or not willing to take. And, this is a good thing. But, it is essential to note, that this has been going on forever. Is there anyone out there who doesn't know what the term, *"The casting couch,"* implies. Meaning, this is such a prevalent form of industry interaction that it actually has been given a name.

Recently, TMZ found some older, major player in the industry coming out of a restaurant. All he had to say was that this had been going on for a hundred years. It was known and it was accepted.

For all of those A-List players out there claiming that they knew nothing about it, I call bullshit. They are lying! Even Tarantino, in his recently interview on the subject, dodged his responsibility in this issue. At least he said, *"Anything I say will only sound like an excuse."* But, think about this, if you watch his films, either the character he plays or another primary character sexually assaults a woman (or man). I have always found this very offensive. Though he is undoubtedly a great auteur, this behavior is just wrong and it should never be glorified in a movie! Plus, virtually all of his films were produced by Harvey Weinstein (the man at the center of this controversy). In fact, when this crisis broke, one of the news networks rightly stated that there has virtually been no Academy Awards Ceremony, in the past twenty years, where someone has not thanked Harvey Weinstein. He is responsible for making some incredible movies. In fact, a couple of his accusers thanked him at these ceremonies. What does this tell us?

Personally, in the independent industry, I have known so many actresses who would tell me things like, *"I had to fuck him to be in his movie."* Or, *"I don't want to be in any more of his films because I would have to fuck him again."* And, these are not major A-Films like Weinstein produces. These are crappy low-budget pieces created by ugly, fat, old men. Even my *Zen Filmmaking* buddy Don Jackson was like this. If an actress wasn't forthcoming with sexual favors he would take them on what he called, *"The Don walk."* I always found that so disgusting. I felt so sorry for the actresses. But, at least, he was not forceful, they could say, *"No."*

On the other side of the of the issue, there has been times when an actress, when I was casting a movie, has done things like reach her hand across the desk, take a hold of my hand, and say, *"I will do anything to be in this movie."* Though tempting, as these were beautiful women, that is just not who I am. There was only one time when I walked down the road of romance with an actress in one of my films but that was based on mutual attraction. But, unfortunately, due to various circumstances, as is the case with many new relationships, that one never had the opportunity to mature.

#metoo. Women are not the only ones who are sexual exploited in the industry. As has been well documented, men too encountered sexually inappropriate behavior. There are two instances, in my career, that come to mind. The first was with a high-powered casting agent. She was a bit older women, who, in her youth, was probably very attractive. After I had gone to the casting session, I was outside getting on my Harley. She ran out to talk to me. What occurred is that she invited me to go to a coffee house with her. I politely declined as I could see what was on her mind. Her facial expression immediately changed. *"You know, I'm your only chance or you're never going to work in this industry,"* was her statement. I smiled and rode off. But, she was right. My budding career in the A-market pretty much ended at that moment. Certain people, in Hollywood, have massive power.

The second time occurred with a manager; a woman, who took me on as her client. Again, she was somewhat older and had recently broken up from a relationship with a younger actor who she had guided into starring roles in a few A-films. I quickly came to understand what she was expecting from me but me, being nice and naïve, I thought I could sidestep this industry requirement. At one point, she invited me to watch a Hong Kong Kung Fu movie with her, which were beginning to become cult-mainstream at that point in history. Me, I showed up with my girlfriend. Well… That ended that. No more manager.

The fact is, most people in Hollywood are willing to do whatever it would take to enter into a position where they would be given the chance to star in an A-film. That is why this has gone on for so long. #metoo. Believe me, if one of those women would have said if you have sex with me I will give you a starring role in a major A-film, I would have happily done it. But, the sad thing is, Hollywood is all about the illusion and the power-play. And, like I have long said, *"The number one rule of filmmaker is that everybody lies."* So, you can't trust anybody!

Mostly, the people that have been in the news, on this subject, are the major female A-players who have been blessed enough to climb to the top. Were they in Weinstein productions? Yes, several of them. What they had to do to climb to the top of the ladder, I guess we will never truly know. But, they are there. We can only speculate if it was worth it.

The other people out there talking are those who did not reach any level of known success. Thus, they are trying to grab a moment of PR. God bless 'em! But, as history has shown us, there is always the powerful at the top and those who desire to be there. From this, some exert their power, while others are willing to do whatever it takes to gain that power. So, what does this teach us? What it teaches us is that the majority of people base their life upon desire. If you do base your life upon desire, then you are going to encounter those people who also base their life upon desire. From this, comes desire attempting to overpower other desire. So, from a Zen perspective we can conclude, remove desire from the equation and you are free.

Are you free enough to be free? Or, do you desire? If you desire, then the result(s) of your life, and those you will encounter, are obvious. Your life, your choice. Desire, and there is a price to pay. No desire, you are free.

Pure Cinema Cinéma Pur

As I have been making movies for a lot of years by this point in my life, I forever find it interesting how people perceptive cinema. We all begin watching a particular movie with a concept of what we are getting into. This definition is based upon what we are told to expect. Then, we base our judgment of that particular cinematic production upon if our personal vision of what we were told to expect was met or not. *"I liked it." "I hated it!"* And, so on…

People have the tendency to project their own perspective onto whatever they are viewing. They have come to like a certain type of cinema so they base all of their viewing experience upon that belief. The problem with this formula is, however, (though it is pretty much the only formula in practice), is that by viewing cinema in this manner the viewer can never understand the cinematic philosophy that the actual filmmaker was practicing. From this, something is truly lost.

As the years have gone on and I have gotten progressively more-and-more into embracing the tenets of Pure Cinema (Cinéma Pur); i.e. taking filmmaking to its most elemental core of simply focusing on visually interesting images, movement, and music, I have witnessed how the focus of those who watch my particular brand of cinema *(Zen Filmmaking)* has not evolved. People are still discussing films I made twenty years ago or more. Why is this? Because, in those films, people find story structure (as minimal as that may be in my films). They find something to talk about. But, in all this talking, again, they have missed the point of what is actually taking place in front of their eyes because they are basing all of their thoughts and discussions upon personal definitions and judgment. This isn't right or wrong—it is simply the way it is. But, by living your life defined by what you have already come to expect, you miss all of the pure and elemental beauty of what is going on in front of you.

For me, filmmaking has always been a spiritual process. Whether my films have been dialogue driven or simply a vision moving across the screen, what I have attempted to do is to harness an elemental image of life and capture it in its essential perfection that existed for only that moment in time. Most people don't get. I understand. That's fine. I am sure that the majority of the people who have watched my films; loving or hating them, have never seen the work of Cinéma Pur filmmakers like Léger, Ray, Richter, Eggeling, Chomette and the list goes on. In fact, if they watched their work they may not even like them as they are so ethereal. But, again, this goes to the elemental nature of cinema and cinema viewing; if you are there expecting something, if you are there judging something, if you are not there in the meditative purity of the moment than your absolute experience is lost—there will be no cinematic satori.

As always in life, let go and be free. See everything as if you are seeing it for the first time and never view anything through the eyes of preconceived judgment. Believe me, if you practice this philosophy, your everything will become better.

Perplexing...

You know, it has always been immensely perplexing to me how people speak about me, maybe discussing my creations, believing they know what I think, how I think, and why I do what I do. But, they never talk to me. I have had articles written about me: my films or my books without the author ever giving me a phone call. I have had academic dissertations written about *Zen Filmmaking* by people who never asked me anything. I have had documentaries made about me without the filmmaker ever communicating with me on any level. People have talked about me in books, articles, and on the internet without ever confirming their facts. And film reviews; forget about it... Some of them have been so wrong it is not even funny. But, if they would have just asked me, I could have straightened out any misconception.

Some people love me and have done really positive pieces about me. That's cool! Some have been just the opposite. But, what is missing in all of these equitation is the, *"Me,"* factor. Nobody talks to me. I'm alive! I'm not dead!

Now, I am not saying this is universally the case. A lot of people, since the dawning of the age of the internet, have reached out to me. If they were cool, I was cool. I have had some great discussions via the internet. If they were not cool, then the dialog ended before it ever began. But, more than that, I'm a person; I am approachable. I'm just a guy who does what he does... No better, no worse than anyone else. But, due to all of these previously detailed factors, where people have spoken about me who do not actually know me or understand why I do what I do, people have all of these misconceptions about me. And, some lies have been perpetuated. But, why? The answer is, they have not reached out a hand to know me. I am knowable! Maybe you will like me, maybe I will like you, maybe it will be just the opposite. But, if you don't try you will never know.

And, all this goes to the whole reality of life. Why do you spend your time not knowing? Why do you spend your time guessing and maybe perpetuating a lie? Why do you not go to the source? If you do not go to the source you will never know the truth. Do you want to live your life not knowing the truth?

How Much of What You Have is Because of Someone Else?

How much of what you have—what you do and what you have become is because of someone else? And, do you ever think about this fact—do you ever give them thanks?

As we pass through life each of us is taught, influenced, and provided things, both physical and mental, by other people. From what we receive, our life is shaped. This certainly goes to both the positive and the negative elements that we receive but whatever the case, none of us are wholly created by ourselves.

Take a look at your life. How did you get to where you are today?

Most of us come from a defined family. How did your family influence who you are at this moment of your life? In most cases, they paid for your upbringing, put a roof over your head when you were a child, perhaps they paid for you to go to school, and so on. As they are your family, as you do see them and think about them on a regular basis, you commonly can easily define what they did for your life that guided you to whom you have become; maybe you even thank them. But, beyond your immediate family what and whom has guided you to becoming who you are at this moment.

We have each had teachers that have encouraged us and guided us on our path. Through these teachers we have become motivated to become whom we have wanted to become. But, one of the key things to study as you analyze whom you owe what to is, understanding the fact that the teacher you learned from also taught others. What did others do with that knowledge? For example, in my early years, there were a few martial arts instructors who truly helped me on my path. But, they also taught other students. Yet, few of those other students continued their progression and evolution in the martial arts as say I did. So, what was the influence of that teacher on those people? This is the same with myself as a teacher—whether this was in the martial arts, filmmaking, or on other subjects, some of my students have moved into their own, while others did not. Thus, this all comes down to the interpersonal emotional make up of the individual and what they do with what they have learned.

What have you done with what you have learned? Who influenced you to become who you are? And, what do you owe that person?

More than simply the people who have taught and influenced us to be guided in a particular life direction, there are also those people who do material things for us. Maybe they are the person who gave you the job you applied for. From their action you were allowed to make a living. Do you ever think about what you owe them and what their action did to touch your life?

As we pass though our existence most people never think to the subtle elements that came to shape their life. Yes, they may love or hate a person based upon emotions but those are not refined elements, they are simply sensations based upon passions.

Who you actually are and what you have actually become has been shaped by particular people. Some you may know and have studied from personally, while others may be distance in time and in space. But, you did not become who you have become wholly by yourself. You need to realize this. Then you need to look to whom gave you what. I would say that you should thank them from what they gave you but that is a personal choice—a choice that few people choose to make. But, at least you should credit them, in your own mind if nothing else, for their helping you find yourself, in the space and the place, where you live today.

All It Costs is Money

In life, a good percentage of what we all want is based upon money. Maybe you want a specific car, home, camera, guitar, bicycle, suit, dress, purse, pair of shoes, vacation, you name it—all based upon if you do or do not have the money to buy it.

Some people base their life upon credit cards. Don't do it! Not only do you pay insane rates of interest—meaning everything you buy costs you way more than its actual price but having unsecured debt is life debilitating—it holds your everything back from becoming.

Same with student loans... Every person I have ever known who has taken one out was all happy about it, believing they found a way to get over on the system and climb to the top of the heap via a college degree but all they did was bind themselves to a seemingly endless/never ending payment at the end of every month.

But then, there are those people with money. Again, it takes money to get what you want to make things happen. You can't be a filmmaker without a camera, can you? I have watched as many people I have known, by whatever method, purchased their camera, computer, and filmmaking equipment, all with the dreams of making a movie but then nothing... They did not make a film. ...Even though they had the money to buy the necessary items, they did not possess the focus and the drive to actually get out there and make it happen.

I think back to a funny story... When I was teaching a course at U.C.L.A. this one young lady student of mine bought the top of the line DV camera of the time. We got to be friends and as I was putting together a new film I asked her if she wanted to be the DP (Director of Photography). I thought it would be fun to have my movie filmed from a new and different perspective; that of a woman. She accepted my offer. On the night before the shoot was to begin she contacted me and wanted to have a sit down. Sure, that was normal. I thought we are going to discuss some of the shooting style. When I arrived we sat down and began our conversation. She said, *"I have one question, how do you focus the camera?"* What! Obviously, I had to push back the production and find another DP. It's funny now. But, it's things like that can really mess up the scheduling of the cast and the crew and make the filmmaker lose credibility.

But, here we are… She had the money but not the determination to learn the craft. For example, me, when I get a new camera I immediately drop everything and learn all about it. But, not all people operate from that perspective.

And, this goes to the point of all this… Have you ever really wanted something, found a way to buy it, and then never used it or it did not equal the pathway to your fulfillment as you had intended? I believe that most of us have had that experience to varying degrees. So, what does this tell us about desire and the price of that desire?

Desire costs money. More than just money, desire costs you Life Time. Meaning, you must find a way to buy your desire, pay for the ongoing costs of your desire, and then pay for the consequences of your desire.

Most of us what to do something in life. Many of us what to create something in life. Almost universally these things cost money. You should really calculate the long-term cost(s) of your desires before you set about on the course of purchasing that desire. Desires are never free.

It is Easy to Criticize When You Haven't Lived the Life

Having been involved in the film industry for almost three decades at this point in my life I can say with certainty that most people who are not here in Hollywood (and I use Hollywood as a generic term) have no idea what is actually taking place. They have not tried to get an agent, they have not paid a lot of money to get their headshots photographed and run, they have not been to a casting session, they have not paid a lot of money to take acting classes, they have not had people lie to them; promising them the world. They have not even cared enough to move to Hollywood and actually give the industry a try. Yet, they have all of these ideas and opinions about what is taking place. But, they have no idea! They have no basis for their thoughts. What is taking place in the Midwest in a film class at a college campus is not what goes on out here.

Some people want to believe that their opinions matter. And, maybe to them and their friends it does. But, as in all areas of life, if you have not lived it, you do not know what you are taking about.

Having grown up in Hollywood (literally) I saw a lot of what the industry did to people. That's why I steered my life away from it initially. But, when I did get involved, I jumped in head first. And, just like all the others, who come from all across the globe, I too fell prey to a lot of the illusion Hollywood has to offer. But, that's why I can comment on the subject. I have been here. I have lived it. Have you?

When I evolved into being a filmmaker this is also why I developed *Zen Filmmaking*. As I state over-and-over again, I did it to simplify the filmmaking process so people could actual get their films made. Again, as I state over-and-over again, this is also why I generally cast unknown actors and actresses in my films, I want to give them the chance to actually be in a film—a chance that no one else will offer them. To all the critics, what are you offering them but words?

Hollywood is all about the promises. It is about the, *"I will do this for you."* But, this very rarely ever happens. What Hollywood is really all about is the lie. Most people come out here believing the dream and eventually leave to go back home very disappointed. I say this, as someone who actually knows. And, I say this to make people understand the reality.

Now, you can criticize me all you want. You can love or hate my *Zen Films,* I don't care. But, if you have not been here, if you have not lived the life, you <u>do not,</u> you<u> cannot</u> understand what I base my words upon. So, before you start throwing shots, live the life. Then, you will have a basis for what you say. If not, you are just like every other armchair quarterback who believes they have all of the answers to the game but has never even been on the field.

Every Creator Says the Same Thing

It always strikes me that whenever I see or hear a musician, a filmmaker, or an author being interviewed they each discuss the same issue. That issue is how they are frustrated with the way people believe they have the right to take their creations, utilize them as they see fit, and even, in some cases, redistribute them and make money off of that item without ever paying for that service. They each believe the same thing, (as do I), that if the people who are taking the creations of others, for free, actually were they ones who created them they would have a very different perspective as to what was taking place.

This phenomenon of, *"Digital Stealing,"* began very recently when one looks to the overall view of human history. I mean, just a couple of decades ago it was far too expensive to do any of that. People could not make a copy of a film, even duping large scale copies of video tapes was far to expensive. To rerecord and then repress a music album cost far too much money to make it a viable commodity. Books… Forget about it. To actually copy, type set, and then print a book was very expensive so it wasn't done. But, in the digital age this has all changed.

When I taught classes on filmmaking in the late 1990s and even into the early 2000s I used to warn my students about placing their screen credits in white on black cards at the beginning and at the end of their production. As what used to happen, particularly in the Asian market place, was that unscrupulous distributors would take the film, remove the screen credits and add their own. It happened to me. This is why I told them, if they could afford it, to put the credits over picture as this was a way of assuring that even if the movie was stolen the true credits would remain intact.

But now, here you and I sit at our computers. The world is our oyster. And many, if not most, people do not even care about what they are doing to the creative works of others as long as they can do it for free. Some have even found a way of making money off of the creations of others. Do you ever think about this as you walk through your pathway of life and you take advantage of what others have created? Do you ever stand up for the rights of the creator?

I believe that each of us who walks the path of creativity wants to get our creations out to the masses. If we didn't, we would be creating them in the first place. Nobody writes a book with the hopes that no one will read it. But, throughout history there has always been an exchange for goods and services rendered. This hasn't always been via money. But, this system has always been in place. It has always been in place until now—in this current time frame we are living within.

It has always been the youth of society that has pushed the levels and understanding of human consciousness forward. This is because when you are young you have the time and the freedom to explore new realms of possibilities, as you are not yet burdened by many of the responsibilities of latter life. But, this is also the time period when many people make the biggest mistakes in their life. They set themselves into a course of action that will come to define the rest of their life. Good or bad, this is just the way it is. But, also good or bad, in youth few people have the ability to look at the big picture and see or care how what they are doing is setting the stage for not only their own life but the lives of others.

If all of the people who are actually the, *"Creators,"* of things have the same problem with what is taking place, doesn't that tell you something? Doesn't that make you think?

The fact is, not everyone takes what is out there in cyber space for free. Some people are very honest. How about you? Do you take for free and feel that you have the right to do it? Do you take for free and feel that just because this other person you know is doing it, that it's okay? Or, do you actually make money off of the creations of other people? If you do, don't you feel you own that person something? Wouldn't it be the right thing to do to pay them, in some shape or form, for what you have taken?

I always go back to the point that all of life begins with you. What you do has the potential to affect the entire world. The small things you do can progress and equal the big things. So, what do you do? Do you take for free and not even care about the consequences? Think about this, if you care enough about the person who created that thing you are stealing to make them the focus of your actions, don't you think that you should care enough about that person to not steal from them in the first place?

Think about what you do. Care about the creators.

Black Hawk Down

Over the past eight or nine months there has been a few stations on FiOS that have been playing the movie, *Black Hawk Down* over and over again. So, whenever I'm flipping channels and/or there isn't anything else to watch I catch bits and pieces of it. I am sure in the past months I have also actually sat down and watch the whole movie from start to finish, as well.

Hands down, this is one of the best movies ever made. Not just one of the best, if not the best, war films ever made, but in terms of overall movie making this film is unparalleled. Ever since I saw it in the theaters, when it was first released, I was simply amazed how Riddle Scott achieved what he did with this film. I mean, the amount of coordination between the helicopters, the movement and interaction between large numbers of people in the air and on the ground, not to mention the movement of animals, people, cars, and the cinematography is exceptional. This is just a great movie!

Sadly, Riddle Scott's brother Tony Scott, also an exceptional filmmaker, took his own life by jumping from a bridge not far from where I live. No one may ever know the reason why, but that was his choice and this is a choice we each have the right to exercise if we need to. But, gone is a great man who also made great films.

But, back to the point... The reason I write this is that whether you are a filmmaker or just a film viewer, you really need to see this movie. I truly cannot even conceive how Scott did what he did, watch for the subtleties, you will be amazed. Though he has long been one of my favorite directors and he has made films since this movie, this one is a pinnacle of exceptional filmmaking.

What You Are Looking For?

Each of us comes at life defined by what we expect. Expectations are what drives us to quest for what we desire. From a humanistic and/or spiritual perspective, one will say that you should never enter into any situation with a predetermined judgment but instead allow all things to be as they are—new and fresh. From this, each of these things are allowed to be perfect in their own essence. I would say this too. But, the fact is, most people do not have a highly develop mind. In fact, they don't want to develop their mind. They don't want to, because their mind is already made up.

With a made up mind everything a person enters into is defined by what has taken place in the before. Everything they see, everything they witness, and everything they choose to do is defined by the experiences they previously possessed going into any of these activities. Not good, but this is the way most people encounter their life. Do you?

The problem that exists, when you live your life from this perspective, is that nothing is new or fresh. It is not free. And, as such, you will never enter into one of those peak experience moments where *Satori* is allowed to overtake you. Thus, your life becomes stagnate and the same.

Think about the last time you went to a movie. What were your expectations? Were you expecting it to be as good as that great movie you saw last week or last year? Or, were you going into it knowing that it could never be as great as that movie. In either situation, you entered the movie theater defined by what you had previously viewed. Thus, unless something truly shook you to your core, you were doing nothing more than comparing that experience to a previously lived experience. Thus, you brought all of your mental baggage along with you. From this, any perfection of the moment was lost. How often do you do this?

I used the example of a movie, but this same predefined judgmental mindset can go to all areas of your life. From surfing, to bowling, to going to the supermarket, to going out to dinner, to reading a book.

...Speaking of reading a book, I can tell you a couple of funny stories...

Recently, in my blog I discussed how a person made a very opinionated documentary about me about five years ago and recently re-released it causing me to receive undeserved hate mail and stuff like that. In that documentary, the documentarian quoted from two of my books on filmmaking. I guess the person got pissed off at me and took those books and some of my films and sold them to a local used bookshop. A university student who was into what I do noticed the transaction, altered me to it, and I own the aforementioned books. I just relooked at them and it was very enlightening to me in that I could see what passages this person had highlighted in yellow. As I stated in a previous piece, those books were designed to help the independent filmmaker but what this person had done was to remove passages from the greater text, which not only made me look bad but completely distorted *Zen Filmmaking* and what I was hoping to present in those writings. Looking at this person's highlights I could totally see what they were doing. They were not reading the book(s) as a method to learn new knowledge or to be helped in the practice of filmmaking but as a means to find a method to use my own words to make their preconceived notions about me a reality and to make me look bad. Not cool! But, it was/is truly interesting to witness how this person's mind works.

The fact is, this is how many people's minds work. They go into a subject with a preconceived notion about what is presented and they never step out of their own opinions to the degree where they can find a new and perhaps better way of thinking.

Another revealing story, in regard to me, is that when I was in my later thirties I had decided to go back to grad school and earn another Master's Degree. I was taking a course on Comparative Religion as Presented in Literature and one of my assignments was to write a paper about this one teacher/author. Going into the assignment I had never really like the method of this man's presentations as he took a little bit of this religion here and a bit of that philosophy there and then intermingled them in his writings. I read the assigned books and, complete with footnotes, I detailed my appraisal of this man's writings. My instructor rejected the paper, however, and told me to rewrite it as what I had written was far too opinionated and at the graduate level this style of writing was unacceptable. Thus, I had to reset my mind and prepare another twenty-page paper. What happened during this process, however, was I turned off my previously decided upon opinions. When I did, I found that the man had a lot of interesting principals to present. Thus, through my being force to rethink my original beliefs about the man and his writing style I was allowed to come to a new and deeper understanding about life, philosophy, and the way in which we each interpret our lives and the lives of others. It was very enlightening and I am so thankful my instructor forced me to rewrite that paper. If I can find it, perhaps I will present it here somewhere on scottshaw.com.

The point being, if you go into any subject—anything in life with a preconceived notion then you rob yourself of all that situation has to teach you and the sheer beauty and the newness of that experience is lost. This is what I teach in *Zen Filmmaking* and this is what I suggest in all levels of life. Allow yourself to be free. Allow your mind to not already be made up. From this, a whole world of NEW is allowed to be given birth to. Check it out. You may like it. ☺

If You Want Me to Be in the Conversation Let Me Be in the Conversation

Whenever I create a narrative-driven film I allow my actors to speak the way they would naturally speak—say what they would naturally say. From this, I believe it provides their character with a sense of realism.

In times gone past, Donald G. Jackson and I would feed our characters their lines in our *Zen Films*. But, I left that ideology behind long ago, as it is not as real as real.

In my *Zen Films,* what I do is allow the actors to say whatever they want. I give them a bit of framework for their character at the outset and then I let them run with it. The only time I interrupt is if they are going totally off storyline. Then, I leave it to the editing room to find the best of the best. That's the great thing about cinema, you have time. It's not like TV that has to be cut down to a very precise period of time. The filmmaker has freedom, if they allow themselves to embrace it. Thus, I want my actors to be a part of this process of cinematic freedom.

When it comes to life, I also think this is the best practice—let people say what they will say. From this, you are allowed to see into their psychic; as what they say and the way they say it can provide you with deep insight into how they truly feel about you, life, and themselves. What a person chooses to say and how they choose to say it is very revealing about who they truly are on the inside.

As an actor, on the sets of other director's films, in many cases, I have been given a script with lines to memorizes. That's fine but is that person me? No, it is a person I am pretending to be. In some cases, in small parts in A-Films, I have been given an on-set line or two to speak. But, I always find those words are forced and predictable. How often do you only say one line? I always felt if they wanted me to speak, they should let me speak. Then, like in the case of *Zen Filmmaking*, a natural conversation would evolve. From this, the audience would be treated to a condition of naturalness.

The one exception to this was the film I did directed by Robert Altman, *The Player*. I arrived on the set to play the role of, *"White Guy."* Yes, in all truth that is what my character's name was given in the actual script. I still have the original script so I can prove it! In that case, as we begin to shoot second part for my character on the stairwell of the Rialto Theater in Pasadena, I didn't like the line that had been written for me. I told this to Bob. He said, say whatever you want. *"You got the wrong guy, man."* From this, it caused a moment of reflection in the film. I remember being at the premier of, *The Player*. With great cinema creation and story development, the filmmaking team had built my charterer up to the degree that after my character's set up in the movie theater, watching the movie the Bicycle Thief, the audience all gasp when I said that simple line. And, as the person who created it, that was a really good feeling!

Most of the time on the set, the actors don't have that freedom, however. They are forced to speak words that have been memorized from a script. This is just like in life; you are trapped in an environment where you must be defined by what you are defined by. Thus, you are not allowed to say what you actually feel. This is why the internet has taken off to the degree that it has—anyone can say anything thing. And, hidden by a screen name, no one knows who you truly are, so they can't confront you face-to-face about what you have said—thus there is a veil of protection.

Yeah, yeah... This is the coward's way out. I agree! But, for all those with no voice, here they have a voice.

But, more to the point, think about when you speak to people... Do the people you know, (the people you actually associate with in real life), allow you to speak in the manner you truly desire? Moreover, do they hear you? Do they listen to what you have to say, consider your point of view, and perhaps change their mind to give your point of view room to grow in life?

Truthfully, most people's lives are not like that. Most people do not want you to speak. If you do speak, most people do not want to listen to what you have to say. At best, they pay you lip service and then continue on their path of self-induced righteous.

Life is a complicated pathway. As I bought up the internet, I can say, there is no true dialogue out here. No one says they're sorry, because no one care about the consequences. At least they don't care about the consequences to others—only themselves. But, this is a shallow place to live your life from for at the end of the day what will it equal? Only you saying what you said, somebody else saying what they said, but no interaction and growing of the minds of multiple people. Thus, evolution is halted. There is only you and no one else.

So, back to the original point, if you want me to be in the conversation, let me be in the conversation. Just like an actor in a film, let me speak in a natural way. Then, you will know me, I will know you, and we can create a new evolution of life and understanding.

The Guy Who Never Made a Movie
The Guy Who Never Wrote a Book

I find it rather interesting/amusing that every now and then someone will heads-up me to the fact that this one guy is out there attempting to cast shade on me as a filmmaker—criticizing my films and/or me in one derogatory way or the other. The funny thing is, and the thing that anybody who reads his posts does not realize, is that it was like ten years ago or so the guy first contacted me directly saying something negative and telling me he could and has made a better movie than I ever could. I gave him my address and told him to send me a copy. Of course, he never did, as he has never made a film. Yet, there he is, still out there, throwing around negativity focused at me and I imagine other people, as well. But, who is he really angry at? Me for making movies or himself for never making one?

Maybe twenty years, when my first book on Hapkido came out, I was contacted by this school owner telling me how terrible the book was. I suggested that he write one. He told me, of course he would, and it would be so much better than mine. Great, I told him, I look forward to reading it. But, that book was never created. I guess he either never wrote the book or he found out how impossible it is to actually get a deal with an established publishing company. All these years later, still no book on Hapkido from him…

You know, when I first began putting the formalized foundations for *Zen Filmmaking* together; the words I spoke, the classes I taught, and the writing that were published were all designed to help the person who may be having a problem getting his or her film actually done. The teachings were put together as an inspiration. This is still the case. But, back then, all the so-called, know-it-all, wanta-be filmmakers were saying *Zen Filmmaking* was all wrong. A film could never be made without a script. But, that was never the point. The point was, JUST DO IT! Simplify and get it done! Since that time, I have still received the same words of criticism. Sure, there are a lot of people who have made a lot of indie films since I first came up with *Zen Filmmaking* almost thirty years ago. But, there are also a lot more who have failed. ...Failed for whatever reason. Mostly, as I have said so many times, the reason people fail in their filmmaking process is their expectations. They want their movie to look like a several million-dollar production when all they have is a few hundred dollars. Or, they wait and wait, hoping the big bank will come their direction but it never does. But, if you let go of your expectation, if you let go and allow yourself to be free in your vision, you can actually get something done. You can actually make a movie or create anything else that you want to create.

  This is the same with all things in life. Maybe you have a vision. Maybe you even dislike what someone else has created and want to do it better. But, until you have shown what you can actually do it and put it on the same chopping block of public opinion—exposing it to the same damnation, then all you are is voice speaking words that holds no true validly.

  Maybe you don't want to make a movie. Maybe you don't want to write a book. And, that's great. That's who you are. But, if you do, then do it. Sitting around telling someone else/everyone else how bad they are, how bad what they are doing is, means you are doing nothing.

Partners in Crime and You Think You Know What You Never Know

As I have been discussing for many years now, some of the most influential martial arts practitioners of the twentieth century have all but been forgotten. Out of sight, out of mind, and all that… I think this is very sad as if you had the chance to meet them and perhaps train with them; they really had a lot to teach. But, unlike people like Bruce Lee, who wrote books and was seen in films, most of them never cast that large of a shadow. Thus, their knowledge was more secretive. Now, it is all but lost.

I have witnessed this to a degree with my *Zen Filmmaking* cohort, Donald G. Jackson, as well. Very few people knew him. Most who did, did not like him or he offended them. But, those who did pierce the veil and actually come to be friends with him understood that he was a unique and very creative individual. *"I'm an artist, god damn it,"* as he would joking exclaim. Together, we instigated *Zen Filmmaking*. Without his and my interaction, *Zen Filmmaking* would never have come to be. Certainly, there are those out there who may wish it would not have been created. ☺ But, with art at its heart, it was. From this, I have been allowed to formulate it into a relatively cohesive ideology and continue to follow the path he and I initiated, guiding the participant(s) towards cinematic enlightenment.

Once upon a time, people asked a lot of question about him. Now, zero… The only people who ever contact me, regarding him, are people that want to make money off of his movies by distributing them. No Thanks!

Sad, I think, he had a lot to say. Though, of course, he was completely self-centered, out of control, and crazy. But, he was a good friend and a visionary.

I have recently been contacted by a U.K. team that I am told is going to do a documentary on *Zen Filmmaking*. They didn't ask me if they could, they just decided to do it. ☺ They did ask me to do a little talk for it, however, but as I told them, I'm a fairly soft-spoken guy and I wouldn't want to bring down the intense energy of their production—as I have seen a trailer and it is great chaotic, psychedelic, anarchy. It sounds like they are going to use stuff from some other *Zen Filmmakers* out there. So, it will be interesting to see what they come up with and if they capture the essence of *Zen Filmmaking* or not.

In actually, I pretty much turn all requests for interviews down. Like I jokingly told my friend a number of years ago when we was giving me grief about turning down a TV spot, *"Hey, if it was Charlie Rose asking I would be there."* But now, sadly, even Charlie has fallen from grace.

A production team did do a big documentary about *Zen Filmmaking* and me in Hong Kong a number of years ago. I saw it in a theater over there. It was great. Big! Hong Kong style. But, it kind of went away. I don't really know what happened to it. I also lost track of the producers. So, it is in the wind somewhere. If you know where it is or have a copy, let me know.

But, this brings me to the point of all this… Back in the days when Don was still alive, it was so much more fun. It was fun to have a partner in crime. It was fun to not have to be the All and the Everything of every production. Though I certainly have worked with other filmmakers before and after Don, they all had agendas. They all wanted something other than the naturalness of Zen. They all had this idealized image of what a production should look like and what a finalized movie should be. A lot of the actors I have worked with totally got it and loved coming back for more. The so-called filmmakers, on the other hand, not so much. Thus, we all went our separate ways.

And, this is the thing about *Zen Filmmaking*, Donald G. Jackson, and Scott Shaw; what do you really know? Do you really know anything about me, him, or it? There are a few filmmakers out there who I am told I have influenced. Some large, some small. Some honest about their influences, some will never mention my name. In fact, maybe a month or so ago there was this guy who had obviously read my books and articles and his team had posted a doc about how he guides his actors with no script. He never mentioned *Zen Filmmaking* or me, but it was such an obvious rip off that it made me smile. But, that's okay, what can you do?

All you can do is do what you can do. That's what I do. I used to go at *Zen Filmmaking* with a much bigger scope of vision. But, as all that is left is me, (I have no partner in crime), I got tired of holding the weight of the All and the Everything on my shoulders. Thus, my vision became smaller, more abstract. Born was the *Non-Narrative Zen Film*. And, here's the thing about life; we all are here, we all are doing what we do, while wanting to do something else. But, what you are doing/what you can do is <u>all</u> you can do. Do you create art in your moment as much as your moment will allow you? Or, do you let the immense gravity in the ALL of life keep you from doing anything?

Let's face it; creation is all any of us have. It is all that will be left when we leave this life. Whether your creations are loved or scorned, they are your creations. So, what are you going to create? What can you create alone when you don't have a partner in crime?

Watching the Evolution AKA Everyone's Dead

There is a new breed of TV stations, offering television series from the early days of TV, that have cropped up recently. Certainly, reruns of old TV shows have been around forever: *Gilligan's Island, I Love Lucy, Gunsmoke, Perry Mason, Bat Man,* and *Star Trek* have never really gone away. But, there were so many other great TV series that, if you weren't there, you would never have known that they existed. These stations are playing some of my childhood favorites like: *Have Gun Will Travel, The Cisco Kid, Rawhide, Wagon Train, The Lone Ranger, Johnny Straccato, Lost in Space, The Rifleman, Naked City, 77 Sunset Strip, Route 66, High Chaparral,* and *Maverick,* onto shows like *Dennis the Menace,* and *Roy Rogers.*

...Did you know that though the *Roy Rogers Show* was supposed to take place in the Old West one of the characters drove around in a jeep? Very strange...

These stations go on to broadcast episodes of shows that shaped my later childhood years, my adolescence, and onwards... Series like: *The Mod Squad, The Green Hornet, The Man from Uncle, It Takes a Thief, The Rat Patrol, Combat, Dragnet, Adam 12, Mannix, The Twilight Zone, The Name of the Game, The Streets of San Francisco, Ironside, Hawaii Five-O, Beretta, The Rockford Files,* and *Hill Street Blues.* Again, if you weren't there, you weren't there and if you don't take the time to watch these shows you may never realize how truly influential they were and how depictive of a time and place in our human history they portray.

But, as I watch them, the one thing that comes to mind is that virtually all of the actors and all of the filmmakers who worked on these shows are now dead. Few, are still alive.

Certainly, this is a condition of life. We all pass on to wherever it is we pass on to. But, if you think about it, these people who are only a generation or two removed from us are now gone. The one factor that allows us to clearly remember who they were is their image having been filmed, which casts their memory to eternity.

Recently, my *Zen Filmmaking* brother, Conrad Brooks passed away. The day he left us, I begin a piece about him, but I just couldn't bring myself to do. A great man lost. The good news is, if you can call it that, I have told stories about our filmmaking odysseys in other places like in articles and my books on filmmaking and *Zen Filmmaking*. But, just as in the passing of people like Roger Ellis, Donald G. Jackson, and Robert Z'Dar, the core team of *Zen Filmmaking* is diminishing rapidly. I'm pretty much all that's left. Most of the others that are still around have left the game altogether. Thinking of these loses does make me sad.

I certainly understand that this is what sets forth evolution. Those who do. Those who take the time to focus and create. Those who for, whatever reason, set about on a path that creates something that is unique and then passed that something onto the masses. Us, we, those of us who do this chronicles a place and a time in history and then set it to something that lasts for more than the moment it was lived within. Thus, it defines a moment of time. Combine this was a life-philosophy, as in *Zen Filmmaking* or the foundations that created early television, and then there is something that can be looked back upon and, even if you don't appreciate it, you can understand that it defines a something.

For many people, it is hard to watch old television series, as they are not made with the same technological advances and rapid pace of story development that can be seen in today's TV episodes. But, it is like art. For each of us we like what we like, defined by whatever non-rational definitions that rattles around in our brain. But, if we don't take the time to study the evolution, we can never understand why we are where we are and what has brought is to this moment in history.

Been There Done That

Have you ever had the experience where someone comes up to you and they are so excited about something that they are doing? Due to the fact that they are so excited, they want to bring you into their project. Maybe they think that because you used to do something similar, that you will be as excited as they are. But, you are not. Why? Because you've been there and you've done that and you've moved on.

I forever find it interesting when this happens to me, especially in the film industry. Due to the fact that, once-upon-a-time, I was the king of doing things on a no-budget budget, people believe that is still who I am. They invite me—they want me to go to their sets and watch them steal a location or setup a great backdrop for a shot without getting any filming permits, production insurance, or anything like that. Sure… That's great! I did that more times than I can even remember. But, it is essential to note, when I was doing my *Zen Films* on that level, I was never really excited about it. I was never enthralled with the getting over on someone or something or society in general. For me, it was always about getting the best project out there that could be had. It was about the endgame not about the doing. In fact, I really did not like that part of the no-budget filmmaking process, as it equaled too much paranoia.

Now, for anyone who has ever made a low or no budget film, you can immediately attest to the fact that your film will find many a critic. But, how many of those people have gone out there and actually made a film? Few, I would wager. Yet, they voice their tone of hatred to the world. But, people do that all the time. As I so often discuss, there is a certain type of person who looks for something or someone not to like. They do not seek the positive, they do not attempt to find the good in the lacking, all they want to do is expel their inner demons onto the vastness of society. Bad! That is just the wrong way to live.

But, for all of those people out there who want to create, who are trying to create, who are doing whatever it takes to create, I salute you. Maybe you will be the one to make something truly great and long-lasting that will change the all and the everything. If not, at least you tried.

For me, as a filmmaker, as I have shifted my focus to the more surreal realms of cinema over the past decade, the *Non-Narrative Zen Films* as I have titled them, I have held onto to the essence expressed in the doctrines of *Zen Filmmaking* that I formulated—of just getting out there and doing it. But, in this doing, my focus has shifted to the visually abstract. And, from this and within this, I have created some *Zen Film Mind Rides* that I really like, while others I have created, I just do not like that much. Just as at the root of my character driven films, some turn out better than others. Currently, I am simply enjoying creating visual images without the need for personality—not mine, not others.

So, when that person who loves what I have done in the past wants to take me into their excitement, it makes me happy that they are happy. It makes me happy that they are creating. But me, I'm walking a different path these days. I prefer the silent and the abstract, lost to the realms of its own visual suchness, compare to the driven that is attempting to piece the veil of commonality. A place I never truly understood.

Enlightenment Through the Arts

The other night I was watching a production called, *Unseen Cinema,* on TCM. What this program presented was short films that were created in the early years of filmmaking that truly pushed the boundaries of what was then considered mainstream filmmaking. Obviously, this was right up my alley. ☺

One of the films they presented was a 1924 piece titled, *Ballet Mecanique.* I had not seen this film in many-many years. But, as I again watched it, I was reminded what a groundbreaking piece of cinema it truly was—especially for 1924. Had it been done in the 1960s, it would have been expected. If it was done in that era it may have been called an, *"Acid Flick,"* as by then LSD was a common thread that avant-garde filmmakers embraced. But, it was made long before LSD was even invented. It is an amazing piece of cinema. What motivated the filmmaker(s) to make this piece, I can only imagine. Watch it if you can. It is inspiring.

Way back then, like now, there was a mainstream that permeated society. There was the accepted norm. Even though cinema was a fairly new art form infiltrating society, there was already a small group of filmmakers who were pushing its boundaries to new and unexplored levels. Most of these people did not find a large audience. Yet, they had an artistic and a spiritual purpose in all that they did. Thus, it rose to the level of true art.

Most people, especially in an art form like filmmaking, do what they do inspired by a desire for fame, recognition, and/or monetary reward. Think about the majority of people that enter the field of filmmaking as actors and filmmakers. Why do they do it? It is not for the art. It is for the ego, the fame, the perks, and the money. The stories I could tell you...

How many people do what they do solely as a means to create art? How many people live their life by that code? Very few.

After that program was over, I flipped the channels and, amazingly, I happened upon a documentary on the great jazz musician John Coltrane broadcast on a PBS station. Immediately, the deep inspiration of this man's music struck me. If you have not listened to John Coltrane you are really missing out. He was a master of unparalleled talent. Even though in my early years I was never a fan of the sax, he is the whole reason I bought a sax and took it up in my early twenties. When I did the soundtrack for the original (not the wide release) version of *Samurai Johnny Frankenstein* I based my sax playing on his style—though it was a poor imitation. But, what Coltrane did was artfully amazing. You should really listen to him. It is magic.

The documentary took the viewer through his life up to his death. In his later years, he married the musician Alice (McLoud) Coltrane. I knew her. It was fun to be reminded. How I met her is after the passing of Coltrane, in grief, she became a disciple of my teacher, Swami Satchidananda. But, at some point in the 1970s she had an interpersonal revelation and she anointed herself, Swami Turiyasangitananda. From this she began wearing the traditional orange robes of the sannyas order and the like.

There is no disrespect meant in this next statement, on any level, but I clearly remember this one time when we had gone with Gurudev to LAX to see him off and Turiyasangitananda was flying with him. She was there with her orange robes, big smile, and big personality. He looked to a few of us disciples and said, *"She's gone a little crazy, hasn't she?"* This was just after her transformation. But, the fact is, she found her wisdom and her art in her own way. And, this is something that she never left behind. I remember on late night TV, back in the days of UHF, she had a late-night TV show, on one of those poorly broadcast networks, where she would chant with a harmonium. She spent the rest of her life teaching and chanting at a spiritual center she created. Art, equaling spiritually, by her own definition.

And, this is the crux of the point, the people that push the boundaries of human understanding and acceptance are the ones who take the chances—do the unexpected and the unseen. Most people pass through their life based upon a precept of preconceived judgment. But, what comes from that? Nothing. Nothing new is enacted, created, and no one is inspired. But, the few who stretch the limits of the accepted norm, they are the ones who inspire change and spiritual enlightenment throughout time, space, and society.

Roller Blade Seven: The Unseen Scenes

As I have discussed a million times, it forever amazes me the amount of discourse and discussion that continues to take place around the first *Zen Film, The Roller Blade Seven.* What I am also always amazed about is the fact that people continue to come to all kinds of conclusions about the film. And sure, I'm right there with you, it is a weird and bizarre movie. But, as I have said a million times, whatever Donald G. Jackson and I did by creating that film over twenty-five years ago, we did something right, as it is still at the forefront of discussion.

All this being said, the amount of unfounded discussion that takes place around this film continually reminds me about how people like to come to all kinds of conclusions about everything and then spout their supposed wisdom out to the world but they do this without ever basing anything they are saying upon actual fact. They don't know, yet they speculate and talk and talk and talk.

Understanding all the things that are told to me by and about what people think and say about the film, I clearly understand they have never researched the facts about the film. Just one example it the Zen Documentary I made about the movie, *Roller Blade Seven: The Unseen Scenes.* I mean there is so much dialogue about what went into the creation of the movie, behind the scenes interviews, and yes, unseen scenes, that I find it very interesting that all of these people discuss *Roller Blade Seven,* but they do so without ever having watched that film. ...Or, they discuss the movie without having viewed the books, *Zen Filmmaking*, where there is a chapter devoted to the

288

film or *Roller Blade Seven: A Photographic Exploration* which also provides deep insight into the film's creation and metaphysical mindset via photographs.

I guess what I am saying here, and these goes to all levels of life, if you don't know, you don't know. And, if what you are saying is based upon not-knowing, all you are doing is spreading lies out to the world while presenting them as facts. And, this certainly goes to all levels of life. I'm just using *The Roller Blade Seven* as an example.

In life, in many cases, the essence of knowledge, where it all came from and how it started, is not available. But, in other cases, you can go to the source, you can learn the actual goings-on, leading to you comprehending the factual truth. Then, at least, what you think and what you say, based upon what you believe, will have some level of authenticity.

Go to the source—study the source. This is the only way to speak the truth.

The Outside That Will Never Happen

I am always made to smile when I hear about the new/next breed of person who has arrived here in L.A., or maybe they have just graduated from film school, and they have the all-knowing discussions about the film industry, whom is or isn't good, talented, or whatever, and how they are the one on the road to making it. They discuss the acting class they go to, the headshots they've just had taken, the auditions they've been to, and the extra work they have done. Of course, they always make that extra work sound like so much more. Mostly, they talk about how they are the one who is destine to make it. Having been in this industry for so long (and growing up in Hollywood) I have heard the same story, told a different way, so many times that it is not even funny. Awh, the promised illusion…

Personally, I am always truly impressed when someone out there in the somewhere else actually makes a film. I think that is where the true film art is born; out there… Not here. I mean, there is a person (out there) who sees themselves as a filmmaker and without any of the hoopla and false promise that is inherent in Hollywood actually makes a movie. That is great! And, that is something to be very-very proud of!

Being active in the industry, I hear all kinds of the same stuff all the time. Mostly, what I hear is what will happen but what has not happened. I hear everyone's critique of everyone else but I do not see people getting busy and actually accomplishing anything. Again, this go to my respect for those people out there who actually get it done.

Since my early days as a filmmaker, I have always tried to help people. Whether it was giving them a role in a film, as that is what they truly desired, or helping them learn the truth about the independent filmmaking game; I have done my best. That is also why I became a college and university instructor on the subject. I have always tried to tell people the truth and what to be careful of. Some have listened but many have not. From this, some of those people ended up walking down a dark road and have been used, hurt, or shamed. And, that is sad. The truth of this industry is that it is a very dark and selfish place, mostly based upon personal desire and personal ego.

But again, what I have tried to do is help. I have always believed that was part of my job. This is why I find it curious when the people in the out-there attack me and the others I have worked with. My associates and I have made movies, we have given people a chance, and we have helped them to secure their dream, even if only in a very small way. What have the critics done for the dreamers? How many people, who traveled to Hollywood with the dream of being in a film, have they given a role?

Again, this all goes to the perception of Hollywood and the film game in general. The critics, out-there, don't know what is going on in-here. As they are not a part of it, as they have not witnessed the ongoing, goings-on, they can never understand. Yet, they want their voice heard. And, this goes to the original premise of this piece. People talk, people dream, people desire, but what do they do? Most do nothing. Wherever you find yourself located in life, Hollywood or anywhere else, instead of talking about a movie, go make a movie. Then, you will have created art.

Who Goes To Nude Beaches?

Ever since I can remember there has been talk of nude beaches and nudist colonies where the modern person could go, leave their clothing behind, and enjoy the sun and/or the whatever. Whenever you see pictures or documentaries of these locations, however, I always question why would I want to be naked with a bunch of people that look like that? They are not young and pretty… ☺ That's apparently not always the case, of course. You do see photos of some topless beaches in Europe where apparently the model-set hang out. But, I never go to the those kind of places. I always try to avoid the sun.

This has not always been the case though. Back in the 70s there was still a freedom in the air. If we were at a secluded beach we would tear off our clothing and jump in the ocean. Same in Yosemite, at night, at the pool at the base of Yosemite Falls. Freezing cold but we would loose our clothing and jump in. There was even a so-called nude hot springs up in the high desert here in So. Cal. I would occasionally skip going to high school and, with my older friends, go up there and hang out, loose the clothes, talk about spirituality, chant, and bask in all that nature had to offer. But, I always got sunburned. It always turned out to be a bad experience for me. Don't you hate getting sunburned?

By the early 80s times began to change, however. I remember this one time when I had met this girl who lived in Ojai. On our first date she suggest we go to this spot she knew of, up in the Ojai hills, where we could lose our clothing and lay around and be naked. Weird first date but I was game. We were laying around in the nude and this weird old biker, hippy looking guy came up. He just started to stare. At her, me, or both; I don't know but it was weird. I was thinking I may have to go to blows with this guy to protect the girl but I knew I was at disadvantage. I was naked! The girl sensed the danger too. We got dressed and left.

Skip forward a decade or so. Now, I'm a filmmaker following one of the key rules of indie filmmaking, nudity is one of the cheapest special effects. Yeah, yeah, I know… It has become very politically incorrect to say stuff like that. But, that was then, this is now.

Anyway, Don Jackson and I used to go to this legally nude beach a bit North of Malibu to film. It was a nice, secluded, very visual location, surrounded by rocks on one side and the sea on the other.

This one time we took this actress with us and we did some nude production stills with her and filmed a couple of in-water scenes for a movie we planned to do. But, we were not alone. There was this guy gawking at the girl. I even noticed him wacking off by the rocks. That's something you don't want to see.

It was getting dark, so it was time to leave. We packed up our crew and equipment and headed for the cars. The only other car in the parking lot was a white convertible corvette which I took notice of.

The next planned stop was in Hermosa Beach, which is no short distance from where we were. I drove, keeping my eye in the rearview as I always do but I saw nothing. Then, all the way in Hermosa I see that guy and his car sneaking behind us. Now, that guy was talented. He followed us all the way to Hermosa Beach without me seeing him. And, I am trained. I would have thought no one could do that. But, he did. Scary...

What this reveals is that, at least some, of the people who go to these nude beaches are psycho. If this guy could follow me, he could easily follow some unsuspecting woman home and then who know what would happen? Of course, after our filming in Hermosa, I eventually lost him on the way back to our offices. But, it just goes to show you that there is a reason that some people go to nude beaches and that reason is not the 60s or 70s mindset of spiritual freedom.

Always be aware of your surroundings. Always study your surrounding. Always be aware of the people you encounter. Always know why you are doing what you are doing. And, always question why another person is doing what they are doing. Be safe!

Torrent and Damn It People Give Me Something!

Like I long ago realized, *"Everybody wants something from me but nobody ever gives me anything."* Now, this may come off as a bit of an egocentric statement but, in truth, it is anything but. And, more than just a statement about me, this is a mindset that goes outwards to a lot of the everybodies who exist out there in the real world.

Think about the people you think about. Why do you think about them? For the most part, you think about them because they do something for you internally when you think about them. Maybe you love them. And, that causes an emotion to react in your body and your mind. Maybe you hate them. And, that causes an emotion to react in your body and your mind. Maybe you judge them. And, that causes an emotion to react in your body and your mind. Maybe you desire them. And, that causes an emotion to react in your body and your mind. Maybe you have all kind of brewing fantasies that are talking place only in your mind about what you hope will happen between you and them; either good or bad. And, that causes an emotion to react in your body and your mind. Whatever the case, you are thinking about them for a reason. You don't think about anybody for no reason. Thus, not only is there, most probably, something you want from them but there is something you already are receiving. Maybe what you are receiving is only in your own mind.

But, you are receiving something that you are not paying for. Again, you don't think about anybody for no reason.

Of late, a lot of people have been asking me for a lot of things; large and small. In reality, this is nothing new. Perhaps it is one of the interwoven conditions of my life that I never really signed up for. You know, one of those deals you make with the devil that you never knew you made. I mean, as a young aspirant on the spiritual path I was taught that Karma Yoga (Selfless Service) was one of the greatest goods. And, I believe it is. I traveled up and down the West Coast doing the sound for my guru for years and I was never paid a dime and that was fine! I taught Hatha Yoga and Meditation for years for free and that was fine. I formally taught the martial arts for more than a decade and never made a dime all so my teacher could make his way through Western Society. I was fine with that.

As my later life has come on, the asking for something from me for free became far more subtle. Whether it was putting girlfriends through college, buying them a car, giving people a place to crash, appearing in films for free, directing films for free, giving people roles in my films they desired, teaching people how to make movies, and people using my name and credentials (both in a positive and negative way) to make a name for themselves and/or sell their product became much more frequent.

On a side note: Keep in mind, the publicity people claim they are providing my creations or me by talking about my films and me; forget about it. I don't need it! It hurts more than helps. Anyway…

I mean, even look at the people who upload movies (my movies among others) to the realm of torrent. They are not doing that just for the hell of it. That realm does not exist in the eternal space of FREE. Somebody is making money from it or it would not exist. Thus, somebody is getting paid but not me. That's why internet piracy is not a victimless crime and that is why I NEVER watch torrent stream films. I care enough about the filmmaker to care!

I am asked to teach a lot of classes on filmmaking. But, the fact is, there is just no money in it. I mean, at the college level they pay for shit. At the university level they pay well but the backstabbing politics that go on is just unbelievable. And, at the seminar level, the promoters always cheat you. I have written about all of this in the past. But, at one point I just decided, why do it? Sure, I can do it for free and/or for Karma Yoga. But, I have bills to pay too.

And, this is what I think nobody understands or at least nobody chooses to think about… I'm a person just like you. I have to find a way to live. For whatever karmic reason I am a creative person but if you are stealing the me in me—if you are stealing from me via torrent, duping, or anything else, then how am I supposed to survive. Moreover, if I wasn't here, than you wouldn't have anything to think and talk about. Yet, do you ever truly consider about me? I know, I am constantly asked to do things for people, give things to people, and not be upset when somebody steals something from me, but damn it people give me something!

Again, this is not some egotistical bombast. I am simply using me as an example because I know the facts.

When you are thinking about somebody else, do you actually think about that somebody else? Or, do you just mentally rob their existence with your thoughts and/or your actions?

If you don't care, you really should care. If you think you have the right to take for free, given to you by some divine purpose or because somebody did it before you, think again, for someday it may be you being robbed. If you claim intergalactic rights and/or poverty and feel you deserve the all of somebody else for free, you are just lying to yourself and creating negative karma that will one day find you.

Life is about giving. Karma Yoga *is* a divine pathway. Taking for free, however, is just the opposite. Care enough to give to the person you think about and the person who causes you to think.

Honoring People's Wishes
and What You Can Do About What You Can Do

For people who create things, they have a specific desire for their creations. For most they hope to get their creations seen, read, heard, or whatever by the worldwide masses. That's why most people create; they have a unique vision or take on a specific art form and thus they want to get what they create exposed to as many people as possible. Though this is the norm, for anyone who creates, they will also understand that there may come a time where you have a different and/or new take on what you have created. At this point, you may no longer wish it to be consumed by the world. You want it to be lost and forgotten. Yet, there are those out there who will not allow this to happen. They refuse to listen to the wishes of the creator(s).

For the creations that the non-creator(s) did not create, this whole mindset becomes a very selfish and/or self-motivated process. They may have liked something (or not) but for whatever reason they want that creation to remain active and alive. They refuse to let it be forgotten, even though that was what the creator wanted.

Case in point; my *Zen Filmmaking* Brother, Donald G. Jackson made a number of movies. As he came closer to his death, he had a change of heart about a few of them. Specifically, those that portrayed violence directed towards women from the male characters. Of which there are two specific examples: *Roller Blade* and *Roller Blade Warriors*.

Don, in his later years, became a very devout Christian. Now, this is not an unusual attitude embraced by a person who knows that their death is eminent. He had leukemia, he knew he was dying. This is a time when many/most people seek a spiritual bedrock. Don's was Christianity.

Ever since I knew Don, he did not like the sexual violence in those two films. He claimed that it was there due to the screenwriter. I don't know if that was true or not. What I do know is that he wished they would fade away as they projected an attitude that he did not ultimately agree with.

For better or for worse, Don assigned all Rights, Title, and Interest to all of his films to me before he passed away. He did this because he knew I would be the best person to keep his legacy alive and to protect his body of work. Though it was not right away after Don's passing but people began to contact me about reissuing some of his films, most notably *Roller Blade* and *Roller Blade Warriors.* Knowing his feelings, I always tried to explain to these people that those titles were not available. In some cases, people did not listen and attempted to release them anyway. Thus, all the legal nonsense began. From this, the only people who befit are the lawyers who make the money. As I explained to a person today, this forced my hand. I had no choice but to release these films so that the unauthorized versions would not flood the market.

I did not want to. I am completely against sexual violence in films. I have never made a film and never will make a film that uses that in its storyline. But, when people have dollar signs in their eyes, they do not care about the way anybody but themselves is feeling.

The thing is, the entire motivation of these people who wanted to release Don's films was money. They wanted to make money off of his creations for free. They didn't create them. They didn't pay for their creation. They just want to copy and sell them and, from a moral standpoint, that is just wrong! And, I am a moral guy.

Today, a man who is doing an event in the near future where a couple of the actresses from *Roller Blade Warriors* will be in attendance, contacted me and asked if he could do a small run of VHS copies of the movie for the signing experience. Wow! I was amazed that anyone would be honorable enough to ask me. And, I told him so. I, of course, said sure he could. I wish him, the actresses, and his event the all the best. But, here is the fact; Don hoped that movie would die. People are not letting it die. Thus, they are not respecting the wishes of its creator.

Do you ever think about this subject when you watch, read, view, listen, or talk about an artistic creation? Do you ever think about the wishes of the creator? If you don't, maybe you should.

The Effort That You Make

Recently, I was told about a podcast that a team did about my *Zen Film, Samurai Vampire Bikers from Hell*. First of all I want to say, *"Thanks,"* to those guys for taking notice of the film, taking the time to watch it, and going to the effort of creating a podcast about it. If you are interested, you can find the podcast by searching the film's title on Google. That's how I found it once I was made aware of it. But, that's not what this piece is about...

It always dumbfounds me why people take the time to do anything like that at all. Now, this is not a criticism, it is simply a question. I mean, the podcast appears to be one hour and forty-six minutes in length. The movie, *Samurai Vampire Bikers From Hell* is only like sixty minutes. Though a couple of the other versions are a bit longer. But, here are these guys talking for an hour and half about a movie that was made over twenty-five years ago. And, it was made for literally zero dollars. There was no budget! SV was absolutely a No Budget Film! And, what was *Zen Filmmaking* then is not *Zen Filmmaking* now. This is one of the biggest mistakes that people who take the time to talk about these films make. *Zen Filmmaking* has evolved!

Again, *"Thanks guys,"* but I really do not see what there is to analyze about it.

Now, I am not one of those people who can listen to podcasts and those kinds of things about films. My interests lie elsewhere. So, except for a quick scan through, I don't really know what they are saying about the film and or the filmmaker (me). Good or bad, that's fine. I get it; you need to have something to talk about when you are doing a podcast.

The issue I have, and the question I always pose in these situations is, why doesn't anybody talk to me? You want to know what went on in the film and why, I am the source! I am the filmmaker! Instead of guessing, speculating, and talking about the maybes; why don't you ask me?

Now, don't get me wrong, I don't want to be on your podcast. I don't want to be in your YouTube presentation. But, the fact is, every time I listen to even a little bit of these productions or when I read a review, a discussion in a book, or whatever, much of what people are saying is totally wrong. To you creators of these productions out there, doesn't that bother you? It would bother me.

Anyway… Again, thanks for the thoughts. But people, you want to know the facts, go to the source!

And, just for the record here… This seems like as good as place as any for me to say this… I believe there is some misnomer going on out there. At least there seems to be, as it is something that I have heard and/or have read when people discuss my movies and/or myself. For some reason, some people seem to think that I hold my movies on some sort of cinematic pedestal and I think that they are the greatest things ever. I have never said that, nor have I ever even thought that. All I have done, as a filmmaker, is to try to bring my cinematic vision to life defined by the circumstances and the budget that has surrounded each project. I have attempted to make cinematic art defined by the constraints of whatever reality has surrounded the individual project. And, as any filmmaker knows, each film possess its own unique blend of actualities.

Do I think my narrative films are all great? No. Most were made for zero dollars and because of that fact alone they could never have achieved what I truly hoped to create. In other cases, some of my films did realize what I hoped to capture to some small degree and in some abstract manner. But, the fact is, I believe most of them are not that great—particularly when seen by the outside viewing public who wants to compare and contrast everything to high-dollar productions. If you weren't there, you weren't there. You can never understand the fun and the excitement we possessed when they were created. At best, with any of my films, what I came away with was a small portion of what I hoped to truly accomplish. But, that is the reality of all art; cinematic or otherwise. You care enough to create art, whatever that art may be, and then you do it defined by what is available to you.

Sure, I'm glad when some people see the art in my films and find them enjoyable. That's all any filmmaker can ask for. But, if you don't like them, you don't like them. That's fine with me. I get it. *Zen Films* are not everyone's cup of tea. Overall, you should really stop trying to analyze and compare them to anything but what they are, as what they are is in a category all their own.

Again, go to the source and check your facts before you make your assumptions.

Cameras Everywhere

I had lunch in San Pedro yesterday. Afterwards, I took a walk down the street to this local record shop to see if there was any vinyl I wanted to pick up. Directly following me into the shop were three people: two women and a chubby middle-aged bald white guy with a beard. He had a camera around his neck and was carrying a cheap tripod.

Inside the shop, me I went to search the bins of vinyl. The trio started to set up the tripod. I though maybe they were going to take some photos of the young, blonde girl who was part of the team.

I continued to flip through the records as I heard the blonde girl taking all of the chitchat that I hate that takes place on movie sets, *"Oh, I auditioned for this…" "I auditioned for that…" "We were doing scenes from whatever in my acting class…" "My agent says…"* I tired to ignore it…

I didn't realize it at the time but I guess they were waiting for me to leave. In any case, I had a handful of records and I went up to pay. I made some small talk with the cashier and she asked me, "What are you filming this for?" I guess she thought I was with the other three because we entered the shop around the same time. Before I could give her an appropriately rude answer, the chubby guy chimed in, *"It's for a web series."* Awh, Jesus…

Anyway, what I would've said, initially anyway, was I would never shoot anything with that kind of camera… It was a few years old, bottom-of-the-line, Canon DSLR. They weren't even using a microphone. Probably because those cameras do not have a mic input.

Now, I have written articles about the technological fact that DSLR cameras are not really designed to shoot video in the past. Yes, they can but they do not do it as well as a dedicate video camera. And, their on-board sound is not very good. So, shooting without an external microphone is just not the right thing to do if you plan to capture dialogue. But, there the team was, waiting to shoot their, *"Web series."*

Now, I get it, this is the digital age, everybody wants to make movies. So, they were doing *Zen Filmmaking* at it's purest. They were out there doing-it with whatever they had—even if what they had was a cheap, old Canon DSLR. But, if you're going to shoot something on that level, I think it is far better to shoot it on your iPhone. The image would be just as good, if not better, as would the on-board sound. Plus, it is way more Punk Rock. *"I shot it on my iPhone!"*

Here we are in the midst of the digital age. By this point, a lot of people have made a lot of films using a lot of different methods. Good for them! Plus, here I am in Hollywood... The stories I could and have told and all the warnings I have given to young, pretty, blonde actresses. It was and is all the same.

So, some people are out there doing it by whatever method they have available. *Zen Filmmaking*, baby!!! Others just sit and dream and talk about what others have done and what they will do someday... But, doing is only really doing if what you are doing has an art, a purpose, and a philosophy. Other than that it is only chasing on the coattails of what has already been done.

Find your philosophy. Know why you are doing what you are doing.

How Little the Critics Know

Kinda interesting… I was listening to the radio today as I was driving and the DJ and a music critic began talking about one of my friend's recent album releases. The critic stated emphatically that the unique sting sounds on the record were obviously loop samples. This made me smile. Nope! What they were was music created by a lute and a harp that I had loaned my friend. Yet, there he was, the all-knowing critic, stating fiction as fact.

I forever find critics a curious breed. Sure, I get why they do it, they want to be seen as, *"The Knower."* But, so often they are wrong! I've even confronted a couple of them over the years; telling them of their mistake(s). Did they change anything? Nope… I guess some people just don't care how being wrong makes them look really stupid.

I've written a couple of semi-joking articles about critics. You can get to them from the *Zen Filmmaking* page on this site if you feel like it. Or, click on the titles: *Film Reviewers: Fact or Fiction* and *Film Reviewers: Getting it Right. Getting it Wrong.* And, like I always say, *"What is a film critic? With very few exceptions,* (i.e. Peter Bogdanovich), *someone who doesn't have the talent or the dedication to make a film."* But, it is really much more than all that. These people try to shape public opinion based upon their opinion and that is just not a good thing to do. Let people think for themselves!

Awhile back, I was shown where some jerk-off troll had been ripping on a bunch of my music and he said about one of my composition, *"No one wants to hear your recording of a Chinese wedding."* This made me smile. Nope! That was me playing a piece of traditional Chinese music on a Pipa and a Erhu. The whole point of that collection of music was to make it sound distant and ambient. He got it wrong! Does he care? Probably not. Do I care about what he thinks? Not at all.

I think most critics can't do what the creative do. They can't create. What's the next best thing? To get famous off of speaking about the creations of others.

Anyway, that's just my critique of critics. My advice, find out the facts and think for yourself!

Roller Blade Seven The Music Video

Over the past several months there have been a couple of people who have taken footage from *The Roller Blade Seven* and used it to make music videos. This is not the first time this has happened. Back in the '90s there were a couple of bands that did this. One was an electronica group from Sweden (I believe). Their music was very good. This was back before YouTube became the massive force it has become and the video was uploaded to a different platform. I forget the name of the band and I never downloaded the video. I guess I thought it was going to be up there forever. Obviously, I was wrong. If you know who that band was and/or have a copy of the video, let me know.

More recently, a couple of people have followed suit. I'm not going to name band names here, just to keep this simple, but the first time this happened (recently) I thought it was done by the band themselves so I contacted them via their website as I always liked their music. The leader of the band got all pissy with me asking if I was trying to promote my movie by using his music. As I told him, *Roller Blade Seven* needs no publicity. I even told him how he could do a Copyright Take Down on YouTube if he wanted to. But, at least so far, he has not. So, I don't actually know who combined their music with RB7 footage or why?

Overall, I have mixed feelings about this whole process. On one hand, it is kind of flattering, as the fact is we made RB7 over twenty-five years ago and there is still a lot of discussion surrounding it and a lot of footage being appropriated. On the other hand, it is all kind of weird because no one has ever contacted me asking me if it is okay to use footage from one of my films to make their music videos. And yes, I do own all rights, title, and interest to the film. So???

From a certain perspective, this is all fine, great, and interesting but it sets me to questioning, *"Why."* One of the main issues is that I have moved on so far as a filmmaker since we made RB7. Everything about my filmmaking style has evolved. Yet, people are still looking to the past. They are not coming to me and asking me to make the kind of music video, for a specific song, that I would do today; they are just grabbing footage and running away with it. And certainly, no one is paying me any money for the use of my footage, which is one of the whole points of Copyright Laws, nor is anyone even asking me if I like the music that they are using *Roller Blade Seven* footage for—which I believe should be one of the elemental criteria. So again, I have mixed feelings.

For example, the most recent band that I have found using RB7 footage for their music video, I am not really about. I don't really like their music. Initially, I thought to do a Copyright Take Down on it but then I realized that would be a bit disingenuous as I am sure some people like their music.

For anyone who has read *The Story of Roller Blade Seven,* they understand that the movie cost my life a lot. So, to not even ask me if it's okay to use the footage is a bit discourteous. If you love the movie, great! If you like the footage, great! But, you should at least have the reverence for the filmmaker to ask him (me) if it's okay to use the footage in association with your music video or any other visual project before you just grab it and run.

For the record, I don't work cheap. But, I can be hired. So, if you want to do it right, you should contact me and maybe we can make a *Scott Shaw Zen Film Music Video,* twenty-first century style, for your song. Yeah, yeah, I get it… You want to grab RB7 publicity (as shoddy as that is) and you want your footage for free and you don't want to have to work too hard to get your music video out there. But hey, if you like *Roller Blade Seven,* think about the filmmaker first!

This is all kind of like when you're in a room and someone is talking about you and you know they're talking about you and you want to say, *"Hey, you realize I'm standing right here."* But, you don't say anything and you just let them speak. ☺

Zen Filmmaking: Don't Miss the Bus

It is kind of interesting... People forever perceive the everything else of the everybody else based upon their own point of view. If they operate from a space of positivity, they see all things as positive. If they operate from a space of negativity, they see all things as negative. Most operate somewhere in between. That's just life. But, here we all are. We are all attempting to operate our way through our life in the best and most beneficial manner possible.

Some people create things. It may be paintings, drawings, photos, music, poetry, literature, films, programs, businesses, children or... Other people do not create. This is not bad or good; this is just life and the definition thereof.

As everybody comes at the everything else of the everybody else based upon their own point of view, some people who do not comprehend the process of creation want to base their life upon judging what another person creates. I mean how many times have you heard people criticizing the art created by someone else? How many times have you heard someone criticizing someone else—meaning that they are criticizing the parents of that person as those parents not only gave both to that individual but raised them into adulthood, as well. But, all this criticism is just mind junk. It is just someone attempting to find something to do with their mind and the time that they have here in life instead of actually getting out there and creating and understating the process of inspiration equaling creation.

Okay, to the point... *Zen Filmmaking* is based upon the most spiritually pure source of energy that there is; instantaneous creativity. No definition, no judgment, no negativity, simply pure, in-the-moment, cinematic realization placed upon film or video or digital memory cards or whatever come next... It is about grabbing a visual instance in the purity of the meditative moment and realizing it upon film. What it is that is captured doesn't matter. Whether it is perfectly framed or not, in or out of focus—if it captures a moment never seen again throughout human history or it is completely meaningless is unimportant; what it is, is just that—it is what it is.

Zen Filmmaking is about operating from a space of mental and spiritual purity. Yet, there are people out there who want to place their own definition upon *Zen Filmmaking*—based upon their own dominate emotion: be that positive or negative. But, by doing this, they completely miss the point. And, by missing they point, they miss the point! Thus, all they have done is to damn an elemental process geared towards generating enlightenment into the realms of interpersonal, self-defined, mind junk. Which means, they don't understand it at all.

Free yourself of definition and criticism leaves your vocabulary. What happens next? Satori.

Zen Filmmaking: The Final Definition

In the first exploration of *Zen Filmmaking:* 1992 until approximately 2005, the *Zen Films* were based upon character-driven dramas. Though always visually illuminating, by the mid-2000s, Scott Shaw began to redefine this Cinematic Art. Born, was the *Non-Narrative Zen Film.* These films initially held descriptions such as *A Zen Film Mind Ride, A Zen Film Meditation, A Zen Film Acid Flick,* and *A Zen Film Movie in the Moment.* In 2009, Scott Shaw created the last character-driven Zen Film. Thus, evolved was the final stage of *Zen Filmmaking* with all works being free of dialogue and focusing solely upon moving visual images and holding the titled, *"A Zen Film."*

Freedom of mind is the ultimate definition of *Zen Filmmaking.*

You Never Know What You Don't Know

I was recently contacted by a student at an Eastern University, (names shall remain nameless). He is a dual-major: journalism and film. *"Wow,"* as I told him... He had just read my new works on *The Guns of El Chupacabra Screenplay* and *The Roller Blade Seven* and he wanted to interview me for his school newspaper. I said, *"Sure."* After the piece is published, I'll put it up here on the site if it offers any new insight into *Zen Filmmaking* or just who the hell is Scott Shaw.

Anyway, we spoke of all things filmmaking and *Zen Filmmaking*. But, the point of this particular piece here is; a question he asked me about using, *"Name Talent,"* in the independent film. The thing is, I have heard this same question asked so many times and the understanding of it misconstrued in so many ways by so many people, that this offers me a good opportunity to answer it to all of you would-be and will-be filmmakers out there. And, to correct all of you people out there who have gotten my filmmaking ideologies totally wrong...

First of all... The, *"Name Talent Scenario,"* was really a technique employed in independent filmmaking in and of times gone past. Back in the 1980s and into the 1990s, filmmakers would put an actor with a known name into their film in order to hopefully help market the project and/or to generate additional sales. In some cases, this worked. In many cases, it did not. But, the truth about this technique is, and something most people who are not actually in the Hollywood game never understood, there is an actual list, created yearly, about which actors or actresses can be used in order to help generate sales. If an actor is not on that list, forget about it; they do nothing for the film and they will not help sales. In fact, they may actually hurt the sales of the film.

The names on this yearly list, (and that list still exists today), are really up there. They are not low-budget actors or actors who have done a lot of low-budget films. They are known names that commonly work in the A-Market. What occurs is that a production will bring one or two of these actors onboard for a high-fee for one or two days of work. They will then give them high billing and put their name prominently on the poster, even though the real stars of the film will be placed farther down the casting list. The problem with all this is, however, the moment an actor starts doing these lower-budget indie films their name value diminishes very quickly. Thus, if they are not soon cast into another major motion picture or TV series, their name value rapidly decreases and they are removed from the list.

As indie films came into their own in the early part of the twenty-first century, (and I'm talking about the high dollar indie films), the use of, "Name Talent," came to be a detriment to the overall organic, independent standing of a film. Thus, this practice became looked down upon among the people who seek out the true avant-garde and revolutionary cinematic vision.

One of the questions the author of this interview asked me was about the, *"Name Talent,"* that commonly appeared in Donald G. Jackson and my films and did they help sales? The answer is, *"No."* These people were our friends. And, it was much more common for them to be calling us and/or me, asking for a role, than us calling them.

They needed money too. Sure, I was always happy to work with them as they were (and in some cases still are) very talented people. Plus, I like working with people I know. That way I know what to expect. But again, they were our friends. That is why Don and/or I used them.

The fact is, and this is something to really take into consideration for all of you new-filmmakers; if you put an actor known to commonly do low-budget into your film, their name will, in fact, keep you from selling that film to the mainstream market. Sad, but true. So, in answer to the question and for all of you people out there who have wondered, most of the so-called, *"Name Talent,"* we used, hurt our sales more than they helped them. This is the reason why on all of the films I did without Don during the 1990s and since the passing of DGJ, I commonly only use new talent and people I have worked with on previous films. As, *"Name Talent,"* is a dangerous game to play in the arena of filmmaking.

In closing, normally I turn all of these internet ramblings into some kind of philosophic discourse. Today, I will not. I will just leave you with, *"You never know what you don't know,"*

But hey, now you know. How Zen is that?

The 70s Were Great but They Ain't Ever Comin' Back AKA You Make What You Can With What You Have

I was kicking around in the late night, last night, flipping channels, and I noticed that the film, *Jackie Brown* was just beginning. I hadn't watched the entire film in a number of years so I sat back with a couple bottles of the grape and settled into the cinema. Good movie.

As is the case with many a Tarantino film, the 70s are heavily referenced. The 70s were a great era for film and music. This was especially the case for independent cinema. There was some really revolutionary stuff accomplished. Tarantino, who is just a years or so younger than me, grew up in that same era and he often makes reference to the 70s in his films. Me too... Of course, due to budgetary constraints, certainly not on the level of his films. *Jackie Brown* is an ideal example.

And, that's the thing; you do what you do with what you have...

Certainly, I have my share of fans of *Zen Cinema*. I also have my detractors, who always seem to be way more vocal. But, like I often say, *"Let's see you do what I have done. Make a film with the scope of my Zen Films for a budget of $300.00 (or less)."* Because that was/is my formalized budget. Sure, it can be done. I did it. But, do you have what it takes to get it done?

As the years went on my focus in cinema changed. For those of you who know me or know about me, about ten years ago I stopped doing narrative films and shifted my focus to pure cinema. Cinema for the sake of cinema. No dialogue;

characters but characters in their natural state. With visuals as the driving force.

Though many/most of the people who discuss my films speak of those I did before this point in my cinematic evolution, it is essential to note that they did not even start talking until I stopped making—making narrative films. So, what does what they have to say, say about anything?

This being said, it is essential to note that there was not a big, fast, and/or immediate break in my filmmaking style. I was doing non-narrative films long before that point in my cinematic evolution. It was simply that they were not as widely viewed as my other cinematic works.

All this being said, I am often asked what would cause me to do another traditional film? …Well, at least traditional in my sense of the word… ☺

I thought about this last night as I was watching *Jackie Brown.* One of the things would be to be able to make that 70s style film with actors from that era like Tarantino accomplished. But, the sad fact is, they are all so old now, if they are even still alive. So many of them are gone. Though the cinema of that era will live on forever. The people who created the cinematic art of that era are rapidly waning. Thus, the talent pool is forever diminishing and will soon be eternally lost.

I guess this is like life. There are those who do what they do, done in an era. There are those who rise up in that era and are forever defined by that era but then life is gone. We all get old. We all die. There are forever those who will discuss what others have done. But, they are not the doers. They are not the knowers. They are not the livers. They are not the creators. They are simply the talkers.

But, once it is gone, it is gone. The life, the people, the era. So, all we can do is what we can do. All we can do is make what we make defined by what we have available to us in whatever era we live.

I Make Weird Movies! What?

I always find it interesting how in the Independent Film Industry people find easy targets for their criticism. This is especially the case in the No and the Low Budget Arena. This lack of understanding and appreciation goes hand-in-hand with something I have talking about literally forever whenever I speak with new filmmakers in my classes, seminars, or face-to-face. ...You cannot become lost in attempting to imitate a film with a large budget when you have no budget. ...You cannot expect your film to come out looking like a film with a million dollar budget when you have five dollars.

For the actual filmmaker, this concept is much more easily comprehended. For the viewer and the critic, not so much.

Most film viewers go into any film watching experience with preconceived expectation based upon what they have viewed in the past. Most of what they have viewed in the past is based upon a film with a substantial budget. Even most Independent Features are bankrolled with a fairly sizeable budget. But, then there is the whole other area of the film industry, the area of the industry where people are making movies for the love of cinema. Though they may have no money at all, they make their movies anyway.

Now, at this level of the industry some people do attempt to mimic what they have seen in the High Budget Arena. Most fall very short of this. Of course, there have been a few films made with no or a very small budget that have broken though. The most obvious examples of this are perhaps the original *Blair Witch Project* and *El Mariachi*. But, it is essential to note, that the versions of these films that went to wide-release were not the original versions of these films. They had major dollars poured into them for reshoots, editing, and sound tracking before they found their way into the mainstream.

All this being said, the viewing of any cinematic project is about the viewing of that particular project itself and it should not be about comparisons. Yes, this is a philosophic concept that most people will never understand or put to practice. But, just because it is not understood does mean that it is not true.

From a personal standpoint, I've watched over the years as people have compared my features to other pieces of cinema. They have gaged my work in comparison to the works of other filmmakers. They have tried to make sense of my work by placing labels on it. But, by doing this, in and of itself, they have missed the point. They have tried to place definitions and judgments on my work when they have not possessed the mindset to even understand it.

This does not bother me particularly. That's just the name of the game in art. People gage things through their own level of realization. They want to find a reason to love or hate a project.

Also, this does not cause me to change. I mean, any artist who adapts their work simply because people criticize it is not an artist.

This being said, artists do evolve. I certainly have. My film work certainly has.

For example, I used to make abstract cinema attached to a verbally driven storyline. But, as I have long said, the stories have all been told. I don't care about the stories. Leave that to the filmmakers with big bankrolls behind them. Though there may have been a subject matter in my films of the past, the story-driven dialogue was never the focus. And, this is where many critics got what I was doing all wrong. The words were just there as an abstract koan to take the viewer into the mind of Zen. The words never meant anything. They were nonrepresentational. They were just people taking about the nonsense that people normally speak of in life. I mean really, how much of what anyone says really matters?

But then, I left all that talking behind. I moved forward to focusing solely upon images.

The fact is, I have not made a dialogue-driven film since 2009. That's almost ten years ago. Yet, most the people who talk about my Zen Films are not even aware enough to be aware of that fact. What does that say about them? Yes, I've made tons of movies since then, but they are all unspoken. They are simply nonfigurative images moving across the screen. The reason? Again, to guide the viewer into the meditative mindset of Zen.

So, next time you see a film, especially an experimental film, try to move beyond what you already know—what you already think you know. Leave behind your judgment and maybe you can understand what the filmmaker was actually attempting to portray. Maybe you can encounter Zen.

Cinematic Enlightenment

When I discuss filmmaking, and particularly *Zen Filmmaking,* I often reference the term, *Cinematic Enlightenment.* From this, I often receive the question, *"What is Cinematic Enlightenment?"* I believe for the true filmmaker they already know the answer to that question. But, for the novice or the non-filmmaker, they wonder what I am speaking about. To explain…

As a filmmaker, you are constantly attempting to capture that perfect image. The ideal representation of what you are seeing with your eyes. You want to bring what you are physically viewing, via the pathway of your mind, and capture it in a filming format that then perfectly presents that image to the viewer. This is a process of body, mind, and camera continuum. Much of the time these elements do not come to together to find a perfect harmony. Yes, as a filmmaker, you may adequately capture the image. But, it is only in those moments of interwoven camera, body, and mind perfection that the image is captured perfectly.

For many, in fact most, they do not understand that filmmaking is based in philosophy. They see it simply as a means of entertainment. Thus, a movie is just something that they like or they do not like. Some may even understand that filmmaking is an art form. Most, however, do not comprehend that true; actualized filmmaking is based in the unique philosophy of the individual filmmaker. As each true filmmaker possesses (or at least should possess) their own unique philosophy, this means that they interpret the filmmaking process by their own set of standards and guidelines. Thus, they seek a particular outcome for each scene that they hope to capture with a camera.

Just as in Zen Buddhism we learn that *Satori* (instantaneous enlightenment) happens in the mind of the individual in a moment of perfect realization, this is the same with *Cinematic Enlightenment*. It is the perfect combination of combining what the eyes see, with what the mind visualized the scene to be, and then perfectly capturing that scene and ultimately projecting it onto the screen. Thus, *Cinematic Enlightenment* is the filmmaker finding instantaneous perfection, realized in their own mind, via the medium of eye, camera, and mind coordination.

To conclude, just as it is understood in Zen Buddhism, there is no absolute pathway to achieving *Nirvana* and there is no one Enlightenment. Enlightenment is realized by the individual in their own unique manner. Thus, there is no school for *Cinematic Enlightenment* and there are no techniques one has to practice to realize it. It is a natural process that the true filmmaker is allowed to recognize when they let go of their physical aspirations, they remove desire from the filmmaking equation, and they allow their body, mind, eyes, and the camera to form a cohesive unit that establishes a perfect reality that is allowed to harness an image, if only for a moment, and then project that image onto a screen. From this, perfect realization of the outside world blended in coordination with the internal world of the mind's eye is realized and Cinematic Enlightenment is experienced.

Buy a Camera and Make Your Own Movie

Recently, a guy contacted me and wanted to fly me into his city to make a Zen Film. He explained that he really needed my sensibilities in a movie he hoped to create. Initially, I thought that might be fun. Working with an entirely new and unknown group of people who were into *Zen Filmmaking*. But, then I started to see the flaws in this guy's hopes and ideology. Though *Zen Filmmaking* is entirely about freedom—about simply getting out there and doing it, I was being asked to come to a city I had never been to and basically do everything. I mean everything. I decided to pass on the offer and I suggested to the guy, *"Why don't you buy a camera and make your own movie."*

In today's world, you can literarily make a movie with your phone. I have. Or, you can use any number of relatively inexpensive cameras that are on the market. The fact is, it is very doable if you have the focus and the dedication. But, I believe that is the issue, the focus and the dedication. There are a lot of people who want to DO but very few people who will DO.

Sure, I have my advice for budding filmmaking. ...Like don't try to mimic what has already been done. Make your own movie, using your own cinematic philosophy, and so on. But, it can be done. And, it can be done relatively cheaply. Not like in times gone past.

This all kind of struck me as interesting when I gave that guy the advice, *"Why don't you buy a camera and make your own movie."* That was something I had said to someone else, way back in the way back when, under entirely different circumstances.

The story, I was making a movie and this guy/my friend (I surmised) was helping me out. He was an actor. I had met him working on the set of someone else's film. And, like so many others, he wanted to break into the Hollywood game. Me, being me, I was charting my own course to achieve that goal. In any case, we were filming one day and I was realizing that we were running late and we were having some technical issues and we should not film this girl he was crushing on very hard that day. He completely freaked out and started yelling and screaming. This obviously really messed with my small cast and crew. It wasn't that I was not going to use the girl. It was just that I realized her scenes would be better filmed at a better location I had in mind and on a different day. In any case, we finished the day. Once home, I left him the message, *"Why don't you buy a camera and make your own movie."*

Though he apologized, we finished the movie, and remained in contact over the next several years; I knew I could never trust him again. That style of reactive behavior is just not healthy for the emulation of art: cinematic or otherwise.

Certainly, on sets, I have seen this style of behavior before and after that occurrence. But, it is just not good. It poisons the fruit. I mean, in worse case, if you are not liking what is going on, leave. I know I have done that. I have done that even in the case of one big A-film I was cast in and on a TV series. ...That one was an interesting one... I was cast to do a role in the last (short-lived) sitcom that the great actor James Garner was doing. In any case, we were on the set, we had done the rehearsals, and then Garner shows up. We started to do rehearsals with him and what an asshole! I mean this guy was a total jerk! That was sad because I had always really liked him as an actor. We shot the scene as Garner continued to go off at me and everyone else. They called lunch. I left and never came back. The production company claimed I ruin the story by leaving.

My agent got really pissed and dumped me. But me, good or bad, I stood my ground. I didn't throw a fit. I just left. ...And, you wonder what happened to my career in the A-Market. There's your answer. ☺

Anyway... That's just kind of a side note to the story and the point of all this. If you want to make a movie, why don't you buy a camera and make your own movie. Use your phone. Use whatever it is you have. Get out there and film something everyday. It doesn't have to have story structure. Lord knows, my films don't. All it has to have is you doing something. Film it, take it off of your phone or your camera, edit it if you want, and make something! Make art!

This is the same with any art you desire to create. Do it! Draw, paint, write.

Art is based in one person doing one thing. Again, do it! Because if you don't, all your life will be left with is all of those artistic projects you envisioned in your mind but never created.

What Would You Do To Be In a Movie?

I believe it goes without saying that pretty much everyone has, at one time or another, dreamed of being a movie star. Growing up in Hollywood, I saw all kinds of nonsense, related to that issue, throughout my youth. When I got into filmmaking in my thirties, I witnessed it from an entirely different level. There/then, I saw what people were willing to do to get a role and/or the things the people who claimed to filmmakers would do to get people to do the things they wanted them to do. It wasn't/and isn't a pretty picture. That's why when I developed *Zen Filmmaking* it was all about the essential element of providing a positive/conscious give-and-take relationship between the actors and myself.

When people have come to Hollywood chasing the Hollywood dream, very few of them have made much progress except for paying a lot of money for classes and headshots. Maybe they even went on a few auditions that equaled no role. Some have jumped on the extra bandwagon—being as they are now politically correctly called, *"A background performer."* But, that leads to nothing—nothing at least in terms of the pursuit of stardom. In fact, it is detrimental to that process. But, at least as an extra they may see themselves on the silver screen. It may be the first gig or it may take a hundred times on the set, but maybe they will be seen. That's something, I guess?

But, for most who pursue the dream of acting, they want to actually be noticed for who and what they are. They want to actually act. They want to be a star. But, how does someone get there?

I was watching the film, *The Tattooed Stranger,* the other night. It's a fairly obscure, sort-of Film Noir from 1950. In that film, Jack Lord (of Hawaii 5-0 fame) had a small speaking role but he was uncredited. That has happened to me in the A-Market, as well. It's kind of crushing. But, it is not uncommon. I believe that my career may have taken a different turn if that had not happened in a couple of instances in the early stages of my immersion into acting. As no one knew who was playing the role, no one could seek me out. But, that's life in the industry. That's the life of being an actor. You have no control. But, just like Jack Lord was in, *The Tattooed Stranger,* I was in those films. Screen credit or not, you can't deny that fact.

The thing is, and this is what I have always warned people about when they come to Hollywood with hopes of stardom; you have to expect the unexpected. This is especially the case on the indie film level. You've got to be careful. As I have said so many times to so many people, there are a lot of people who claim to be filmmakers out there. There are a lot of people who want to be filmmakers out there. But, having the dream of making a film and actually being able to complete a project is very different. Many films never get finished. So, all that time, hope, and energy equals nothing.

The thing about acting and about filmmaking is, it should be seen as an art form. Art as the filmmaker sees it and art as the actor interprets it. That's why I allow my actors to improv. With this, they are adding to the process of creating a piece of cinematic art.

Another important point to keep in mind is that, especially on the indie level, few films make money. At least not the level of money that most people imagine. It is like myself being an author; everybody believes that the minute you get a book published by a major publishing company you are a millionaire. That is anything but true.

I know some people have criticized filmmakers, including myself, for not always paying their cast in dollars and cents. Though this has only sometimes been the case with my films, the fact is, do the people who launch these criticisms realize how much it costs to actually make a movie? Do they realize that the return is generally very small, if anything at all? I don't believe that they do. Because if they had ever actually made a film then they would possess a completely different perspective of actualized understanding.

Moreover, as the title of this piece questions, *"What would you do to be in a movie?"*

Admittedly, some indie filmmakers expect their cast to be locked in for days, weeks, or even months. That's why I always shoot the dialogue-driven part of my narrative films for a maximum of two days. I do not take much of an actor's time to make them a star. Plus, as I complete all of the films I begin, that actor does get an actual role in an actual film. They do get their names in the screen credits. They do get their name on the Internet Movie Database in association with the film; which is invaluable. They do get a copy of the movie to use as a demo reel—which as any newbie actor knows is essential. ...Many pay thousands of dollars to have faux-demo reels produced. (Me too... I foolishly did that via the insistence of a manager way back in the way back when).

So... The point being... They are getting paid. Just not with money.

As an actor, I sometimes worked in the indie market for free when I was getting started. I learned a lot. So, that was the price I was willing to pay to be in a movie. What is the price you are wiling to pay?

Though I am speaking about movies here, because that's one of the things that I do; make movies, this same concept can go to whatever it is you are pursuing in life. What are you willing to do to get what you want?

You really need to define that in your mind as each person has a different set of standards just as each person has a different set of morals.

Know what you want. Know what you are willing to do to get. But mostly, know what you are going to do if you don't get it, because that is the fact of life for virtually all of us.

Film Distribution:
Understanding the Rights and the Rules

As a filmmaking who has created a large number of feature films and has written about the subject of filmmaking quite frequently, I am often either asked about film distribution or confronted with the fact that someone is illegally distributing one of my films via the internet. To the average film watching individual, they may never even question where, why, or how they are receiving the film they are watching. In fact, in many cases, they do not even care. But, to the filmmaker, this subject matters as illegal distribution truly robs the income of a film's creator.

Again, as a filmmaker, having created a lot of films, I am also frequently contacting by people who want to distribute a film that I own the rights to. I appreciate those people who have the honor and the business prowess to realize that they must first legally obtain the rights to a film before they can sell it. Therefore, this piece is geared towards those individuals, as well, as they understand and appreciate that to legally distribute a film, without any worry of legal repercussions, they must obtain the assigned rights.

Internet Piracy is Not a Victimless Crime

To begin, it must be stated, in this age of the internet, all rules have gone out the window. This was first illustrated by Napster in association with the music industry. But, Napster was a company with a name and a location. Though the owner did encounter legal objections to what he was doing, he was a person and there was a place. Thus, it all played out in front of a judge. In many cases, however, the person who grabs another person's film to distribute is either a non-existence entity or a business located in some country where copyright laws are not enforced. Moreover, they are a person who does not care about the repercussions on the filmmaker. I would say, *"This is wrong and a person should not behave in that manner,"* but I am sure that statement would fall to deaf ears as a person who follows the path of illegal film distribution only cares about themselves and the money they are making.

This also is an important fact to keep in mind if you are one of those people who scours the internet to find a movie for free. The people who are offering those movies did not create that movie—they did not pay to have that film created, yet, they have stolen it from some source and are offering it to the world. Many sites claim they are free but they are never free. If they were not making money, they would not be in existence. Thus, that film thief is making money off of another person's creation and another individual's financial outlay. This, in and of itself, should make you think about where you get your movies. But again, I imagine, to the uncaring individual, all they care about is watching a film they want to watch. But, you should be more than that and think before you watch.

Okay, with all of the foreboding forewarnings out of the way, let's get down to the business of film distribution…

Creation of Content

A person comes up with an idea for a movie. They create the movie. Who owns the rights to that movie?

This question is both simple and complicated. For if a person comes up with a movie idea and then creates that movie with their own money, they own all the rights. But, if a person seeks money from an investor, depending on the contract, there can be more than one person who owns the rights to that film. This is why contracts are essentially important during the creation of any film as it defines who owns what—whether this is by percentage or partial or whole ownership. I have seen many a filmmaker begin a film, run out of money from one investor, and then turn to another financier. From this, ownership becomes very convoluted if everyone involved was not present and in agreement every step of the way. This has caused many a completed movie to be lost from distribution as the legal implications of ownership are so convoluted.

Therefore, to a film's creator, be very conscious of whom you bring into your production and be very precise of any contractual agreements you enter into as it can truly affect your ability to distribute your film.

Film Distribution

This brings us to the subject of formal film distribution. You have created a film; how do you get it out the viewing audience? First of all, it is important to look at the times gone past.

There used to be only one way to get your film out to the viewing public and that was via a film distributor. What a filmmaker would do was to get a copy of their completed movie out to the various distributors and then make a deal with the distributor that offered them the most upfront money.

In no uncertain terms, film distributors have always been notorious creatures. In times gone past, they would at least pay you for your film upfront. From this, at least some of the financial outlay would be repaid. But, that would generally be it. Though you very possibly would have a contract promising you a percentage of the film's sales, receiving a penny was virtually impossible. It fact, many times a distributor would give the filmmaker a, *"Charge back,"* claiming that the filmmaker owed them money for distributing their movie. As most filmmaker, (especially independent filmmakers), do not have the finances to employee savvy legal representation, the distributor would simply keep all the profits.

As first the video age and then the digital age came upon us, and everybody became a filmmaker, distributors ran away with this. As there was so many films being offered, they no longer had to pay the filmmaker anything upfront to represent a movie. I cannot tell you how many filmmakers (including myself) I know that have made a movie, witness it be released on VHS, DVD, and offered via established download and streaming services, and have never made a dime. Yes, they were promised money but they never saw anything. The distributor obviously kept all the money. For the most part, distributors are snakes. So, if you are a filmmaker and are lost in the dream of making millions from of your film, and you give it to a distributor, think again.

Online Distribution

Today, there are so many services where you can distribute your own movie and get it out there without employing a formal distributor—for the indie filmmaker that is absolutely the best way to go if you hope to make any money from your movie. Amazon Media On-Demand is currently one of the best options. You can monitor sales in real time and they pay you at the end of every month.

Ownership

Now, to the modern distributors… I have encountered both the unscrupulous and the honorable distributor who have crossed my path. I have watched as some people have attempted to just take a movie that they liked as a teenager and believed it was out of print so they digitized it and released it. From this, they got sued big time.

It is essential to note that just because a movie does not have current distribution does not mean that the title is not owned by somebody. If it is owned by somebody, they own all the rights to that title. Maybe, they simply no longer want it to be in formal distribution. Maybe there are other factors attached. But, these are all factors that a distributor who just grabs an old VHS and runs it through their computer cannot know or understand. All I can say is don't do it! I have witnessed more than a few people, even one very successful filmmaker/distributor, be driven to financial ruin by this practice.

If you do not formally own the rights, you have no right to release a film. Just because you like it or believe you want to get that film out to the public who has never seen it, or just because you believe you can make some money off of it, you <u>do not</u> own the rights. Thus, you have no right to release it.

Copyright Infringement

A side note here for the new breed of internet film reviewer who takes small or large amounts of footage from a film and then discusses it in an on-line presentation. Though some of your productions may be fun to watch, you <u>do not</u> own any rights to that film or to that footage. Thus, it is illegal for you, under U.S. Copyright law, to use that footage in your review. If the owner of that footage chooses to do so, they can take legal action against you, and you will lose. Do not believe the lie that many non-legal experts speak about when they invoke the term, *"Fair Use."* The moment you make one penny from using the footage from someone else's film, Fair Use, goes out the window and you are infringing on copyright. Even if you are not making money but you are using the footage from someone else's film they can still take legal action against you and sue you for damages. In other words, using footage from someone else's film without consent, for any reason, is not only illegal but dishonorable and you should not do it.

Honest Distribution

This brings us to the scrupulous distributor who has the same motivations for getting a film out to the public and actually contacts the filmmaker. I salute you. You are doing the right thing.

There are some filmmakers who do not have the technological or the business savvy to get their film out there. This, particularly, may be the case if they are from a previous generation and are not up on what is going on technologically. To those individuals, a distributor may be able to get their film out to the public.

To the honest distributor, they must be very careful in whom they approach to gain the release rights to a film, however. If a film is no longer in distribution, there is generally a reason for this. This is especially the case if a film was fairly successful, once upon a time. The thing is, if the rights were signed away to a production or a distribution company in the past, then the rights or ownership to that particular film have become convoluted. From a personal perspective, in years gone past, I have had people steal the masters for a couple of my films and sell the rights. They did this with no release from me but they did it anyway. Then, they disappeared with the money. Which caused me to have to take legal action. But, legal action is something nobody wants to do. It is expensive and it is time consuming. It is just not worth it. So, to the honest distributor, be sure you are contacting the person who actually owns the whole and complete rights to a film before you take on the distribution of that film because it could lead to legal consequences.

Payment

When it comes to money, it always gets complicated. Have you ever noticed that when you play the game Monopoly with some friends, the person who is the banker always wins? Why? Because they are cheating. They have access to the money, you do not. This is very much the case with distributors. To the honest ones, sure you may plan to pay out money to the person from whom you got the rights to a film. But, then comes your rent, your expenses, and the things you desire… Then what? You may plan to be honest but in most cases honesty and the film business do not go hand-in-hand. So, all I can say to everyone, on all sides of the distribution issues, is be careful as any deal you make will probably not turn out the way you hoped that deal would be actualized.

In closing, filmmaking should be solely about art. The fact is, it is not. Filmmaking, is based, (as is so often stated), in the, *"Film Business."* Filmmaking is a business. From the low/no budget filmmaker to the ultra high-end production, people are in it to make money. And, for the artistic and the honest, they are commonly the ones who come out on the low end of the equation.

The Roller Blade Seven: The Story of the Production

Fade In:

To begin, there is a chapter in my book, *Zen Filmmaking* on the creation of *The Roller Blade Seven* that I believe provides a lot of insight into what went on behind the scenes and has a bit of a different focus than this discourse. I wrote that when Don was still alive and he really liked it. It was up on scottshaw.com for a while—way back in the way back when. I recommend you read it if you really want some additional insight into the making of this film.

To be truthful, I have long thought to go back into my production notes and write a detailed book about *The Roller Blade Seven* as it was such a long, mind-bending experience. In fact, it was complete fucking chaos! And, I may still do that at some point in time. ...In the meantime, for all of those of you who have wondered, I will tell you what I can tell you... I imagine that even this piece will end up being fairly lengthy. If you can get through it, I believe you will have a deeper understanding of what this film and this film's filmmaking process was all about and you will probably see why it would take an entire book to actual detail all of the finite goings-on.

There are a few prerequisites to the telling of this story that you readers should know about at the outset. As all movies are, this film was created based upon a conglomeration of personalities. Some of these personalities were good; some were not. So, I am going to tell this story as truthfully as possible. But, there are a lot of secrets. For those of you out there who are worried about what I might say; don't be. Though I am going to tell a truthful story here, your secrets are safe with me. Mostly, this piece is a study in psychology more than simply a fact-based dissertation on filmmaking.

To begin, there needs to be a little bit of a backstory about me.

...I truly do not know what caused me to decide to enter the film industry, as an actor, when I was in my early thirties. Having grown up in Hollywood, I had truthfully seen the downside of it all. Throughout the 80s, I had run a martial art studio, went to grad school, played music, painted, wrote poetry and novels, traveled the world, spend many a late night at underground Hollywood nightclubs, and was in relationships with a lot of various psycho bitches of one flavor or another. As the 80s were coming to a close, I had met a nice young lady, who I am still with to this day, and my life's focus began to change. Again, I cannot give you an absolute reason why.

By the early 1990s, I had thrown my hat into the acting ring. Though my early onscreen appearances were mostly small, they were in the A-Market, I had my SAG Card, and was frequently being hired as a Featured Day Player in Under-Five roles. Thus, I would be given my own trailer, treated very well, and was paid at that time a base-rate of $455.00 for eight. I was what may be called, *"A working actor."* Things were moving along in my career... I had been active for less than a year and I was doing pretty well. Out of nowhere one day, I was called on my voice mail, (we all carried pagers back then), by Donald G. Jackson. He had received my headshot and he was about to do a movie.

I have told this story before but we never figured out who sent him that headshot. It was a color 8X10 of me holding two swords. Color headshots, being very expensive back then, were usually not sent out. I had a manager and an agent but they both said that they had not sent it to him. So, I guess our meeting was some weird destiny thing that may never be explained.

In any case, I called him back and he inquired if I could actually use the samurai swords. I, of course, could. So, he asked me to meet him at Gower Gulch in Hollywood the next day. As I was an inexperienced actor, making many of the mistakes that an inexperienced actor does, I agreed to meet him.

The next day, I arrive at Gower Gulch; which is basically just a strip mall on Sunset Blvd. and Gower. I was on time, as I always am. I began to stand there and wait. Sometime later, an African-American man with a jheri curl mullet began standing around, as well. I eventually inquired if he was there to meet Donald G. Jackson. He was. He was a strange little guy who I was told was into Wing Chun.

Normally, I only wait for a person for fifteen minutes. If they are not there by then, I'm gone. But, as I was an aspiring actor and all, I waited... Forty-five minutes late, here comes Don: a balding, portly, middle-aged man, dressed in camouflaged clothing. Every bone in my body told me to walk away. But, I did not.

Don had arrived with two young ladies in tow in a car driven by another man; who I will get to in a moment. He came up to me and the other guy that he knew. His first question to me was, *"Where's your car?"* When I pointed out my 1964

Porsche 356 SC his eyes popped out of his head. Don loved vintage cars. Instead of going with the man he came with, he asked me to drive, stuffed the two girls into my very small backseat, climbed in the front, and we were off. We headed to various Hollywood film equipment locations for him to check out some stuff he needed for the upcoming production.

Weird! I could not believe I was doing that...

A bit later that afternoon, we arrived at the aforementioned guy's apartment. He was a recent film school grad and had hooked up with Don somehow??? He had written a script for Don called Roller Blade 3 and he was Associate Producing it with Don directing. The premise of the script was moving forward from Don's *Roller Blade* and *Roller Blade Warrior* films. We went into the rear small patio area of his apartment where I was asked to demonstrate samurai sword usage. The man with the jheri curl was to be my judge and jury. This both amused me and pissed me off. Again, I thought to leave...

The man impressed... I mean, why wouldn't he be? From there, within a few minutes, other members of the cast arrived and I was training them how to do combat sword techniques. I had been hired. I was to be the male lead of the film as well as the sword choreographer.

I do not want to get too sidetracked into what went on with that film. I recently did a documentary about it called, *Roller Blade 3: The Movie That Never Was*. I recommend you check it out as it does provide deep insight into the life and mind of Donald G. Jackson. I will say that it too was complete cluster fuck. The film student seeing this, high-jacked the production, stole Don's investor, but the movie was never finished. I have written about it in a few essays.

After that, Don continued forward attempting to find financing for his next film. I continued following the path of an actor and did a few roles, which additionally laid the foundation for my evolving career. Don and I communicated over the next year, mostly via voice mail, and we met once or twice. Then, upon the completion of *Frogtown 2*, Don called me, invited me to his office, and said he really wanted to work with me and I should be in his next film, *Roller Blade Seven*. My course of destiny was set into motion.

Before I go any farther, I need to say that the moment Don got into my 356, as I was driving him to the hospitable for the final stage of his life in 2003, he said, *"I really want to apologize for what happen to you on Roller Blade Seven."* I will get to his reason for saying that near the end of this piece. But, keep that essential statement in mind as it is very revenant to my involvement in RB7. I will continue...

There was not a lot of money backing *Roller Blade Seven.* It was to be financed by Tanya York who had tapped into financing from an aging Hollywood insider. The first film she Executive Produced was *Divine Enforcer,* which she asked me to appear in, then *Frogtown 2,* (which I turned down), and now RB7. Don wanted me to be the lead, do the martial art choreography, write, and produce it with him. The only probably was, as we only had a $30,000.00 dollar budget and the film was to be shot on 16mm film, there was not enough money for me to be paid. He would be paid but I would not... (Though I was promised big money on the back-end.) Initially, that seemed okay, as it would be a good opportunity for me. Don was a known filmmaker. He was a friend of Jim Cameron, which I had confirmed when I had a small role in *Terminator 2*. His film, *Hell Come to Frogtown* was frequently on late night TV, and I thought it would be a good progression for my career. As we were only scheduled for a one-month preproduction and production window, I thought I could easily make it through that timeframe without getting paid.

Again, I need to go into a bit into the backstory here... When I signed up to do *Roller Blade Seven,* I had never seen any of Don's films. I was not into that style of movie. As a dude, I enjoyed the action-flicks of Seagal and VanDamme, which were big at the Box Office during that moment of time, and the movies that came out of Hong Kong. B-Movies, Cult Movies, and the kind of films Don made, I had no idea about... I was into Film Noir. My mistake, I should have researched what I was getting into.

Anyway... On the very first day we began preproduction, I arrive at what would become our production office and I was ready to go. Niceties were exchanged, we talked about a few things, began to set up casting sessions, discussed ideas for the film, and the like... Around lunchtime, Don doesn't say anything, gets up, and walks out the door of the office. Initially, I didn't think anything about it as I thought he might be going to the bathroom or something. Time ticks on... He doesn't come back. I sat there for over an hour, starring off into space, when Tanya comes by—as our office was in her suite of offices, she inquired as to where was Don. I told her I didn't know. I told her he got up and just left without saying a word. I could see the anger rising her eyes, *"You two are working together! Tell him to stop behaving like that!"* Tanya who had a long relationship with Don, knew of his shenanigans, and I guess was trying to warn me.

Here's the thing... And, something I did not know at the time, Don loved to test people. He would always fuck with people's mind, just to see the reaction he got out of them. But me, I'm not easily pushed, nor am I easily tested. Though my first thought was to say, *"Fuck this,"* and leave the production all together, instead, I walked across Hollywood Blvd. and went to *Bushido McDonalds,* as Don liked to call it, and got a Big Mac combo. Awhile later, Don reemerged in the office after I heard Tanya going off on him from another office. With her as the money, he did not treat me like that again.

The rest of preproduction went as preproduction does. We would meet at the office each day, do casting sessions, and the like. We would go scout locations, check out equipment, and we became closer as friends. But, underlying all of this was this innate tension that Don emanated throughout his career. He was constantly testing and pushing people. He really treated most people like shit. This really worked against my mindset as that is not the kind of person that I am. He would even subtly fuck with me on various levels, during those early days, by bringing in other people and offing them prominent positions in the production or in the cast and so on.

This was one of the major faults of Donald G. Jackson throughout the years that I knew him and something that got him into a lot of trouble with a lot of people. For example, if a person said that they were a screenwriter, Don would tell them to write a script and promise that he would produce it. If they were an actor, he promised them a starring role. As Hollywood is all about dreams and the promise thereof, he made a lot of enemies via this practice.

For me, within a few days of preproduction, I was ready to walk. It was just a mind fuck mess! There was so much unnecessary tension... There are so many stories I could tell and maybe someday I will... But, not today.

The problem with my mindset and who I am is that I am not a quitter. If I say I am going to do something, I am going to finish it. I believe that this (my mindset) was the entire reason that Don and I remained co-filmmakers for all of those years; I got things done, when he could not.

There are a few preproduction stories I can relate to you that may add to your overall spectrum of understanding.

As the movie was based upon Don's concept of, *Roller Blade*. ...It is essential to note that he came up with the title before the Rollerblade skates were even invented... Anyway, we were looking for a cast of people who could skate very well. (Obviously, I could not.) One afternoon, we were out in the back of the building that held our production offices, in the parking lot, testing the skating ability of a few potential cast members. Afterwards, we went back up into the office. Tanya called us into her office, which overlooked the parking lot. Very rudely, she tells us that we are not allowed to do that in the parking lot. I mean, she really went off...

A side not here, I am not dissing her when I say this as in her own book she states she was always a very bossy person. But me, I do not take well to authority. Be nice, and I'm all-good. Be rude and I react. I mean, I was already an accomplished person by that point in my life; okay. She was twenty-one years old. Treat me with the respect I am due!

Again, that is another one of those moments where I almost said, *"Fuck it,"* and walked out the door. I didn't need it! But, before the words could even finish coming out of her mouth, Don began to apologize. He went into a whole discourse about how when he worked at an auto factory in Michigan he had a manager and he did what the manager said and so on… The way Don reacted provided me with deep insight into his hidden personality.

Another thing that was going on was that I had developed a number of actor friends in the year or so I had been involved in the industry. As this was my first big-film producer position, I wanted to bring as many of them into the production as possible. I invited them to the office and we would have talks. Some of them decided not to do the film due to their union status. A SAG union actor cannot be in a non-union film. I could skirt that fact because I was a producer and the union cannot keep someone from producing their own movies. Others wanted to get paid but as we had a low budget; payment wasn't an option. I even contacted my agent and she sent a few people over; one of which we cast. Mostly, what occurred was that through this process, I lost a lot of friends due to Don's behavior. He just loved to fuck with people and he found a way to fuck with me by messing with the heads of my friends. But, one or two of my peeps did get on board.

Regarding the screen story and its development... It is true that *Zen Filmmaking* is all about not using a script. But, in the early stages of *Roller Blade Seven, Zen Filmmaking* was not yet in existence. Don told me that he had shot his then unreleased film, *UFO Secret Video* without a script and that *Roller Blade* was largely done without a script but Don truly relied upon a screenplay throughout his career. Plus, Tanya wanted to know what we would be doing. Thus, it was decided that I would be the one to write a script. So yes, *Roller Blade Seven* did initially have a script, though it was never used. I wrote it!

If you feel like it, you can read the treatment I wrote for *Roller Blade Seven* in my book, *The Screenplays*. You will see that what we planned to shoot and what we did shoot were very different.

Preproduction was scheduled to take about a week. By the time we finally got ready to go up, we were over a month into the process. All this time and I had not been paid. Again, I should have seen the writing on the wall and left.

One of the interesting things that occurred, a day or so before we were to go up, was that a young, beautiful actress came in to audition. Before we could get very far in our conversation, she reached her hand across my desk, took my hand, and said, *"I'll do anything to be in this film."* We all understand what that means... Me, being me, I was about to walk her into the closed off back section of our building, where we had production stages, and well... You know... Just at that moment, Claudia, the girl who played Kabuki, literally burst through the door, sees our hands intertwined, and blurts out, *"What the fuck is going on here!"*

Claudia was a very interesting person. From Germany; she was an outspoken stripper by trade, a smoker and a drinker. She loved the *Crazy 8's,* as we call them on the street; *Old English 800.* A nasty street beer almost universally only partaken of by African-Americans. But me, I was right there with her. I was the only one who would drink that swill with her. Whenever she came by the office, which she did quite a lot, she brought a forty once bottle or two and we would pass it back and forth.

What would have happened between that actress and I given the chance? I guess I will never know??? But, she is in the film. Guess who she is?

On the first day of production, in the early AM hours, I loaded up all my swords, my Rollerblades, and stuff into the back of my 356 and headed over to Mark's house in Downey. Mark was to be an actor in the film as well as our Art Director. Good guy! He had done a lot of work with Troma. Plus, he was a great rollerblader and had several friends who were also great rollerbladers that he brought onboard.

You have to understand, by the first day of the shoot, I had no idea what was going to happen next. Though I was the only other producer on the set, Don had created such an anxiety-ridden preproduction that I didn't know if I would quit, be the star of the production that I was promised to be, be replaced, or what was to take place next??? This, even though I had brought some of my friends on board—one in a principal role. But, me being who I am, (the non-quitter) I played along.

The fact is, this was one of the ways Don used to manipulate people—always keep them guessing. But, the truth was, (as I realized later), his mind was so chaotic that he too didn't know what was going to happen next and due to his very deep rooted insecurities, he was always afraid of being rejected, so he power-tripped to such a degree to keep anyone from having the ability to hurt him. But, that's life... Creative people are generally the most fucked up.

We had a lot of people there on the first day of production. Mark had a lot of costuming at his home. He handled getting the cast outfitted. Then, Don and I gave the final approval.

Mark lived within very close access to the L.A. Riverbed basin; which is where we planned to shoot. This is why we staged from his home.

Before I go any farther, if you care about the *Roller Blade Seven* and its behind-the-scenes, you really need to see the documentary I did titled, *Roller Blade Seven: The Unseen Scenes*. There's a lot of very revealing stuff in that doc that begins at this point in the production.

Just as we are about to begin shooting, it began to rain. Rain is a great, free, special effect. It is not, however, great for roller-skating. In the aforementioned doc, you can see my character being the first to take a fall on the slick path that we were skating along. For me, who had only been on rollerblades once or twice, it was a scary and dangerous experience. Even our RollerCam guy, a GREAT skater, took a dive with the Bolex in his hand on that day. You can see that in the doc, as well.

The first shots of the day were the *Roller Blade Seven* skating as a team. Next, were the villains. We finished the day up by doing some of the martial art confrontation. Here is where a lot was revealed to me about Donald G. Jackson...

Obviously, I was a well-trained martial artist. My agent had sent me a well-trained female Kempo stylist that we cast for the film. Plus, I brought on a few other people who knew their stuff. Don suggested I go and set up the fights. I figured I had some time so I was first working with the girl and her opponent. Maybe ten minutes into the session Don walks up, *"Okay, let's shoot."* But…

Here's the thing, Don didn't even care that the people weren't ready. All he cared about was getting something/anything on film. So, all of those one-on-one fights you see in the film were choreographed on the spot. I told them do this or do that, and that was that.

Now, here was Don, a guy who loved the martial arts and samurai films. Though he never trained, he was constantly referencing all things bushido. But, there he was, making a martial arts film but he did not care about the most elemental component of the film we planned to make, the fight scenes. Plus, he had no idea about how to shoot angles so that the fighting techniques looked like they actually connected. Mostly, I think it was once again his insecurity and his fear of someone, (i.e. me), taking his power away.

There was a high point to all this that came later in my filmmaking career, however. From this experience, I realized that on the indie level of making a film that employs the martial arts, it is better to just choreograph one technique at a time; film it, then move on to the next. That way, no elaborate choreography is needed to be learned by the cast members.

The Saturday and Sunday shoot ended.

The following week, we took the film to *Fotokem* to be developed. We then had it telecined.

Don hated what he saw. Being on the other side of the camera, I was a bit more forgiving; understanding that the actors had virtually no direction from Don, the director. Don was like that, he never really directed his actors. But, I too saw the flaws.

We were in the office, discussing the results of the pervious weeks endeavor. Don was fuming as he often did. Blaming others, as he almost always did. We decide that we needed to let go of all the structure and throw all of the plans that we had for the film out the window and just go out there and film. It was then and there that I came up with the title, *Zen Filmmaking*. *"Let's just be Zen. This is Zen. This is Zen Filmmaking."*

The next weekend, we reconvened at Mark's house. Again, we had a very large cast; though many of the people, especially the friends I had brought on board, had quit. As we weren't shooting any dialogue on that first weekend, they felt like they were just being used as an extra. And, Don refused to call all but three of the original *Roller Blade Seven* back; one was Kabuki, the other was this great rollerblader and friend of Marks who play several roles including the banjo player and Fukasai Ninja, and the other was one of my friends, a highly trained martial artist.

Once everyone was suited up, we went down into the river basin and Don called everyone around him. There and then, he blew up. He began screaming at everyone. Telling them what horrible actors they were, how they had cost him and I thousands of dollars, and that they were total pieces of shit. I was in disbelief. I had never seen a director treat people like that. He went on-and-on insisting that they were all ruining his and my movie. Wow!!!

He went up to one guy, who had been using nunchucks the first weekend, grabbed them away from him, threw them on the ground, and told him he was an fucking idiot and didn't know how to use them. Now, this guy was a trained martial artist and I expected him to react. I mean if someone had come at me like that the least I would have done is told him, *"Fuck you,"* and walked away. At the worst, I would have kicked his ass. But, this guy took it. Did nothing but stand there. I could not believe it. The whole scenario I could not believe!

Eventually, Don was finished and we began to film. We shot the first words of dialogue recorded in the film—my character laying on the ground saying, *"I can't believe she made me wear these skates."*

We filmed all day. We did the big skate oncoming, leading to the big fight scene. We also did a little trick that Don suggested—individually killing off all of the main characters so if we saw their face in the final cut, we could show their character dying and thereby keep the story sound.

As the day was coming to a close, there they came, the police officers. Someone had reported us. As we obviously didn't have a filming permit, this presented a problem, as what often occurred back then is that the police would confiscate your film. Don had actually been arrested once. But, that was because he was filming a naked girl handcuffed to a fence.

What we did was to give all of our exposed film to our RollerCam guy and have him skate off into the distance. Don, Sergio (our AC), and I got the cameras and walked off into the sunset. As the cast was just the cast, we left them there to deal with the repercussions of which there were none. What could they be held responsible for?

That was the last weekend of big production on *The Roller Blade Seven*. After that, all things were kept smaller and more controlled. Though we did have a fairly large number of cast and crewmembers on several of the shoot days, there was never the massive amount of cast and crew as on those first two weekends.

As we moved farther into the production, we needed dialogue for the cast to speak. Don loved my books: *Essence: The Zen of Everything* and *Time*, which was later published by one of the Bigs as *Zen O'clock: Time to Be*. There it was, our script. People like Joe and Karen took to it immediately. They could just choose their aphorism and that was that. We were set to go…

In the past, I've spoken a lot about cast members like Karen, Joe, Bill, and Frank and their involvement in RB7 in interviews, articles, and the like. For Joe, Chris Watson asked me to write the introduction for his book on Joe, *Wiping off the Sheen*. There, I pretty much spell out our meeting with Joe and his involvement in RB7. The one cast member I have not spoken that much about is Don Stroud. So, I will do it here…

I first met Don Stroud on the set of *Divine Enforcer*. I could not understand why an actor of his caliber would be doing a movie like that. I mean he had a GREAT career from the 1960s forward. In fact, ever since I saw his film, *Angel Unchained,* in my early teens, he was my idol. I forever watched his career evolve. So, to get him in RB7 and to get to work with him was a dream come true.

For those of you who have seen RB7 and Return of the RB7 you will know that Don plays the congas in those films. That was all his idea to bring his congas along. And, a great idea it was as that really added a lot to the films and gave us something to really build around. For those of you who have seen the 1978 movie, *The Buddy Holly Story,* you will know that Don did a great job of playing the drums and bongos in that film.

Though Don did play the congas live in the film I actually had to loop his playing when we were in post. Thus, that is me you are hearing not Don. I will explain the reason for this in a moment.

A funny note, Don is a great and humble person. When I first met him he was living in Brentwood but he later relocated to Manhattan Beach when I was living in nearby Redondo Beach. Every now and then I would bump into him and he would be all excited to see me and say, *"Hey Scott! It's Don... Don Stroud."* Like I didn't know. In fact, sometimes he would call me up and invite me over to his place or to go out to lunch with him or something. But, I just couldn't do it. I could not hang out with my idol. It was just too weird for me. Though every time I ran into him, I was very happy to see him.

That's the story, in brief, about my feelings about and interaction with Don Stroud... Great guy!

Anyway, with my two books as a basis for dialogue, the movies got made. There are a million stories I could tell you. But, that would take a book...

It is essential that before I get any farther, I detail a known fact about Don Jackson... At least, known to those of us who knew him. Don was a very dark individual. Though he referred to himself as, *"The Master of Light,"* and he could quote you biblical passages left and right, he truly embraced a negative energy. An energy that spread to all of those around him if you were not very careful. Basically, he was one of those spoiled children who never really grew up. He was probably allowed to throw temper tantrums as a child with no discipline as that is how he behaved as an adult. If he wasn't getting his own way, he went off. While we were doing RB7, I allowed his negativity to enter my life and I was doing things completely against my nature like barking orders at cast and crew and just not caring about people and life. Being involved with this movie truly took me to a really dark place. But, I ended up paying the price. Read on...

Anyway, we went into postproduction. But, not without a terrible toll having been taken on both Don and I. Due to all the chaos he invoked in our lives by the time we got to that stage we were both eating Xanax like baby aspirin—stressing massively. Me, who has had chronic anxiety problems from my adolescences forward, due to living through one of those childhoods that you never quite get over, was particularly susceptible. So, it was bad...

Plus, I went to the doctor somewhere around this time period. I had gone into the production weighting my standard weight of one hundred and fifty-five pounds. When I got on the scale and the doctor told me I was one and eighty-five pounds I could not believe it! ...The thing was, Don ate all the time. We were constantly eating burgers, candy, chips and junk. With no time to work out, as RB7 was pretty much twenty-four-seven, I had put on the pound. Plus, Don had a hiatal hernia that he never had treated. Thus, he barfed all the time when he was eating. It just all added to the fucking mess that was this production.

As detailed, in my earlier writing on this subject, we went into the editing of RB7 expecting to have one of Don's previous editors do the job. Each day we would show up and try to guide him but he just wasn't onboard for what we were trying to achieve. We wanted something really crazy, artsy, psychedelic, and abstract. But, he was trying to take it mainstream. He just didn't understand our vision. As stated in the past, he taught me how to use the editing equipment and I instantly took to it. Thus, we fired him, moved to a large editing suit, and I got down to business.

A side note here... Don made one of the cardinal mistakes of filmmaking while we were at the original editing facility. He arrived one morning. With him was all of our original audiotapes from the production where we had recorded our dialogue. We were recording our sound for the film on the then new DAT tape system. He went to the bathroom en route to the studio. There, he forgot the tapes. They were all in a paper bag. I was already guiding our editor when he arrived at the editing studio. He sat down for a time and then remembered he forgot the tapes. He went back to the bathroom to get them but they were gone. Someone had stolen them. He, of course, massively freaked out. We searched for them, asked people for them, put up notes, but nothing. They were gone. You have to admit, that is a pretty fucked up thing to do—to steal something that important from somebody. But, that was all just part and parcel to the RB7 experience.

The only thing that saved us was the fact that we had much of the dialogue recorded on our ¾ inch edit tapes. Without that, we would have been fucked beyond belief. The whole movie would have had to have been looped.

You can see, in the aforementioned doc, *Roller Blade Seven: The Unseen Scenes,* several of the scenes that did not make it into the final cut of the film due to the fact that we did not have the original audio recordings.

Big mistake on Don's part! In any case...

We moved to a new editing facility. It was a fun and interesting time at our editing suite. There were drugs, alcohol, and women in there all the time. It was a massive orgy. True hedonism.

Though we partied, I did do the edit.

One of the things that I realized doing the edit on RB7 was, though I have edited a lot of movies throughout the years, editing is not good for my brain. For after I would spend a whole day in the editing suite, looking at and cutting footage, I began to see life as an edit. It really messed with my psyche.

In terms of the footage used, we put all the best of the best into RB7 except for one very good fight scene. The rest of the footage we used for *Return of the RB7.*

Once we were done with the off-line edit, as it is called, we took it to an on-line editing facility. For those of you who may not know, making a movie on film is a complicated and expensive process. First, you have to buy the film, shoot it, develop it, telecine it, sync the dialogue, transfer it to time coded tape, do the edit, then take the footage to a facility where they can match the time code numbers to the original masters, and then create the final edit of the film. This final stage is called on-line editing. Though on-line has a very different meaning in today's mind.

We went to the on-line facility and did our final edit. By the time we had gotten there, we still had no soundtrack. I don't know what Don was thinking but he seemed like he had a plan. As was commonly the case, he did not. As we were closing in on the final construction of the movie, I was handed the task of creating the soundtrack as the budget had all been spent. I was given one weekend. That was it. I had two days to create an entire soundtrack for two feature films and Don wanted music to be laid over every element of the movies.

My girlfriend and I lived in a small flat right on the water in Redondo Beach. Though the location was beyond great, the place was fairly small. And, as it was an apartment, it was not like I could jam out with loud drums and guitars and stuff. And, this was long before the computer age of music when everything got easy. Thus, I came home on that Friday night bewildered; what would I do? The answer, I just did it. I sat down with what I had: guitars, a sitar, a sarod, tablas, a banjo, a drum machine, and synthesizers, and just got it done. I created and recorded the soundtrack on a Teac 4-Track Cassette Recorder that I had picked up in Tokyo. Monday morning, I arrived with the soundtrack and we laid it down.

One of the truly philosophic elements I learned while we watched the final playback of the final edit of RB7, in the on-line studio was, in filmmaking, sometimes you have to accept what you get. There is a scene in RB7 where Alison's characters skates up to Don Stroud, talks to him, and then skates away as Don laughs. When original laid down, we had Don's laugh loudly echoing as Alison skated away. It was really cool. In the final playback, the laugh was gone. The on-line editor had messed up. The on-line editor looks at us. Don looks at me. I look at him. To go back in and redo that track would not only mean a lot of time but a lot of money. Though I thought it was essential; Don just let it go. And, that is one of the sad facts of filmmaking—you may want something to be someway but sometimes you just have to let it go...

That was it. The films were done.

With the films done, it was time to shoot the poster...

As we progressed through the months, pretty much all of the original cast members had fallen away. As they weren't getting paid, they were all gone. I got it. Even by the end, Kabuki was gone and she took her leather jacket with her. Thus, we had to buy another one of the expensive jackets she wears in the film from a shop on Hollywood Blvd. so we could imitate her character in the final poster shoot—which was photographed at a high-end facility in Santa Monica.

One of the funny stories about that photo session is that if you look at the RB7 page on my site or in the Photo Book I create on *Roller Blade Seven, The Roller Blade Seven: A Photographic Exploration,* you will see that there is a poster shoot with Don (Jackson) in the shot. Tanya hated it. She made us go back and get shots were he and the guy who played Heavy Metal were not in the picture. Awh, the power of power...

By this point, we had been up on RB7 for months. I was dead broke. As I have detailed in the past, I had to sell my 1934 D'Angelico New Yorker and other vintage guitars I owned just to survive. In fact, I don't know that I have ever truly recovered from the financial loss I took on RB7 for after all of these years I still have not been able to replace that D'Angelico.

Though the movie was finally completed, the problem after all of this toil and turmoil was, I was about to have salt poured into my wounds. I found out that Don had been paying Alison, our female lead, throughout the entire production. (I wonder why?) Now, it is not that she didn't deserve it. But, there I was: the producer, the casting agent, the location scout, the still photographer, the choreographer, the screenwriter, the star, the soundman, the editor, the soundtracker, the…, getting paid zero.

The back-end money I was promised… I was paid zero. Plus, the movies were released without me signing a release for anything: not the words from my books, not the music I created, not my producing, not my acting; zero, nothing, nada… How illegal and immoral is that?

Then, Tanya stepped in… She didn't like the fact that my name was all over the films. Thus, after she had made in the mid six figures, (that is in the mid hundred thousand dollar range for all of you people in other countries), in other words—a lot of money by releasing the original versions of the films internationally at the 1992 American Film Market, she then had a re-do edit done for U.S. release where virtually all of my screen credits were wiped from the films. I got a lawyer involved. But, lawyers cost big money. Money, I didn't have back then. So, I was fucked. Fucked beyond belief. Thus, answering the question of why Don said on the way to his deathbed, *"I really want to apologize for what happen to you on Roller Blade Seven."*

Don and I fell away from each other after that for a time. I was obviously very pissed. Plus, he liked people he could control and I had already set about making my own films. But me, I was the one who got fucked. Not him. He continued to get financing from Tanya. ...In my life, my Porsche had blown its transmission while we were doing the on-line edit and that would cost big money to be fixed. I had none. And, that is just one elemental example of what was going on in my life. ...Don or Tanya, they were flush, thus they did not care. I was the source of not only their money but a film that has been in public discussion for decades and I was not paid a dime.

I guess the final blow came when I was on my way to pick up this girl on my Harley to go and see Soundgarden at the Roxy. I had just found out that Tanya had me thrown out of our production offices and ban me from entering the building. This, after she had made all of that money off of my creative vision. Me, I was driving and a car hit me from behind. The guy didn't have any insurance, so my fully customized Harley Davidson was toast—gone forever; totaled. I was taken in an ambulance to the emergency room at Cedars Sinai. They wanted to check me in but I wasn't down for that.
So, I checked myself out. This was obviously before the age of instant communication with everyone via the smartphones that exists today. Back then, if you didn't have the number memorized, you were out of luck. I called all the numbers I could remember to get picked up but nobody answered. I called my girlfriend but she was at work and didn't feel it was right for her to leave—she's that kind of person: work before love. So me, my life in ruins, my body broken, bruised, and bleeding, I sat there on the

steps of the emergency room of Cedars Sinai hospital for five hours waiting until I was finally picked up.

That's the story of *The Roller Blade Seven*.

FADE OUT.

THE ZEN

Max Hell Frog Warrior:
The Story of the Production

Fade In:

The *Zen Film, Toad Warrior,* which became *Max Hell Frog Warrior,* was the third film that Donald G. Jackson and I completed as a filmmaking team. The first two were *Roller Blade Seven* and Return of the *Roller Blade Seven.* As we have well passed the twenty-year mark of the inception of *Max Hell,* I though I would take a few minutes and detail a bit more intimate information about this film's ideology and its production facts as there is a lot of ongoing interest in this film and there remains a lot of questions and incorrect speculation about what actually took place during its creation.

The Roller Blade Seven

To begin with, Don and I had parted ways upon the completion of the *Roller Blade Seven* under less than ideal circumstances. The money had run out on the production budget before we were finished. Don being Don had squandered much of the budget and Don, as he tended to be, was very self-involved. Thus, any remaining money he kept for himself and to spend on his girlfriends. ...He kept the money even though I did much of the work on RB7: casting, producing, acting, editing, soundtracking, plus most of the words spoken in the film(s) either came from or were influenced by two books I had authored: *Essence: The Zen of Everything* and *Zen O'clock: Time to Be.* But me, I walked away totally broke. In fact, I had to sell my 1930s *D'Angelico New Yorker* just to survive. That was a terrible loss that I have never been able to replace. (For the record that was one of the Masterpieces created by John D'Angelico himself and not one of the replicas that are on the market today). Plus, my '64 Porsche 356 SC had blown its transmission and somebody had crashed into my Harley as I was driving it on La Brea in Hollywood; totaling it and injuring me. Thus, it was not a good time for me.

The fact is, I cannot discus the creation of *Max Hell Frog Warrior* without referencing *Roller Blade Seven* as the two have a very close correlation. *Roller Blade Seven* was a chaotic production. It didn't have to be. But Don, being Don, made it so.

Have you ever had one of those life-experiences where someone is so based in a negative mindset that they bring out the worst in you? That happened to me, in association with Don, when we made RB7. This was amplified by the negative, petty actions of our Executive Producer. Though we made a great movie, that is still at the forefront of the Cult Film Hierarchy, it left my life a mess. The fact is, during production and post production both Don and I were constantly carrying Xanax with us as there was so much perpetuated anxiety associated with the production of that film. As I have stated in several places, though I have written an extended chapter about the creation of RB7, which is presented in my book, *Zen Filmmaking*, I really want to write an entire book about the film as so much went on during production that understanding the process may truly help other independent filmmakers overcome obstacles and allow everyone to come to a better understanding about human consciousness.

One of the essential things to note is that when Don asked me to come on-board and make RB7 with him, the production was scheduled for one month. One month, I can handle that. So, when I showed up at our production offices at the Hollywood Center Building on Hollywood Boulevard on the first day of pre-production I had no idea the months-upon-months that it would take to complete that movie and its sequel. Now, think about taking months out of your life while making no money. As I am a dedicated, one-pointed person who doesn't give up, I did not leave the production. But, I did pay a very high price for my involvement with that film.

Moving On

By the end of *Roller Blade Seven,* I was ready to set out on my own and make my own films. As the video revolution had just hit and realizing I had the skillset to make it happen, I immediately went up on *Samurai Vampire Bikers from Hell* upon the completion of RB7. Don being Don, got jealous so he went off to work with Mark Williams who was both a part of the cast and the crew of RB7. Then, the Executive Producer of RB7, to play a petty little power trip, had me kicked out of our production offices and banned from the building. This, after she had already made thousands-upon-thousands of dollars on international sales of RB7 and *Return of the Roller Blade Seven.* Though Don and I occasionally communicated over the next few years, I did not have good feelings about him or the Executive Producer as they were both prospering off of my vision and my labor.

Then, in 1995, out of the blue Don contacted me via the Voice Mail system which was the main method of industry communication of the time. We all carried our pagers. He wanted to make another movie and he invited me to his production office in North Hollywood to talk about it. Though I had serious doubts about going, but as I had nothing else on my plate at the time, we set up a meet and I arrived.

To track backwards a bit... Don felt that Mark Williams, (a good guy), had gotten too dependent on the film financing Don had in place. Don hated people becoming dependent upon him. Though Mark was writing all of Don's scripts at the time; including: *Rollergator, Little Lost Sea Serpent, Baby Ghost, Pocket Ninjas,* etc., Don fired Mark in a rage. (Just a note: Don was prone to rages). But, Don was one of those people who couldn't work alone. So, he paid to have friends. As RB7 was already becoming a Cult Fan Favorite in Europe and as he remembered that we worked well together, he decided we should make another movie and, thus, he contacted me.

When I arrived at the production office, I was surprised to see how old Don had become in just the couple of years since I had last seen him. At the time, I didn't know that he had been diagnosed with leukemia—which was probably one of his main reasons for contacting me, as he knew I got things done and he wanted to cement his filmmaking legacy and needed someone like me to do that. We spoke for a while; hung out over the next few days, and I finally reluctantly agree to make another movie with him. Keep in mind, I had a lot of trepidation about working with him again.

But, we set up a weekly pay scale for me that was reasonable and we moved along.

Pre-Production

For the next few weeks we would meet at the office every day about eleven, scout locations, do casting sessions, hang out with other filmmakers, get drunk at lunch, go to private movie screenings, go and see obscure alt country and bluegrass bands in the evening, hit the occasional strip club, (scouting for talent), and do what industry folk do…

In terms of the pending production, we toyed with a few ideas prior to settling on *Toad Warrior*. The reason we finally decided to make *Toad Warrior* was that Don's creative vision had been taken away from him on both *Hell Comes to Frogtown* and to a lessor degree on *Return to Frogtown*. He never really liked the finished films—though, at least at the time, *Hell Comes to Frogtown* was frequency playing on TV and that film had really cemented his career as a known filmmaker. But, as he was never content with the two previous features, he always wanted to make a more free-flowing version of a film with *Frogtown* as the backdrop. Thus, *Toad Warrior*.

Though Don was linked into a company that was financing his films, so money was free-flowing, we decided to keep the production small. And, as we both considered *Roller Blade Seven* to be a true *Zen Film Masterpiece,* we hoped to re-invoke the essence of that film in what we were next to create.

Another factor to keep in mind about the inception of *Toad Warrior* was that by this point in my career I had begun to see myself more as a Producer and Director than an Actor. Don, however, wanted me to star in the film as *Roller Blade Seven* was already gaining Cult Classic status, plus he wanted to capitalize on my martial art notoriety of the time as I was in a lot of magazine, had a very successful Hapkido Video Tape Series on the market, my books were being published, etc... Thus, he suggested that we Co-Produce and Co-Direct the movie, while I star in the film. I agreed and we moved forward with this as our basis.

As RB7 was already a legacy for us, we wanted to invoke that film's sensibilities. Thus, my character again wore a black suit, black shirt, and the elbow and kneepads from RB7—minus the skates, of course.

Production Begins

On the first day of actual production, which was a Saturday, we were scheduled to go up at about noon. We had the entire second floor of offices in a building on Lakershim Boulevard in North Hollywood so we decided to dress the offices and use them as sets to establish the initial character interactions. As for our actors, the first to be cast was Joe Estevez. Also cast was a friend of Don's, (from the days when they both were working for Roger Corman), to play Humphrey Bullfrog, a couple of girls Don had previously worked with in films, (finished or not), a newly arrived couple from New Jersey who we had just met at a casting session via an ad we placed in *Dramalogue* the day before, and one or two other new faces.

The day of the shoot I got up, put on my black suit, and was preparing to go to my storage unit as that is where I kept all of my lighting equipment which I was going to bring to the set as Don only had a couple of cheap photofloods whereas I had a number of Fresnels, C-Stands, etc.

As if a warning sign from the great beyond, the first thing that happened to me was I thought I had my keys in my pocket. I walked out of the door of my apartment, carrying some equipment down to my 356, but when I got to my car I realized it wasn't my keys at all. Thus, I was locked out. A bit nervous about time, I went to find the manager of my building who was always in the office but she was not there. With a bit of freak-out running through my veins, I went on a quest to find her and finally located her in her apartment. She got the passkey, let me in, I got my keys, loaded my stuff, and was on my way. I get to my storage unit but the moment I opened the door I realized somebody had broken in. Someone had rented the storage unit next to mine and had cut a hole through the wall. They stole all of my lighting equipment, all of my costuming, my first guitar, my power tools, and a lot of guitar and amp parts and accessories I kept in the unit. I was upset to say the least...

With the police report made, I sped to the set. Living in the South Bay area of Los Angeles, I was quite a distance from North Hollywood. As I was driving towards the freeway onramp, I see the train gates up ahead going down. Damn! It seemed like the very long train took forever to pass. Again, a sign?

In the interim of waiting for the train, I called Don on my large flip phone and used some of the very expensive cellular minutes of the day to leave him a message on his Voice Mail and tell him of the situation.

As I sat there waiting for the train to pass, me, I really felt like I had failed. Though the theft was obviously not my fault, it made me feel like a liar as I could not bring my lights. And, as a person who is always very punctual, being late made my adrenalin serge. It was starting all over again, the craziness of *Roller Blade Seven*… I thought to just call it quits and walk away… I still, to this day, wonder if that was the life-course I should have taken? But, I drove on…

On the Set

By the time I finally got to the offices, a lot had already been accomplished. Don had brought in a camera guy, Jonathan Quade, that he had previously worked with. Jonathan was actually a gaffer in the big budget industry but he did a great job of set design, lighting, and low budget camera work. (We went onto work with him on a number of films). He, in association with a Production Assistant, had already created the set where Joe Estevez's character is revealed with the parachute covering the walls. But, with my lights stolen, all we had to light the set with was Don's two photofloods.

Most of the cast was wandering around the offices as Jonathan, the PA, and I continued the staging. Don sat in his office, as he liked to do, talking on the phone, joking with the girls, and generally screwing around. Finally, Joe arrives and we get underway.

We took Joe to the set where he was to be seated upon his thrown. Don asks him what he wanted to use as a character name. Joe suggested Mickey O'Malley, as he saw the green, thought of frogs, and wanted to reference his Irish roots. Don immediately hated the name. But, Don being Don, he didn't say anything. Me, I also saw the problem… We had hoped Joe to be a very fierce and domineering character. But, with a name like that...

Taking a Turn for the Worst
There is a point in every film where if you are an observant filmmaker you can take note of where the film all falls into place or where it all goes awry. This was that moment in *Toad Warrior*... Joe deciding on his name and Don or I not wanting to force a change. Thus, the production took a wrong turn that it never recovered from. This, before the first scene was ever shot.

...That's the problem when you are working with someone you really like and who is a really good guy like Joe—you don't want to come off as harsh or condescending. You want to keep them happy.

In any case, the first scene(s) to be shot were Joe interacting with the character Cricket AKA Sandra Purpuro, (the newly arrived actress from New Jersey). We immediately realized that she was a very good actress. In fact, immediately after *Toad Warrior* she moved onto having a very successful acting career.

We also added a couple of adult film starlets to the scene to give it some depth.

The Hierarchy
I was a bit in question about how Don was going to react to my co-directing the scenes as this was the first time we worked together in that manner. Though I obviously had a lot to say during the filming of RB7, I never felt like I was the director and I never crossed Don's boundaries. But, he was totally cool. The thing to note about Don, as a director, is that he never really directed the talent.

He just let them do whatever they wanted to do and say whatever they wanted to say—the way they wanted to say it. Me, on the other hand, I think natural inspiration is great but you need to give guidance to the actors, at certain points, so the storyline will stay on track. That's what I did…

We shot the scenes with Cricket and Joe. We then brought in his two minions: the boyfriend from New Jersey (Kent Dalian) and a Japanese actor, Tom Tom Typhoon. Don wanted the Japanese guy to communicate in English but as I speak Japanese I directed him to speak in his native language as he spoke very poor English. When you see him totally going off at Joe, that was totally his idea. He really got the essence of *Zen Filmmaking* and took it to the next, necessary level. Joe's reactions to him are great. Those are probably some of the best scenes in the film.

We then went and did the Humphrey Bullfrog stuff which I just do not like. That character and those scenes were developed by Don and his friend. They are just stupid and they don't play well. Again, within the first few hours of filming, *Toad Warrior* was set on a wayward course.

As evening was coming on, we decided to go to this nearby park that is linked to an overpass above the 170 freeway. There, we filmed the park fight scenes and the various characters crossing the bridge. While we were filming, we left the Production Assistant to create additional sets in the offices.

Returning, we then filmed the scene where the two girls are in jail: Agent Banner (Camille Solari) and Dr. Trixi T. (Elizabeth Mehr). This set was actually just an enclosed deck outside of one of the office windows. I thought they did a great job constructing that whole dialogue driven scene. And, they did it with no guidance. They were both talented actresses.

After that, we filmed my character's interaction with Joe. We then brought in Selina Jayne, (the Spirit Guide from RB7), who I had remained friends with, to do a Fortune Teller thing with Joe. Though I love Selina and Joe, that scene just did not work. Then, Joe goes into the scene where he does the hokey-pokey with the one actress portraying Dr. Trixie T. Terrible! Terrible! Terrible! So bad, I could not even watch it being filmed. Though, for the record, it was totally improved.

We then filmed the scene with the girl singing in the club where my character gets a drink thrown in his face. That club scene was set up in the waiting room of our offices.

We finished that evening by doing the inner-office fight scenes where my character and the actress playing Agent Banner fights a couple of frogs.

Calculating the Consequences

If you look at the amount of scenes filmed in just one afternoon and evening, and if you know the film, you will understand that a good portion of *Toad Warrior* was actually created in that one day. Though we captured a lot of footage, the essence of what I hoped the film would become, was lost. It had become nothing more than a poorly acted, un-comedic (though it was trying hard to be a comedy), stupid storylined, production that was destine to just remain a mess. Yet, we continued…

Over the next couple of weeks, we filmed additional scenes. Next up was Conrad Brooks. I had never met Conrad prior to the day we first filmed him but I did, of course, know of his previous work with Ed Wood. I immediately realized he was a really nice guy. I liked him a lot. And, I loved his style of acting.

We took Conrad to a location by the L.A. River where he and I interact with a couple of frogs. We then went back to the office and shot the scene in his tent. A tent that was constructed from the same parachute used to line the walls of Joe's lair.

For some reason, Don wanted to bring Conrad back as the character Swamp Farmer from another of Don's films, *Rollergator* and have the talking Baby Gator in the scene with him, as well. I like Conrad's performance but Baby Gator just added additional, unnecessary, stupidity to the film. That is the thing when you are working as a team member with someone, you may not always like their choices but you have to allow them their creativity.

A day or so later we went to do an evening shoot at an old bridge that Don had titled, *"The Bridge of Broken Dreams."* There, we took an actress we had just cast that afternoon. As she was new to L.A. I warned her about doing what she did; i.e. getting in a car at night with men she did not know and was not even aware of where she was being taken. In any case, she is the character that my character continually tells to, *"Shuuu,"* every time she tries to speak. We also did the scene where my character kills a frog at night with the bridge in the background.

Referencing the anxiety that took place during the filming of RB7 and how this same style of emotion engulfs other people... Don had this Production Assistant who had been working with him for a year or so. He did the voice of Baby Gator during the filming of Conrad and myself in the tent. He was also the one wearing the frog mask that my character kills in the aforementioned scene on the bridge.

Don had begun to get increasingly annoyed by this man. I thought he was fine but, again, Don found him becoming too dependent on his money. I suppose this change of heart had a lot to do with my now being part of the team as I was a fully functioning filmmaker and there was a lot of things that I could do that this man could not. As he had begun to annoy Don, Don had become more and more short with him. At one point that evening he yelled at the guy to get something out of the car. Instead of taking the frog mask off, he ran all the way to the car and back with it on. Thus, equaling a massive anxiety attack. It was the next day that Don, in a rage, fired him. The man called me up that night wondering what had happened and if I could ask Don to let him come back to work. I told Don the story but Don was the source of the money for this project so there was nothing that I could do as Don did not want him back.

The Lies Actors Tell

Don and I continued forward hanging out everyday and occasionally filming over the next few weeks. One of the interesting stories, that I have told elsewhere, happened when we cast this girl because she told us she was an avid motocross rider and owned her own dirt bike. We though this would be a great addition to add to the film. We called her character, Road Toad. We meet her up on the dirt section of Mulholland Highway, where she promptly fell off of her bike and broke her clutch handle. Every time she got on, she fell off. Finally, to save any hope of making the entire situation equal anything, my character asks her if I can borrow her motorcycle. From this, we film me riding it for a bit. Keep in mind, I was shifting with no clutch. After that, the girl rode off. (I hope she made it home safely). But, we never heard from her again.

Though we periodically shot a scene here or there, we only did serious filming maybe three or four additional days to create *Toad Warrior*. ...Compared to the days-upon-days-upon-days of full-on production we had previously done on RB7, *Toad Warrior* had very few actual days of production.

Expanding the Cast

I had brought on Roger Ellis who had played the roll of Stealth in RB7 and I had used in much bigger roles in *Samurai Vampire Bikers from Hell* and *Samurai Johnny Frankenstein*. He became Overload War Toad. Roger was a great actor and really added some good stuff to a very faltering film. We did all of Roger's interior scenes at the garage/stage of Jonathan Quade, the aforementioned cameraman, who worked with us throughout the entire production. This is where the infamous spank scene(s) take place, which was the idea of yours truly.

The girl in those scenes was a great up-and-comer named Robin Kimberly. She made her living as an exotic dancer. I remember her telling me she hailed from Alaska and I really liked her as a person and an actress. But, she was one of those people that we never heard from again after her days on the set. She played the roll of Agent Spangle. And yes, the female agents in the film were intentionally named: Agent Star, Agent Spangle, and Agent Banner. That was on Don. ...A sign of his abstract patriotisms.

Next up was Adrianne Moore AKA Jill Kelly, a girl who did her first onscreen performance in RB7 before becoming a major force in the Adult Industry. In the opening scene we find her character being chased by frogs out at the El Mirage Dry Lake Bed. The work we did with her character really adds positive aspects to the overall film.

El Mirage is one of the places where the, *"Magic,"* that I often speak of in association *Zen Filmmaking,* took place. We went there with only a basic idea about what we would film. But, when we got there we noticed a couple with their pair of ultra light aircraft. Don asked if we could use them. They said, *"Yes."* With this, we added the entire opening scene to the film, providing a lot of production value. ...We had no idea this would take place but we allowed the spontaneity of Zen to be our guide and, thus, True Cinematic Magic occurred.

Something to Scream About

Elizabeth, the girl who played Dr. Trixie T., was soon to be moving and she invited us over to her large house to film. Here, we created the lab set. Overall, she is a great girl and a good actress; I really liked her but many of her scenes were too comedic and just added, in my opinion, to the overall failure of this film. This is the case with the lab scene that we filmed at her home. Her and another girl, (one of her friends that we never met before or after that moment in time), go into this whole fake British accent thing, talking about the development of the frog plague. Again, both very nice people, but the scene just did not work!

One of the now-funny occurrences that took place that night was Don had left the set as he had something else to do. We had been there for awhile and I asked if anybody wanted something to eat. Some did, so we sent out. One girl who I had cast earlier that week, a new arrival from Japan, initially said she wasn't hungry but then, all of a sudden, after we had recommenced filming, she completely started freaking about the fact that she was hungry and she wanted something to eat. I told her we were busy and reminded her that she said she didn't want anything but this did not stop her. I told her I would give her some money if she wanted to walk over to a local fast food place but she would have none of it. She really was causing a scene. Finally, I took her outside and firmly explained to her in Japanese how unprofessional she was behaving. She calmed down, told me she was sorry, and she kind-of shut up. This is just a reminded to you filmmakers out there, sometime the people you cast can become a real problem to your production.

Going Nuclear

We also shot exteriors at this one location in the West San Fernando Valley that used to house nuclear silos. That is where you see Sargent Shiva and my character do the Kurosawa influenced, long lens, sword fighting scene(s). I know a lot of people have discussed this scene in their reviews, incorrectly claiming there was only one take that was reused. But, if you actually take the time to study the film you will see there were several takes. We also shot some of the other additional exterior scenes out there that day.

Though there were a few more days of filming small things, here or there, that's what it took to create *Toad Warrior.*

It is essential to note that the moment Don and I began working together again, we did not wholly focus on *Toad Warrior.* We, almost immediately began to formulate, come up with other projects, and begin filming them, as well. Most notable filmed around this same period of time were the films that became *Shotgun Blvd.* and *Ghost Taxi.* Though none of these first, *"Next Generation Zen Films,"* rose to the cult status of *Max Hell Frog Warrior,* at least in my opinion, they were all better films than *Toad Warrior.*

Post Production

Post Production on *Toad Warrior* did not happen right away. As stated, we began working on other films. Finally, as the 1996 American Film Market (AFM) was approaching, we set about editing the movies we had in the can. I did *Shotgun Blvd.* and *Ghost Taxi* and one of Don's friends began to work on *Toad Warrior.* But, he was using some weird system that did not output in a high enough quality format so Don went into one of his rages and fired the guy. He then gave the footage to one of his long time friends, Chris—a true film editor and a man who had edited some of Don's previous features. Don and he sat down and they did what they did.

I don't know if it was the lack of technology at the time, laziness, or just the fact that the editor was more locked into a sense of Traditional Filmmaking than *Zen Filmmaking* but he and Don really missed the mark on the original edit of *Toad Warrior.* The fact is, though they probably grabbed the best of the footage there was, so much more great footage was left unused. More than simply not liking the finished product, the fact is, the film really bothered me. It bothered me that so much footage was left on the preverbal cutting room floor. Plus, the story construction was shoddy. And, Chris knew it. He didn't like the edit either. He asked me if I wanted to redo it. But, there wasn't time. To me, the edited film kind of felt like they were just filling in the required eighty-two minutes that it takes to make a movie viable for international sales.

AFM

As AFM was coming up fast, Don and I gave the edited *Toad Warrior* to a sound design company to finish up the soundscape. We both watched the final product and didn't like it. But, as the hotel rooms that they turn into AFM selling suits on the Santa Monica coastline are expensive, we had to have product. Thus, posters were created, a selling staff was hired, and Don and I hung out at AFM, did some interviews, and watched a lot of movies.

One of the funny experiences we had at the 1996 AFM is when Jill Kelly came by one evening. We walked around the expansive hotel, full of buyers from all over the world, and all eyes were on us. Well... They were actually on Jill. She was a beautiful sight with her long blonde hair, her big platform shoes, and the white, virtually see though clothing she was wearing.

Though we didn't like *Toad Warrior,* three countries did buy the limited theatrical rights we were offering to be shown only in theaters in their country. Japan, Malaysia, and the Philippines being the buyers. After AFM, Don being Don absconded with all of the money from the sales. Lesson: people never really change.

Post, Post Productions

Post the 1996 AFM Don and I buried the film. We planned to reedit it but we were busy and we never got around to it.

By the early 2000s, Don was in his late fifties, getting very sick, and wasn't really able to do too much. Me, I did take the original film and created a Zen Speed Flick Version of *Toad Warrior* titled, *Max Hell in Frogtown.*

For those of you who don't know, a *Zen Speed Flick* is a film cut down to its most essential elements. This re-edit really gave the film a new vision. Gone was all the bad implied humor, leaving only the best of the best. Don loved it and I liked it a lot better than the original version.

Max Hell Frog Warrior

In 2001, as computer editing had become a realistic possibility; I pulled the original edit of *Toad Warrior* into my MAC G4. I begin the process of a re-cut in an attempt to make it a better movie. I removed some of the scenes that really bothered me, tuned-up some of the others, and added a bit of unused footage. I did not, however, go into a full blown reedit. What emerged was *Max Hell Frog Warrior.* Better than *Toad Warrior?* I think so. As good as this movie can be? No.

The Next, Better Version

I have personally sat down, looked through the footage, and started to do a completely new, better edit of the film four times over the past fifteen years or so. I do this, because as stated, there is a lot of great, unused, never before seen footage that could reveal an entirely different and better movie. Each time I have sat down to do this, however, I get maybe a half hour or so into the storyline development and something stops me. …I don't finish. Then, I dump the edit. Though I know I really should complete the process something has always stopped me from doing so. What, I don't know?

Perhaps at some point, I will compete this process as I know there is a better film hidden within the footage.

Though I suppose there is a million subtle stories I could tell about the creation of this film, in this piece I have provided you with an overview of the All and the Everything of *Toad Warrior* AKA *Max Hell in Frogtown* AKA *Max Hell Frog Warrior*. I hope this provides you with some factual insight into the actual goings-on. Any specific questions, you can always ask…

Be positive and smile.

FADE OUT.

THE ZEN

Guns of El Chupacabra:
The Story of the Production

Fade In:

As we have recently passed the twenty-year mark of the beginning of the creation of the *Zen Film, Guns of El Chupacabra* and as I continue to receive a lot of questions about the process of filmmaking used in making that movie, I thought I would take a few minutes and write a little bit about this *Zen Film*. I should begin this piece by stating that there is a chapter devoted to the creation of *Guns of El Chupacabra* in my book, *Zen Filmmaking*. That chapter is a great source for a lot of the inside-inside and the philosophy about what went on during filming. But here, I thought I would spell out more of the A to Z about the film, to give all of you who have wondered a bit more insight into the film's actual creation.

To begin with, Donald G. Jackson and I were friends. That is the best way I can describe our relationship. Being friends, sometimes you are more forgiving of a person's behavior than you would be of someone with whom you are not friends. In brief, Don was a psychologically complicated guy who had a lot of inner-demons. I say this to illustration how and why he and I had a bit of an on-again/off-again turbulent relationship, even during the filming of *Guns of El Chupacabra*. ...We were two very different people. I guess that he had undiagnosed bipolar disorder as one minute he would be fine and the next moment he would be completely freaking out. For anyone who knew him they will instantaneously confirm this fact. With this stated, he always treated me with the utmost respect—at least to my face. From this relationship, even amidst

Don's chaotic mindset, we made a number of seminal films together, including what eventually became *Guns of El Chupacabra*. This film is one of the two films that we made together that Don and I both considered to be *Zen Filmmaking* masterpieces. The other being, *The Roller Blade Seven*. Though I would add *The Rock n' Roll Cops* to that list, as well, but Don never got to see the finalized version of that film.

    The reason I begin by discussing the mindset of Donald G. Jackson is to illustrate what it was like to work with Don. It was not easy. Moreover, it is also important to note that Don was a horrible confiscator of other people's creative ideas: i.e. my idea about doing a film about the Chupacabra or a similar creature which I had relayed to him a few months previous to the beginning of filming. We even started to do my film, Surf Samurai from Atlantis, which was to highlight a Sea Monster—artistically referencing films like *Creature from the Black Lagoon* and *Return of the Creature*. But, we got sidetracked and that film was never completed… In any case, I hadn't seen Don in a few months before we began filming. I had gone off to Southeast Asia and, as I tend to be, was very happy living in Thailand. But, I had gotten attacked by a few knife-wielding foes one night. Bangkok can be a very dangerous place. Though I overcame my five attackers fairly readily, I did have a serious cut down the center of my face which brought me back to L.A. in a rush to see a plastic surgeon. I had been home maybe a week or so and one day, out of the blue, nearing the end of 1996, Don called me up and tells me that talk of the Chupacabra is all over the internet and we should do a film about it. Okay, but didn't I already suggest that a few months ago... In any case, we got together and we started preproduction. The only missing fact was, he had already taken my idea and had started filming. I guess he had hoped to grab my idea and create a film about the Chupacabra without me. But, I didn't find this out until later.

The problem was, as was always the case with Don, he had great creative ideas but he couldn't get anything done. He always surrounded himself with a less than ideal cast and crew. So, in essence, due to his lack of precision crewing, everything he had previously filmed was basically uselessly. ...At least in terms of the technology that was available at the time. And, he had filmed it on 16mm so that process wasn't cheap. Enter, me... My acute focus and my ability to get things done is what made *Guns of El Chupacabra* move forward and finally get finished.

Initially, we called the movie, *El Chupacabra.* With that as our inspiration we went out and began to film.

A friend of Don's, Bob Mizrahi, was living at this great ranch north of L.A. I am told that it was originally owned by Hoyt Axton. The great thing about this ranch was that not only was it secluded but it had hills surrounding the property. From this, we could fire live ammo, (of which a lot was shot during filming), with no worry of stray bullets traveling onto other people's property. Moreover, there were several abandoned bulldozer and other heavy machinery that gave the place a great look. We filmed many scenes at this location over several visits.

Initially, I was not sure about who my character would be or how I wanted to guide that character's development. Originally, I had thought about doing a professor sort of thing. From this, on the first day of shooting, I brought along some old-school desert expedition sort of wardrobe. But, as I always wear a sport coat, slacks, and tennis shoes, I just kind of ended up in front of the camera wearing what I wear. It was shortly after that Don and I realized that we really needed to take the storyline to the next level and not make it simply Earth based but intergalactic. Thus, it was Don who came up with my character's name, Jack B. Quick, Space Sheriff.

As was the case whenever Don and I worked together, we would meet at the office everyday at about eleven, do preproduction, location scouting, casting, and other stuff during the week and film mostly at night or on the weekends. Those were always fun and fulfilling days. This was the same path we followed with *El Chupacabra.*

When we began filming the movie we didn't have a monster. We simply did character development. It was Don who contacted the Executive Producer of Roller Blade Seven, knowing that she was in possession of a monster costume. This suit was originally made for a movie that never was filmed. One Saturday morning we went over to her house and picked up the costume. *El Chupacabra* was born.

While we were there she made Don promise her that he would not damage the creature costume as she wanted to use it in an upcoming film. He, of course, promised her that he would keep it safe and sound. But, I will discuss what came next in a moment…

For anyone who has seen the movie I am sure you will agree that it is a really great monster costume. When it was created, it cost a lot of money. The problem was, it was made for a fairly small and thin person. So, none of the men we knew could fit into the suit. But, the girl who was playing the character Linda Marshall was willing to climb into that costume. Me, I would have been way too claustrophobic to have ever gotten into a monster suit like that, as there was no self-way in and no self-way out. It had to be put on and taken off by someone else. As such, on the first day we filmed with her in the costume, she brought along a friend of hers whom we dubbed, The Monster Wrangler.

The first day we used the suit was a few months into production. We took our skeleton crew, our monster, her Monster Wrangler, and we went to Bronson Cave—which is a great Hollywood landmark that has been used in an untold number of films and TV shows. We filmed the reveal of the monster and my character fighting the creature.

An important note to keep in mind is that in the traditional Monster Flick, the monster is never revealed in broad daylight. The monster is always kept somewhat hidden and allusive to the seeing eye. We totally broke that rule with *Guns of El Chupacabra,* however, and let the monster be right in the face of the audience.

Filming went along for several months. Don and I also did a few other films in the interim. I was also very active in writing books and article about the Martial Arts and Zen at that time, so those projects took up a lot of my time when I wasn't working on the film. I also completed another Master's Degree during this period so it was a busy and productive period of time for me.

Filming on *Guns of El Chupacabra* took us over a year. In fact, it took us close to two years to actually finish the film. I have one of those very prominent memories etched into my mind where Don and I were on the roof of *The Broadway Building* on the corner of Hollywood and Vine, where we filmed many a scene, and Don looked at me, shook his head and said, *"We've been filming this for over a year…"* Yeah, we had… Pretty scary… Where did the time go?

Speaking of *The Broadway Building,* that is where my character encounters the crew of ninjas and martial artists. That team was brought on by a guy who Don had met several years the previous who wanted to make martial art movies. As Don told it, that guy simply walked into his office unannounced one day and said he had money from a guy in prison who could finance films. But, the money never came through but that guy, like so many people who inhabited the world of Donald G. Jackson, continued to pop up hoping to break into the game.

This is one of the things that needs to be said about Don—he promised everybody everything. He told people what they wanted to hear. If they were an actor, he promised them a starring role. If they were a writer, he promised them he would produce their script. But, he never did… Hollywood is a cutthroat place where everyone expects to be a star and when someone promises you this dream… Well, when they don't follow through, things can get sketchy. Don made a lot of enemies.

The martial art troupe that the aforementioned guy brought into the production were all great martial artists and very professional. I think they added a lot to the overall presentation of the film. They guy himself, however… Well, I guess he suffered from a Napoleon Complex as he was very short. The day we filmed those scenes he kept insinuating that he wanted to fight me. Oh please... Get a life...

I only saw him one time after that, a couple of years later, when Don had an office in Santa Monica. He showed up out of the blue, was friendly and kept saying, *"You're like Don's son. Look at you two. That's why you never wanted to work with me, Don. You have a son..."* Again, Oh please... I'm told that guy died soon after that. Though much younger, he died even before Don passed away. RIP.

If I sound all over the place in talking about this film, that is because that is how it was created; very randomly. If I looked at my notes, I could tell you exactly happened when but that is not at all how I remember the creation of *Guns of El Chupacabra*. It went in spurts. We worked on it and then we didn't.

At the 1997 *American Film Market* (AFM) Don showed up having created a twenty-minute trailer for the film. I had been in Hawaii with my lady for a time and returned the day before the '97 AFM was to begin. Don had the tendency of being jealous and vindictive. Thus, he created the trailer without my input and I, the star of the film, was barely in it. Though I suppose I should have been angry, knowing Don I found that very-very amusing.

Don was one of those people who like to subtlety mind-fuck people. He thought that was how he could get over on them. Me, I was at one of those points, that happened several times throughout our partnership, where I was just going to tell Don to, *"Fuck off."* But, he kept insisting that I needed to be at AFM as I was the star of several films and he was distributing a couple of my Zen Film... So, I showed up. Though we didn't offer *El Chupacabra* for sale, we test-screened it to several buyers and they were all very impressed and interested.

Sometime soon after the '97 AFM we went into our second segment of filming. We changed the name of the film to *Guns of El Chupacabra* and we had recruited a few new interesting cast members. This is where the Santiago Kid as well as Maria-Maria came into play. This is also where we recruited a few porn girls to take part in the movie. Which I guess is an interesting story in and of itself to tell…

Don and I wanted to add some nudity to the film. Like the creature, we wanted this nudity to be in your face with no explanation or reasoning. We tried casting actresses for these roles but it just did not work out. In one case, the cast, the crew, he and I arrived at the office early on Saturday morning, we packed up all the equipment, but the girl who was scheduled to do the nude role did not show up. We called and called but nothing… So, all that time and energy had been wasted.

It was at that point Don came up with the idea that we should go to the major adult film-casting agency here in L.A., where he was sure we would easily be able to get some female talent who were willing to work in the nude. As there was no on-screen sex involved, something that these girls did for a living, he was certain we could find the right actresses. We went there, paid the two-hundred dollar casting fee, looked through their books, chose some girls, and got their numbers. Over the next week, we had them come by our offices, take off their clothes, and see how well we would be able to work together. A few girls were decided upon.

As *Zen Filmmaking* is all about living in the moment, we rarely planned what we would do next. On the day we were scheduled to work with the first two (nude) girls, both high-end adult stars of the time, we had them meet us at our North Hollywood offices along with other cast members such as the Santiago Kid and Maria-Maria very early on a Saturday morning. We planned to go to Bronson Cave to shoot. With a few cars of cast and crew following us, we arrived. But, the *Power Rangers TV Series* was filming there. There was tons of star trailers and crew trucks. ...Couldn't film there...

Next stop, we thought to go out to *The Mizrahi Movie Ranch* as we called it. Don's friend's place. We drive all the way out there, cast and crew following us. We pull in and a new owner of the property had taken over. He had evicted Bob. He tells us, *"Get off my property!"* Wow... Okay, now what?

Finally, the Santiago Kid, who lived out in the Palmdale area, suggested the desert ranch of one of his friends. Having already paid for the talent, and with nowhere else to film, we had no choice but to check it out. Again, with several cars in tow, we made our way a hundred miles northeast out to the desert.

Arriving at that desert ranch, it was a visual very nice location. It reminded me of an old run down chicken farm, though I do not actually know what it once was. But, we were free to shoot there.

With no real storyline in mind, we looked around and noticed a few chicken wire cages. Don and I decided that would be a great place to put the girls, detailing that they had been capture by El Chupacabra to be eaten later. Then, my character would arrive to rescue them. Finally, filming was underway.

I can only imagine what the porn girls and their manager were thinking with all of the running around. *Zen Filmmaking* and all… But, they were getting paid their day rate so I guess they really didn't care. Overall, we became friends and used the team in a few other films.

Filming went well at that ranch. We shot there a couple of times. Like *The Mizrahi Movie Ranch,* it was isolated and cinematically very interesting. We did have a problem when we were firing some AKs out there one time, however. Not realizing how far a bullet will actually travel, I guess one of the distant neighbors had a few shells flying by his head and had to drive over and ask us to stop firing in that direction. Luckily, nobody got shot.

The third phase of filming *Guns of El Chupacabra* came about when Don enlisted Julie Strain and her then husband Kevin Eastman, co-creator of the Teenage Mutant Ninja Turtles, to get on the bus. They were and are both very nice, very talented people. And, at the time, Julie had a great PR team behind her. From her being a part of the production we got interviewed on a couple of TV shows and a few magazines wrote articles about the film due to her being a part of the cast.

The majority of the scenes involving Julie and Kevin were shot at a location close to the L.A. River not far from Downtown. This space was owned by an artist who did some great gothic paintings. You can see some of them in the background of their scenes.

All of Julie and Kevin's dialogue was created a few moments before filming by Don or myself. We would roll camera and Don or I would feed them their lines, one line at a time. Then, cut. They did a great job. This is also the place where Julie knights my character, the Revered Doctor Saint Francis Blade.

This is a character evolution that was developed by Don. He thought my character should have some reward upon the completion of his mission. And, that was it, being knighted. Don, who was very Christian and very religious in his later years, wanted to evoke the power of Christianity in all of our films whenever he could.

It would be impossible to discuss the making of *Guns of El Chupacabra* without mentioning Conrad Brooks. Though he did not end up having a large role in the film, he was elemental to several important moments.

First of all, Conrad is a great guy. He comes from that old-school of acting (or should I say overacting) and I simply love his performances.

Conrad is a very nice guy and perhaps that was his downfall—at least in terms of working with Donald G. Jackson. For if Don found someone he could vent his anger upon, look out. Conrad often served that purpose as Don would just scream and scream at him. For example, when we were filming at *The El Mirage Dry Lake Bed* and my character was driving up to meet Conrad and a female cohort, Conrad kept missing his mark as he walked into the scene. Don just let loose on him several times. But finally, Conrad explained that he had cataracts and, as such, the high light of the desert made everything just a blur. From this, he was unable to see where his mark actually was. In the next take, as Don filmed from the backseat and my character drove into the scene, Don said, *"I guess I shouldn't have been so hard on him."* But, he never apologized. That's just who he was.

I believe this abusive mindset was one of the key downfalls to the overall career of Donald G. Jackson. He would test people and if he would find them venerable, he would go after them nonstop. Conrad was often on the wrong side of this abuse.

Though Don was certainly one of the most instrumental figures in relaunching the career of Conrad Brooks, why Conrad put up with it, I do not know? But, he did. In fact, Conrad loved Don. I think back to a time when I was teaching a course on filmmaking at U.C.L.A. and one of my students needed an actor for a scene he was shooting for his class project so I suggested Conrad as his day rate was only $100.00 and, hey, he was in *Plan 9 from Outer Space*. The moment Conrad got on set he thanked Donald G. Jackson. This made me smile, *"Hey Conrad, it was me who got you the gig!"* But Conrad, like so many other people, simply assumed that Donald G. Jackson and myself were one inseparable team, but we were not.

I know I have told this story somewhere before but when Don and I were filming *The Rock n' Roll Cop,* just after *Chupacabra,* we had brought on this one guy who was the godson of actor William Smith. Good guy. I really like him. But, he pissed Don off for some nondescript reason and Don just went off. I was driving in the car behind them and for nearly an hour I could hear Don screaming at the top of his lungs at this guy. When we finally got to the shooting location the guy gets out of the car a bit shell shocked and asked me if Don treated me like that. *"Hell no,"* I said, *"I'd kick the shit out of him if he did."* But, here was this guy; my age, healthy, and I'm sure he could fight, but he let Don treat him like that. But, Don behaved like this all the time as long as someone would let him get away with it. Again, Don made a lot of enemies. That's why he always needed someone like me around—someone who was willing to fight. There was more than a couple of times when I had to step in to keep Don from getting his ass kicked.

In fact, near the end of filming *Chupacabra*, it had gotten so bad, as Don was getting so many treats, that we both ended up carrying loaded guns with us all the time. Don had his Smith & Wesson and I had my Glock. I thought then and it makes me think now back to that Rappin' 4-Tay song, *Playaz Club*, *"I don't need a Glock but I bought one just incase some sucka tries to stop me from pursuing my paper chase."* Don was really afraid that someone was going to burst into the office and shoot him. He always told me if that happened to please just shoot the guy and then give him my gun, he would say he pulled the trigger. As you can see, things got very strange, chaotic, and dangerous due to the behavior of Donald G. Jackson during the filming of *Guns of El Chupacabra*.

But, I have gotten off point... Another interesting moment, during the filming of *Chupacabra*, involving Conrad came when we were filming at the aforementioned space of the artist near the L.A. River. One of our crew had brought his girlfriend along. She was a showgirl from Vegas. This being *Zen Filmmaking*, we, of course, offered her a part in the movie. We put her in a scene with Conrad. Now Conrad, any time he had the chance took advantage of it and shoved his tongue down the throat of any actress in a scene with him. Thus, the showgirl got initiated into the acting technique of Conrad Brooks. The crew guy was fuming. I told him to step in and stop the scene. She wasn't my girlfriend and, as such, it wasn't my call to make. But, he did nothing. Thus, Conrad got the kiss, the showgirl got her major motion picture film debut, and the filming of *Guns of El Chupacabra* moved forward.

As stated, Don promised to keep the monster costume in good shape. As we got near the end of this period of filming, this is where my character kills the creature. For those of you who have seen the film you know that, among other things, I shoot arrows into El Chupacabra. That does not keep a monster safe, sound, or intact. Thus, by the time we were done filming with the monster that costume was pretty much trashed.

Don being Don, as we were about to shoot that scene, he told me that he wanted to, *"Fuck up,"* the costume up so that the person who gave it to us could never use it in another film. Not cool. But again, this goes back to mindset and code of conduct that Donald G. Jackson inhabited.

With the completion of this segment of filming we telecined the film, time coded it, and I sat down to edit the movie. Now, this became a very interesting process. Don and I had a full floor of offices in a North Hollywood office building at the time. We set up one of them to be my editing suite. Don rented an editing bay from one of his friends. It was made by Sony and was not dissimilar to the editing controller I used on *Roller Blade Seven*. The problem was, this system had been developed in some weird way, for some weird reason, in that it only worked in reverse. Meaning, whenever I put the various cuts of a scene together I had to do it in reverse. Therefore, every scene in *Guns of El Chupacabra* was not cut editing from start to finish but from finish to start. Believe me when I tell you, that was not easy to do...

During the editing, one of my sweetheart's from Bangkok came to L.A. I took her by the editing suite and showed her some footage from the film one evening. She immediately assumed that Z'Man (Robert Z'Dar) was wearing a prosthetic jaw. Nope, that's just him... Awh Z'man, you are missed!

I did the first cut and we let the film sit for awhile. The 1998 AFM was still a few months off and we were working on other projects. During that period of time Don and I did *The Rock n' Roll Cops, Lingerie Kickboxer, Mimes: Silent But Deadly,* and a few individual films. As the '98 AFM approached, Don had the idea to add our *Zen Filmmaking* buddy Joe Estevez to the cast which took us to the last stage of filming *Guns of El Chupacabra.* Don envisioned Joe as being the storyteller that comes on and interrupts the movie like in the 1950s and 1960s TV shows in order to narrate and fill in any story gaps. Thus was born, Rocket Ranger Dan Danger.

A funny story here is that Don and I watched the movie and discussed where we needed Joe to fill in the story gaps. I went home and actually wrote out the dialogue that Joe was to say in full screenplay fashion. And, there was a lot of it. I gave it to Joe.

On the day of filming we went to pick Joe up at his place in Hollywood and we headed over to Bronson Cave. Don was doing the camera and I was doing the sound but Joe... Joe didn't learn his lines. He didn't even bring the script that I took all that time to write. ...I am smiling as I write this as it was so amusing. Me, Mr. Zen Filmmaking, writing and giving someone a script and them not even bringing it. *Zen Filmmaking* Forever!!! Don and I did the best we could at feeding him lines that would patch up any story flaws.

Post that, I edited the scenes into the film. We then took the movie to online post. And, that was that, the movie was done. It premiered at the 1998 American Film Market.

Guns of El Chupacabra!

POST SCRIPT:

From the footage we shot during this period of time I was able to construct three individual films making up *The Guns of El Chupacabra Trilogy*. Though the title figurehead of this film group is the most relevant feature, the other films each offer a unique view into the *Zen Filmmaking* legacy of *El Chupacabra*.

A couple of year before he passed away, Don's father died. With this, Don retuned to his hometown of Adrian, Michigan. While there he fell in with a group of Christian zealots who preached, *"A bible in one hand, a gun in the other."* As he was the hometown boy who had made good in Hollywood they heartily embraced him. They even gave him a radio show on their pirate radio station. ...This, until the FCC shut them down and confiscated their equipment. Don was rebaptized and believed he had been cleansed of all his sins. I don't know about that but while he was there he wanted to show the congregation *Guns of El Chupacabra*. The only problem was, there was all that nudity in the film and he believed that the nudity would not be acceptable to a Christian audience. As such, he asked me to edit it out. I did so and sent him that version. This is the PG version of the film that was released much later as, *Crimes of the Chupacabra.* He was very happy with his new group of friends and remained in Adrian for a time until the strain of the relationship with his step mother got too intense and he was forced to leave. I picked him at LAX. This period, and his interactions in Adrian, truly defined the last years of Don's life.

When Don passed away I knew that he was still in possession of the El Chupacabra creature costume. Though I hoped to get it, have it repaired, and do another film featuring it—resurrecting El Chupacabra, Don's wife had discarded it before I had the chance to retrieve it. She did this knowing how much Don disliked the executive producer of Roller Blade Seven whom had given it to us as she had sued Don shortly before his death due to an unfulfilled movie contract. This, in association with the fact that Don's wife and his daughter moved out of the house they had lived in for over twenty years in Canoga Park shortly after his passing, as such they were in the mode of rapidly discarding all nonessential items. Thus, El Chupacabra is lost forever.

FADE OUT.

THE ZEN

The Rock n' Roll Cops: The Story of the Production

Over the past year or so I have written three, *Stories of the Production*. With the completion of each one, I receive tons of asks to do another movie profile. That's great! I'm glad you like them and find them informative. *Zen Filmmaking!*

I first began with one on *Max Hell Frog Warrior*. Then, I wrote one about *Guns of El Chupacabra*. Finally, I did one on *The Roller Blade Seven*. Each one spells out the details of the film in a free flowing, stream of consciousness manner. The one thing that all of these movies, (including The Rock n' Roll Cops), have in common is that I made them in association with Donald G. Jackson. For those of you who have read the previous *Stories of the Production* you will understand that working with Don was always chaos in the making. The fact is, this is probably the last *Story of the Production* I will write as the production of the films I have made without Don were very, (for lack of a better term), boring. Aside from the occasional asshole crewmember or ego-driven castmember, things on my sets generally go off without a hitch. That's just who I am and that's just how I make my movies. Thus, writing about them would provide the reader with very little suspense or melodrama.

This being said, *The Rock n' Roll Cops* was a crazy chaotic mess. Why? One reason, Donald G. Jackson. He used to love to rile people up. I guess that provided him with some sort of a sense of misguided power. I don't know? I do know that of all the films I made with Don, *The Rock n' Roll Cops* was probably one of the shortest in-production pieces we ever did together. We shot it pretty fast. It was only up for about two weeks. None-the-less, it was, without a doubt, one of the wildest and craziest.

As I mentioned in association with the other *Stories of the Production,* if I went back into my production notes I could provide you with an exact date-by-date, play-by-play of everything that took place. But, I'm not going to do that right now. Maybe I will do that at some point in the future.

For the record, there is a chapter in my book, *Zen Filmmaking* that tells the overview account of the creation of this film. In that piece the literary emphasis is placed on a distinctive set of sentiments and events that is different from this essay. So, you may want to check it out. Here, with this piece, I hope to provide you with a more personal understanding of the actual *what-went-on* during the creation of *The Rock n' Roll Cops.*

Okay... Here we go...

Guns of El Chupacabra

The Rock n' Roll Cops went up directly after *Guns of El Chupacabra.* Don and I had been working nonstop on film-after-film for a few years. *Guns of El Chupacabra,* as was the case with several of the other films he and I created, took a very long time to complete. As stated in *Guns of El Chupacabra: The Story of the Production,* there was one point when Don and I realized we had been filming that movie for over a year and we were not even done.

In any case, to tell a little bit of a backstory, as is referenced in one or more of the previous, *Stories of the Production,* Don loved to promise people one thing or another but he never delivered. From this, he created a lot of enemies. Though Don would promise people producing, writing, and director positions, at best he would allow someone to write a script, critique it, and then never speak to them again. One-on-one he would often say to me, *"Let them go find their own money to make a movie. Why should I pay for it?"* Thus and therefore, there was a lot of negative energy being focused our direction from people who were mad at Don so we had to go armed pretty much everywhere we went as Don was receiving a lot of death threats. And me, because I was seen to be his friend, a lot of people wrongly included me in their equation of hatred. Combine this with the fact that Don always talked shit behind the backs of people, as he loved to create havoc in interpersonal relationships whenever possible, thus and therefore by the time we filmed *The Rock n' Roll Cops,* it is hard to believe the amount of pandemonium that surrounded us.

Pre-Production

Due to Don's feelings about financing the films of other people, it came as kind of a shock to me when he told me he wanted to do my film, *The Rock n' Roll Cops.* I had previously told him about my idea for the film and he brought it up one day when we were having lunch out of nowhere. We certainly had co-directed several films together, but when he asked me to solo direct this film with him shooting it, I was very surprised. Though knowing Don as I did, I knew it was not going to be as simple as all that.

The one thing I had going for me, and Don knew it, was that I didn't need him, (or his financing), for me to do my own films. As the digital age was taking hold, I had become the master of the team, as I was the only one who possessed the knowledge of computers, digital editing, and the like. But, what actually made Don ask me to step to the forefront, I guess I will never know. But, none-the-less, he did and so we began pre-production.

As stated, we were just coming off of *Guns of El Chupacabra,* and several other films, so we had a large talent pool to choose from. Throughout all of our filmmaking endeavors over the years, we were constantly casting, so we were always meeting new people to bring into the fold.

We went up fast on this film. At the time Don was having legal issues with the company that had been providing him with film financing so he had ventured off on his own, setting up a film finance company that romanced those people with a lot of disposable income. Hand-in-hand with this came a lot of additional people that wanted to be in the film business in one way or another. From this, we found additional compatriots.

One of the amusing events that occurred just prior to shooting *The Rock n' Roll Cops* was when one of the high-end money people came over to our production offices to discuss possibly financing a film. At that time, Don was very interested in getting the bumpers of his '62 Plymouth Belvedere powder coated. Instead of even talking to the guy he let him sit there as he made phone call after phone call discussing the powder coating process. I could not help but smile watching this guy, who I am sure had never been treated like that before, sit there uncomfortably in disbelief. But, that was Don…

For the record, I want to be a little carful in some of the names I use in this piece because I do not wish to make anyone regret that they are mentioned here. ...Because a lot of shit went down during this production and I don't want those people to be reminded of a negative experience. Anyway... Just keep that in mind.

Back to the storyline...

My vision for the film was to do the camerawork very much like the television series *Cops*. Not staged or set up in any manner. Just in your face cinematography. And, I think we achieved that. I suggested to Don that he mostly shoot in autofocus mode so that the focus would fade in and out like it does on *Cops*. And, to some degree, he did that.

For the camera, we used the then, just on the market, Sony VX1000, Mini DV Camcorder. For the sound we used a Sennheiser ME66 Microphone, predominately on a pistol grip.

In terms of casting, as stated, we had a large talent pool to draw upon.

There is something that most people who are not involved in actual Hollywood filmmaking do not understand. That fact is, if you are a production company, actually making movies, there are a lot of would-be stars and starlets hanging around with you all of the time desiring to get on screen. Not to mention all of the people who are constantly calling you to remind you of their existence—also desirous of being on screen. ...Some, with fairly big industry names. Don and I certainly had our fair share of people who made up that category. So, doing our casting session for *RnR Cops* was pretty easy.

I will say, here at the outset, that we did cast a new face in this film, Ann Marie. We had a casting notice running in *Dramalogue,* the primary indie film casting newspaper at the time, and she was one of the hundreds-upon-hundreds of submissions we received. As I remember, she was a newly arrived transplant to L.A., from Boston, who had come here, like so many others, to find fame and fortune. Unlike so many others, however, she was a truly talented actress and very nice person to work with. She put up with all of the shit that Don dished out without a whimper and was a great-great asset to the cast.

So, with a virtually endless cast in place and plans for filming *The Rock n' Roll Cops Zen Filmmaking* style, we had boundless locations. Thus, the movie went up.

In Production

For our first night of filming we brought in a couple of porn stars we had previously worked with as female femme fatales. We got a limo from one of our castmembers who used to own a limo service. We were set to go.

Don suggested that we use David Heavener as my costar, which was fine with me.

David is an interesting guy. He had set out on his own several years the previous, found financing for his films, and made some high-end indie productions with some big name players. Like Don, however, he had a lot of enemies in the industry. In fact, even my ex-brother-in-law had a beef with Heavener believing that he should have made money from a movie of his that Heavener was distributing. Heavener's side was that he gave the guy ten thousand dollars to finish the film and that was payment enough. Even my sister-in-law would call me up and say, *"Please don't work with David Heavener."* But, David was the same age as me, we had worked together before with no issues, he had never done me wrong, so I was all-good with the suggestion. He was a talented guy and had a big name in the industry at the time.

The first shot of the first night was the limo pulling into the parking lot behind our North Hollywood production offices. Don being an obsessive cameraman did trip on that pull-in shot a bit, making the limo drive around the block and pull in several times. But, the numerous takes, as always, equaled one shot that was eventually used in the final cut.

The next shot was David and I, with the beautiful porn girls, interacting in the limo.

In terms of improv and *Zen Filmmaking,* David was always great. He had his acting chops well honed so with just a minimal amount of story guidance, he was good to go.

The problem with David, as an actor, is that he is a bit of a ham. Meaning, he likes to try to steal the scenes. For me, that was never an issue, however. I really don't have a big ego in that department. As a filmmaker, if someone has something worth saying, let 'em say it and we can work it out in the editing room. The girls, on the other hand, they were a little stiff. But, they were very pretty so it was all-good with me. Finally, after probably three hours with the girl both clothed and unclothed in the limo, and Don obsessing about his in-limo camera work, the scene was shot.

In is kind of funny/interesting to be describing this process in so few words because at the time it drove me nuts how much Don obsessed about him getting the shot just perfectly. For a big film, there is a reason for that kind of enhanced, over-shoot process. But, for the camera-based freedom I hoped to embrace in this production; well, it was not going the way I had hoped. But,

Don was the camera guy, my co-producer, and my financier so I had to let him have his say.

We finished up the evening at about 2:00 AM or so with my character and another actor, who had been in *Guns of El Chupacabra,* doing a scene together. After we were done he complimented me how much he liked the naturalness I emulating in the scene. ...Different from my character in Chupacabra. *"That film was deep cult,"* I explained to him with a smile. *"This film is me on the streets..."*

The Problems Begin

During the production of this film, we shot it almost exclusive at night. I wanted to give it a very urban feel and I think we achieved that.

For the second day of actual production, Don and I showed up at the office around 2:00 PM and begin to plan out the next evening of shooting and whom we were going to call into the process.

The second night of production is where the problems began. Along with a few actors who never made it on screen... ...Don loved to do that to people. Bring them along for the ride but then never film them... But, we had also called in a very good guy named Eric. We had worked with him before, he had a great look, and was a talented actor. He wanted to play his character as a black-influenced white guy. Being an open to input director, I liked what he was doing so we ran with it.

The only problem was, he had another movie set to be on later that evening. One which featured the great actor William Smith who was also in *RnR Cops* and I will speak of him in a bit. Don, loving to fuck with people, kept Eric from going to the other set. We filmed some stuff in

Burbank and aside from being asked to not film in front of a movie theater, all went well. But, Eric had to leave. As we had driven him to the set, his car was back at our offices, so he couldn't leave. Don fucked with him and fucked with him until I finally stepped in and had this one actress, who was being unused, drive him back to the office. With Eric on his way, we continued to film scenes late into the night in Burbank.

A day or so later we decided to film again. We decided that we should establish the relationship between Eric's character and mine. It was Sunday, so we knew there would be very little traffic over in the junkyard section of the Valley. We drove there in the afternoon, got some daylight car drive-by shots, which I eventually used as a backdrop for the front-end credits of the film, and then set up the scene where Eric's character attempts to steal my *1964 Porsche 356 SC*. Though Don did have his share of camera obsessions that day, in that period of the shoot-day, it was not too bad. We got the shots. I also did the gag where Eric is driving off and he hits my character and I roll off of the window and the hood of the car. We then shoot me jumping into my car to give chase to Eric's character. All-good.

A funny side-story here is that we did not shoot the actual, in-car, through the window angle on that gag until late in the evening that night. As the original scene was shot in the late afternoon, the shots did not match at all. We jokingly explained it to each other as we filmed it, *"Filmmaking is the suspension of belief."* But, I never actually used that angle in the final edit.

Anyway, it was time to move on. Then, there, Don goes ape-shit nuts.

We are set up to do a driving scene. Don is in the car with Eric, filming him discussing my character and what just took place. I gave Eric some basic instruction about what to talk about and I am following them in my car. The rest of our crew is following me. Watching the footage, Eric did a very good job. He's a good talker. But, that is not what was weird. Maybe fifteen or twenty minutes into it all, I hear Don begin to yell. Keep in mind, I am in the car behind them. So obviously, Don was yelling very loudly. We drove for maybe another twenty minutes. The entire time I can hear Don screaming at Eric at the top of his lungs. Telling him what a stupid fuck he is and stuff like that. I mean, flat out, I was in disbelief.

We ended up in a parking lot and Don angrily gets out of the car, massively agitated. He is going off about how Eric is a stupid fucked up actor and he is a complete moron. What set Don off, I do not know. I went over to Eric who was standing there obviously shell-shocked. He asked, *"Does Don talk to you like that?" "Hell no! I would kick his ass."* The fact is, I am surprised Eric didn't do just that. I guess it was a combination of surprise at Don's behavior and maybe that he must have been trained to have respect for his elders or something like that, because he certainly could have kicked his ass if he wanted to. He was a young, healthy guy.

This is something that I first realized about Don when we were doing *The Roller Blade Seven*. Don would go off of the deep end at people, especially and pretty much only when he knew that he had someone around that would protect him and fight his fight for him. But, in the case with Eric, that would not have been me because Don was totally in the wrong. Moreover, Don always pushed people to see how far he could get with them. Obviously, he realized that he could treat Eric like shit and get away with it. Thus, another example of why Don had so many enemies.

After that, I sent Eric home with one of the other crewmembers. Don and I set out to film my side of the car chase conversation.

If you look at the *Zen Documentary* I did titled, *Cinematografia Obsesion,* you can see the obsessively insane nature of Don's camerawork. We shot me doing the same scene over-and-over-and-over again maybe thirty times or more times as we drove through the Valley. Even me, a normally very calm guy, was getting pissed. Again, this obsessive style of camera work may be necessary for some high budget productions but I just ended up using one of those takes in the final cut. What a waste of time…

The Turtle Mansion

The next day of production we were scheduled to go to the *Tuttle Mansion* as we called it. This was the Bel Aire home of Kevin Eastman, (Co-Creator of the Teenage Mutant Ninja Turtles), and Julie Strain.

Sadly, just last week, I did an interview regarding Julie and our film work together. She is apparel suffering from severe dementia and is not long for this world. Very sad, she is not that old. …Younger than me.

In any case, we did a lot of work with Kevin and Julie around this period of time. Both great-great people! Like I told the interviewer last week, it was not unusual that Julie would call up and say, *"Let's make a movie."* So, Don and I would go over to their house and do just that. …Julie loved to work from her home and as they had this beautiful house with a gigantic backyard and pool, it was a really great setting to film movies.

On that day, it was our plan was to shoot in the afternoon. But, I get a call from Don at about 10:00 AM. He says that I must rush over to Kevin and Julie's house right away as Eric was on his way.

Eric, was a filmmaker in his own right, and Don, being the very paranoid guy that he was, became worried that Eric would go over there and ask them for money. So, I get in my car and drive, in a rush, from Redondo to Bel Aire. Though Kevin and Julie were happy to see me, we sat around staring at each other for a couple of hours before I get the call that Don had got in touch with Eric and demanded that he come to the office instead. Thus, Don, Eric, David Heavener, and a couple of other people were on their way. Again, another mind game played by Don for no good reason.

A couple of interesting things happened on that day of filming… First of all, this was one of those times when I provided a fuck you to Don—done so for Don being Don. When the cast and crew arrived, I begin to tell Kevin and Julie the story of Don yelling at Eric in the car. It then became like one of those things that happens in a sitcom where Don was standing over to one side shaking his head, *"No, don't let them know I am an asshole and I treat people like shit."* I smiled at him and I continued to tell the story. I figured if you are going to treat good people in that manner, your actions really need to be called out.

Another interesting thing that occurred on that day was the meeting of David Heavener and Julie Strain. It was the strangest thing… They were two of the biggest names in the indie film world at the time and neither one of them had heard anything about the other person. They both went blank when I introduced them. I guessed that was just ego. They were both so self-involved with themselves and their own careers, why should they care or even know about anyone else?

Overall, the filming went very well that day. My character had a fight with Eric's character and threw him in the pool. We established Kevin as another key co-star to the story. And, we filmed that great dance scene with one of Julie's female friends.

Though we filmed a couple of days of *RnR Cops* at the *Turtle Mansion,* this was undoubtedly the most productive of those shooting experiences.

An interesting, telling event, happened near the end of that day of filming. It had begun to rain and I was doing a scene outside with this lawyer that Don had met via his new film finance company who was also interested in being an actor. Good guy. We called him, *"Law Boy,"* as he looked so young. Also, rain is a great, free special effect, so to all the filmmakers out there, I suggest you don't run from it but use it in your scenes whenever you can.

Anyway, I had gotten totally soaked. We left right after that to go and regroup at the office before we went out for a night shoot. But, my clothes were saturated and due to the fact that I was carrying a lot of equipment in my car, I didn't have room for the backup suitcase filled with clothing that I normally carry with me. I decided to stop off at the mall and pick up some additional clothing. I was in the department store disgruntled that I was not finding anything to buy that I felt would fit my character and I begin to receive page after page, phone call after phone call. Finally, I answered my cell and it was Don completely freaking out that I was not yet at the office. I guess he thought that I got pissed and bailed. And, Don begin Don just couldn't do anything by himself. I explained I would be there in a bit and he calmed down…

Praising Doctor Praisewater

It was about at this point that Don began to become the worse version of himself. I guess he became jealous at my control over the film. He deicide that hand-in-hand with *RnR Cops* we would shoot another film that he had the idea for, *Praising Doctor Praisewater*. This was to be a semi-comedic film about a sketchy doctor who was supplying people with illicit drugs.

This whole concept of doing two movies, side-by-side, didn't really bother me because we had done stuff like that in the past. I did observe, however, how this process provided Don with the tools to become a bigger asshole to the cast and crew and attempt extend his control over both projects.

On the high side, as we were using the same cast, it allowed the desirous talent the ability to get more on-camera screen time. Me, I went along for the ride.

To be honest, however, this was the first point where Don began to try to steal *The Rock n' Roll Cops* from me. But, I can be a stubborn person. I was not going to let that happen.

To skip ahead a few years in the future, after Don had passed away, a man who Don had apparently sold the rights of *Praising Doctor Praisewater* to, contacted me. Though the movie was never finished and I told the investor that fact, he asked that I send him the footage, which I happily did. When he received the footage he became very upset as I guess Don had really sold the guy with the fact that the film was something much more than it was. When, in actually, it was nothing more than a jumbled messed of random scenes. That was Don… The investor was obviously pissed. Even though this was the case, the investor, knowing my reputation, asked if I was seeking film financing and offered to finance my next film. I explained to him that is not how I created my movies.

Regarding *Praising Doctor Praisewater,* had I been allowed to keep the footage I probably, with minimal addition pick-up shots, could have put the movie together and released it. But, the footage is gone. Thus, *Praising Doctor Praisewater* is lost forever.

Darkness Falls

It was during this period that I really began to witness a shift in Don. Anger could be seen brewing in his eyes. If you want to see an ideal example of this (on film) look to the scene where Don's character does a scene with Ann Marie's and my character on the stairs of an outdoor parking lot. This is where his character says, *"Did Jake tell you that he's a Rock n' Roll Cop."* This is the one of the few times that I actually felt like I was going to have to knock Don out as the aggression level in him was insanely high and I really thought he was going to take a swing at me in the many-many takes of that scene that we shot. But, I guess he knew what would happen if he did, so nothing ever happened. But, it was intense.

I long believed that Don had an undiagnosed case of bipolar disorder. Combine that with the no sleep, the large amount of prescription drugs he was taking, and possessing the mindset of a spoiled child who is only happy when he was getting his own way and there was a constant chance of everything going South.

As production continued, things got worse and worse. For example, we were filming with David Heavener. We started out in the early evening and did a great scene at a restaurant as we were having dinner. We then went to *Los Angeles Union Station.* We did a great scene with David having a breakdown in a wheelchair as a nurse pushed him through the train station. Like I said, he was a bit of a ham when it came to acting so I just let him run with it… The scene played great.

We shot some other stuff but as the night wore on it was getting really late. For me, I have no problem staying up all night. For David, however, around 3:00 AM he began to say, *"Come on, Don…"* As Don was obsessing majorly about his camerawork, he yelled out. *"Fuck you. You're getting paid."* Here was David, one of Don's longtime friends, yet he said that to him. I couldn't believe it. Though the backstory is, Don always had a troubled relationship with David. Maybe it was jealousy? Maybe it was spite? Maybe it was power tripping? I don't know? But, more times than I can count David was the target of Don's distaste.

The next night we were shooting at *Jay Burgers.* …One of my all-time favorite burger places. Sadly, it closed a decade or so ago but I went there from the early '70s forward. On that night is where Don and I did that great scene where he blows up a blow-up globe and, *"Offers me the world."* The scene played great. But, this was a public burger stand, on the wrong side of the tracks, over in East Hollywood. A lot of gangbangers hung out there.

Now, growing up where and how I did, I know that most Latin gangbangers are not going to give you any shit if you don't come at them. Which is exactly what Don did to this one guy.

Here was Don, a fifty-six year old man, (but looking much older due to his leukemia), and there was this young gangbanger with a couple of friends. Don begins telling him to shut the fuck up and get the fuck out of the shot. Obviously, the guy came at Don.

Again, I guess Don thought that I would step in. But, I didn't create this mess. Had the guy actually attacked Don I guess I would have had to intercede. But, Don apologized and stuck out his hand to shake the others guy's hand. Which he did not do but at least a fight was avoided.

The Shit Hits the Fan

Undoubtedly, the worst night of production came when we decided to bring in my *Zen Filmmaking* brother, Z-Man, Robert Z'Dar into the cast. The shit really hit the fan on that night.

Hand-in-hand with Z-Man, we had the largest cast and crew that we had throughout the entire production. But, in this case, it wasn't just Don who was in a pissy mood, it was several other people who were grinding their teeth due to the behavior of Don. I remember going into production that night with an actual concern about what was going to come next, as pretty much everyone was pissed off, strapped, and ready to fight. By the time we got to the set I stuck my Glock under the seat of my car as if bullets stared flying I didn't want to be the one to blame. I know that sounds melodramatic but that was the kind of emotional intensity that was surrounding the movie by this point in time.

For our set, Don had the idea that we shoot some scenes on the roof of this parking structure in Burbank. That was all fine and good with me but, like I said, we had a large cast and crew, so I was concerned. As Burbank is one of the hubs of the industry, the cops are very aware of *guerrilla productions* and quickly shut them down. I've actually had helicopters zone in on my productions while filming in that city. None-the-less, never one to back down, we staged for the shoot.

On location, immediately, Don went off. Instead of going off on Eric, he focused in on Robert who we brought along as an additional cameraman.

Robert was an interesting guy. I first met him when I was first working with Don on the never competed, *Roller Blade 3*. Check out the *Zen Documentary* I made about that film, *Roller Blade 3: The Movie That Never Was,* if you want to see some behind-the-scenes of early DGJ. Previous to that, Don had hooked him with a production company and Robert had directed his first movie at the age of nineteen. He even directed Z'Dar and me in the movie, *Divine Enforcer.* Though he was very hands-off.

Though Don constantly pitted Robert and I against one another, by making false statements about what we said and stuff, I never let that kind of BS effect me. I always judge a person face-to-face and I had no problems with Robert.

Anyway, Don went off at Robert screaming some of the most demeaning things at the guy. I was in disbelief. Like Eric, Robert was a young, healthy male. He could have torn Don apart. I asked him that night, *"Why don't you just leave?"* I mean, he only lived a mile or so from the location and could have walked home. But, he said, *"I want to prove who is the better man."* Wow, I would not have reacted that way.

In terms of Z'Dar, Don just went after him, as well. At one point he screamed at Bobby, *"I wish I could get a decent actor on the set."* *"I take exception to that Donnie,"* was Z'Dar's only reply. I mean, I don't know how Don could say that to Z-Man, he was a GREAT actor!

After that, Don goes into this whole yelling discourse about how he is in a lot of pain. Which I do not doubt that he was. A side note is that Don was on a lot of medication due to his leukemia. Apparently one of those medications was very destructive to human cartilage and Don had no remaining cartilage in his right hip. This caused him to walk with a pronounced limp and use a cane. Plus, it caused him to eat a lot of Vicodin. So, I am sure that he was in pain. But, that was no reason to take it out on Z-Man.

Side note: We actually incorporated that part of Don and him needing pain medication into the storyline of *RnR Cops*.

Anyway... Don kept pushing and needling and trying to take over the evolution of the scenes and the movie. But, I would not back down. Robert said, *"I've seen him steal movies like this from other people."* My initial thought was maybe that was why Don wanted to do this film in the first place. He was a horrible confiscator of others people's ideas. Maybe he liked my concept and didn't have any ideas of his own. He thought that I would get pissed and bail. But, that's not me. The more you push, the more I push back.

Around 1:00 AM or so we had shot all we could shoot at that location and Don decided he wanted to eat so we headed over to the nearby *Denny's*. Again, it was a crazy chaotic mess. Don had this crazed look in his eyes.

Don, Robert, Ann Marie, and I were sitting at one table. Z-Man and the rest of the cast and crew were at other tables. I guess Don realize he had been treating Robert badly and he asked him what he wanted to eat. Robert told him he just wanted some fries. Give him three plates of French fries screams Don at the waiter. Don then ordered a grill cheese sandwich for himself.

Denny's used to have these great grill cheese sandwiches. Right at that point, however, they had begun to change their recipes. Don found a tomato on his sandwich which caused him to pick up his plate and literally throw it across the room. I could not believe it. I truly thought that they were going to call the cops. But, for whatever reason, they did not.

Another interesting thing that took place that night was that after I ordered coffee, so did Don. The weird thing about this was is that Don never drank coffee. He hated it. Then, he went into a rant about how could stay up longer than anybody. He could film for days and not stop. The man was obviously loosing it.

Shortly after that we sent most of the cast and the crew home. With Z-man and Ann Marie we continued to film until the early morning. What changed, I don't know, but Don began to back off about moving in on my position as director.

Again, in *Cinematografia Obsesion,* you can watch as Don obsesses about filming a shot where Z-man goes and gets some money out of an ATM.

The night and the day of production were done…

The Armor Shop

During the filmmaking of *Guns of El Chupacabra* we had met these people who operated an armor shop where they created some great medieval armor for cosplay, enactments, and… We introduced the team to Julie and they were enthralled. You can see some of their armor in *Chupacabra.*

In any case, they had a shop in Burbank and we contacted them. They were more than happy to let us shoot there. For a price, of course…

We had a pretty big cast and crew that evening and Don was not in a good mood. In fact, he was behaving like a total bitch. But, this was my film so I had to hold onto it tightly. I wasn't going to be driven from my set.

He was treating David like shit. *"Could you get in the fucking shot,"* and stuff like that. The real focus of his anger that evening was on this PA named Dennis that we had hired a week or so the previous. A good guy, who was new to L.A. In addition to being our PA, I put him in the film and his acting was spot on.

In any case, Don went after him and went after him hard. He was ruthless. At one point, we were dressing the guy in some armor so he was shirtless. Finally, the PA had enough and he walked off of the set without his shirt. The only problem was, he walked towards the back of the shop. From which, there was no way out and onto the street. For a long time, literally like an hour, I wonder what happened to him but then he stormed through the set and walked out of the front door, still wearing no shirt. And, this was the winter. It was not warm. So, he had to have been cold.

Like I said, a good guy. A good guy who Don fucked with for no reason. We lost a lot of very talented people over the years by Don behaving in that manner.

We did the shots in the armor shop that night and moved on.

I guess this is as good as a point as any to mention this. Yes, on the set Don was behaving like a total asshole. But, when we were together during the day, planning the next shoot, he was totally normal. We would laugh and joke like we always did...

Let's Play Some Music

During the filming of *Guns of el Chupacabra* we were introduced to this guy who had a large warehouse space over by the L.A. River. We filmed the Kevin and Julie in armor scenes at that location. You can also see some of that guy's great gothic artwork in the background.

In any case, we needed an interior location to further develop the story. So, we contacted the guy and returned to his space. There, among other things, we planed to film a jam session with David and I.

David was a country western singer who had a couple of albums on the market. But, he didn't have access to an electric guitar. So, I packed up my *1964 Gibson Trini Lopez* for him to use and I took my *Gibson, Kris Derrig, Les Paul* for me to play. I would have like to have brought some of my Marshall stacks to use as amps but there was no way that I could fit them in Porsche. So, all I had room for was my '57 Fender Deluxe. One of the other castmember brought a practice for David to use.

Maybe someday one of you people out there with a lot of CGI experience can put a wall of Marshalls behind us. But, that was all we had to actually work with.

What really surprised me when we got down to filming the scene was that I thought that David and I were just going to jam with me playing lead. But, David had actually written an entire song titled, *The Rock n' Roll Cops*. Wow! He really went all in and that was highly appreciated.

In the final cut of the film I didn't use the song, however. We had spoken about actually going into a recoding studio and recording it right. But, that never happened. As, the audio from one Sennheiser ME66 microphone just did not do the song justice, it never made its way into the film.

Shooting Continues

We shot some interesting stuff over the next few days. I don't know how much Don had been sleeping, or what he was taking to stay awake, as he was also doing *Praising Doctor Praisewater*. ...A film, by this point, that I didn't want to have anything to do with.

In any case, I showed up at the office as we were set to go out that night and film. I had gotten to the offices in the late afternoon and Don and/or no one else was there. I hung out for a little while and Don with his cast and crew barrels in. He was mad and agitated. What had apparently occurred is that the castmember, who owned the limo, and provided a great character in *RnR Cops,* was also doing *Praising Doctor Praisewater* with him. Remember, people want that screen time... As I was told, the guy's limo had broken down in this really sketchy part of ghetto L.A. but instead of helping him out Don just told the guy to fuck off and figure it out for himself. Don and the crew just left him there. I mean that is really messed up.

The backstory about that guy was, he was a former gangbanger and a current drug dealer. The guy was always strapped with one of those large, *Dirty Harry,* Smith and Wesson 44 Mags in a shoulder holster. So, he was no one to mess with. As Don drove off, the guy was obviously pissed off big time and was hitting Don with some serious threats. Can you blame him?

Anyway, back at the office, Don and his people all pull out their guns awaiting the arrival of the guy. I mean, what bullshit melodrama. All for nothing. Again, I am left in a state of total disbelief. Don then calls the cops and tells them that he is being threatened by this guy and the guy is on his way to kill him. Unbelievable…

Some people love all that style of adrenaline filled bullshit. Don always did. But, not me. I just don't need it.

I guess the guy got his car started and just as he was showing up the cops arrive. I couldn't even watch what was going on. I went to my office and sat around talking with this one actress who had not been involved in the melee. Luckily, they didn't arrest him, they just told him he had to leave. But, Don should not have done that. Plus, he did that with the full support of the cast and the crew of *Praising Doctor Praisewater.* I refused to let of them film any more scene in *RnR Cops.* Me, I would have stayed there and helped the guy out if his car had broken done. Not Don, he loved the melodrama. Bad, bad, bad…

The Final Scene

Though we shot for a few more days, the final scene of *The Rock n' Roll Cops* involved the great actor, William Smith.

I don't really remember where or why we decided to do it but we chose the famous *Bonaventure Hotel* as a location for his scenes. Don and I went there early in the day and rented a hotel suite. We then went back to the office where Don proceeded to call this insane amount of castmembers to meet us in the room—promising all of them a big part in the film.

We then had a core group of people meet us at the office and Don sent this one guy to the hotel as the Cast Wrangler.

Now, this guy who was also in the movie. …A very good guy and a great actor. He was the brother of an Academy Award winning director. He predominately worked as an extra while he wrote scripts hoping for one to break through. He was given the key to the hotel room and was told to keep everyone in the room and not let them wander the halls.

Don and I then left the rest of the central cast and crew in the office and set out on our day.

I knew what Don was doing. He loved to fuck with people and he just wanted to see how long he could make them sit around doing nothing. We went out and had lunch and later dinner. That tells you how long we were out.

Out, we were also planning to buy Mini DV tapes for the evening's shoot. The thing was, there was none to be found. We literally went everywhere. And, I mean everywhere around Hollywood and the Valley but they were all sold out. Apparently, some big production company had just discovered the format and bought everything. We searched and searched until we finally found some at an electronics store. That was a strange experience and a good lesson to filmmaker; i.e. make sure you have your film stock before you schedule your shoot.

Then, Don had the idea, why don't we film at the *Chateau Marmont* on the Sunset Strip instead of the *Bonaventure?* We went there. Don boldly exclaiming that we wanted to film some scene that evening in a suite for this great film we were making. *"This is the director, Scott Shaw,"* he exclaimed. Again, I could not believe his actions. Whether or not it was true, they told us they were fully booked. By now, it was about 9:00 PM so we headed for the *Bonaventure,* calling the people who remained at out office and telling them to meet us there.

The next thing that shoved me into disbelief was the way Don encountered the staff of the hotel. We pull into the underground parking lot of the hotel and instead of being cool and casual he boldly tells the bellmen how to unpack and load up all of this massive amount of film equipment he had in his very large trunk. I mean, we didn't have a permit to shoot at the hotel or anything like that and I expected the management would come down on us. Don literally had the bellmen unpack two full hotel carts of equipment and take them up to our suite. It is hard to even explain what I was feeling.

Next, we go upstairs. We walk in the room and see that there were at least fifty expectant castmember sitting around. All of them stuffed into this two-room hotel suite. These were all people that we had worked with before. Don goes off, *"Get them the fuck out of here! Why did you let all of them in here!"* Don yells to our Cast Wrangler. In disbelief, people try to speak to me, as I am the nice one. I just ignore them and walk away. It's all too insane for me. There is nothing that I can do. As was always the case, it was Don who made the phone calls and set all of this into motion but it was Don who tried to blame someone else.

Next, Don goes after the Cast Wrangler. He starts screaming at him for not maintaining control over the people. A very nice guy, he looks at me and said, *"I guess I should have seen this coming."* He inquired as to his pay but I told him that was Don's department. He left. But, at least he didn't hold a grudge against me.

Talent on the Set

About 10:00 PM the great actor and Clint Eastwood Co-Star William Smith arrived with his girlfriend, (who later became his wife). Don was immediately pissed that he brought her along. Me, I had no problem with her being there at all. While I was setting up some lighting, Don apparently told Bill that I did not like her on the set and that she had to leave. Which she did. I was told she went down to the hotel bar.

A few minutes later, I asked Bill where she went. He told me Don said I wanted her gone. *"I never said that,"* I exclaimed. With this, Bill goes into the bedroom of the suite, where Don was getting the camera ready, and joking put him in a chokehold. As they were longtime friends, I knew there was nothing to worry about but it was fun to see how the tables had turned on Don in an instant and he was totally incapacitated by a truly tough, take no prisoners, sort of guy.

The next strange thing that occurred is that Don completely stepped back from any interaction onto how I was going to guide the scene. There was no input about camera or otherwise. I talked to Bill to tell him exactly what I wanted him to do. Don said nothing.

Now, this was not the first time Don had done this over the years. On more than a few occasions, Don would leave our sets altogether. But, due to the way Don was behaving over the past week or so, I did not expect it.

In any case, Bill wanted to play the charter with a Russian ascent. Sure. I was good with that.

So, I guided Bill, Ann Marie, and Don through their scenes and that was that. Bill was paid and he went home.

We stayed around the hotel until the early morning hours of daylight shooting filler stuff with Ann Marie's and my character. The noteworthy thing was, Don was totally brazen. He had us shooting all over the hotel, in the elevators, and even in the lobby. This, as stated, with no permits. Ballsy, I thought.

At one point, the hotel security guards even came out and took a look at us. But, they said nothing and just walked on. So, we got the shoots while fully utilizing the Bonaventura Hotel with no permits or anything like that.

And, that was that. Those were the final shots of the film.

The Aftermath

Upon completion of *RnR Cops,* I assumed Don would hand over the footage to me and I would edit the film. We had an editing room set up in our offices where I had done several other of our films and I thought this film would follow the same pathway. It did not.

Almost immediately upon rap, Don returned to his usual, more or less normal, self. I will leave it to you psychology majors to figure that one out. Plus, he also gave up filming *Praising Doctor Praisewater*.

We filmed *RnR Cops* in January of 1998. *The American Film Market* was rapidly upon us and I created a poster for the film as we were going to offer it for sale and international distribution.

One of the weird things that went on during that AFM was that there were people outside actually protesting David Heavener and passing out flyer bagging on him. Thus, Don wanted his name removed from the cast. I thought that was a bit messed up, as Don knew whom he got into bed with when he hired David, but I played along. So, there are a couple of different credit lists on the poster out there.

Though there was a lot of interest in the film from buyer, we didn't have a trailer or anything to show them, so the film went nowhere except for the fact that I was interviewed by *Rolling Stone Magazine* and a few other media sources regarding the film.

But, that was it. Though Don and I talked about the film over the next few years, as I never had the footage, there was nothing I could do to make it become a film.

In 2002, I was teaching a class at U.C.L.A, *The Art of Independent Filmmaking,* and I got to be friends with one of my students, Rich Magram. A great guy, we decided to make a film together.

For that film, what I hoped to embrace was that same feeling of the TV show, *Cops* that I hoped to capture with the original *RnR Cops*. I wanted to it to be in your face cinematography. As I believed I would never possess the footage for the original *RnR Cops*, I titled this new film, *Rock n' Roll Cops*. We shot it very documentary style, like I had hoped to do with the original film.

Filmed and edited, it was then released.

Very soon after this, in 2003, Don became very ill and asked me to take him to the hospitable. His time was almost up. Knowing this, and knowing that I was the only one who would keep his filmmaking legacy alive, he made sure that his wife gave me all of the footage to all of his and our movies. There was literally hundred of hours of uncut footage. Immediately, I located the *RnR Cops* footage and began editing the movie. But, Don passed away before I could finish.

One of the first things that I noticed when I began editing the film, and something that I did not previously realize, was the fact that we had shot a lot of very usable scenes. Some of these played out very well for a very long period of time. For me, as a viewer, I don't really like movies that stretch on for more than ninety minutes, however. So, there were a lot of scenes that I substantially cut down and a number of intact scenes that I did not use in the final cut. I believe that there is enough unused footage that I could actually create another full-length movie. But, unless there is a reason, I doubt that I will do that.

As I had already released a movie with the title *Rock n' Roll Cops*, I released the original film as, *Rock n' Roll Cops 2: The Adventure Begins* on VHS.

During that period of time, DVD was rapidly taking over video and I said, *"Fuck it, I am going to retitle and rerelease things as they should be."* Thus, *Rock n Roll Cops* became *Hollywood P.D. Undercover* and *Rock n' Roll Cops 2: The Adventure Begins,* became *The Rock n' Roll Cops.*

Thinking back, as I write this, I don't actually know how much *The Rock n' Roll Cops* actually cost to make but it was not cheap. All of the established talent had their day rates and we paid the other castmembers about one hundred dollars per day and the crew about two hundred dollars per day. Me, I was on a five hundred dollar a week retainer plus four hundred dollars a day for each day we were in production. Don, I am sure, was making way more than that. Plus, a few of the locations we actually rented and that was not cheap. So, this movie did cost some money to make. The exact amount, I will never know.

As to the *Zen Filmmaking* legacy, Don and I always felt we made two masterpieces as a team: *The Roller Blade Seven* and *Guns of El Chupacabra*. But, I would add *The Rock n' Roll Cops* to that list. Even though it was a crazy, mind bending experience due to the behavior of Don it, none-the-less, is a true embodiment of *Zen Filmmaking.*

That's the story... The story of *The Rock n' Roll Cops.*

FADE OUT.

FADE OUT.

The Zen

www.ingramcontent.com/pod-product-compliance
Lightning Source LLC
Chambersburg PA
CBHW031610160426
43196CB00006B/85